THE COMPLETE COMEDIES
OF TERENCE

THE COMPLETE COMEDIES
OF TERENCE

Modern Verse Translations

BY

PALMER BOVIE, CONSTANCE CARRIER,

AND

DOUGLASS PARKER

Edited and with a Foreword by
Palmer Bovie

RUTGERS UNIVERSITY PRESS
New Brunswick, New Jersey

Library of Congress Cataloging in Publication Data

Terentius Afer, Publius.
    The complete comedies of Terence.

    I. Bovie, Smith Palmer, comp. II. Carrier,
Constance, tr. III. Parker, Douglass, tr.
PA6756.A1B6   872'.01   74-5264
ISBN 0-8135-0775-8

Manufactured in the United States of America by Quinn & Boden Company, Inc.,
    Rahway, New Jersey

CONTENTS

FOREWORD

Formal Roman literature essentially began in 240 B.C. when a Greek slave from Tarentum named Livius Andronicus produced Latin verse translations of a Greek tragedy and comedy at the festival held in Rome a year after the defeat of Carthage in the First Punic War. In 264 B.C., almost inadvertently, Rome had declared war on Carthage and embarked on the program of military expansion beyond the peninsula of Italy that was to determine the future of the world. By the end of the Second Punic War (218–201 B.C.) she was the dominant power in the Mediterranean, and by the end of the Third Punic War (151–146 B.C.) had brought Macedonia, Greece, and Asia Minor under her control. At the beginning of the third century B.C. such a result would have been unpredictable: any one of the leading nations, Macedonia, Syria, Egypt, or Carthage might have prevailed, especially Carthage, the prime sea power, wealthy in trade and controlling vast agricultural resources while strategically located in command of the coast, with territory in Sicily and Sardinia. But by the middle of the second century B.C. Rome had successfully invaded every one of these territories and by means of tactics devised through trial and error, rather than because of any long-range strategy, had gained the leadership of the western world.

The Roman comedies by Titus Maccius Plautus (254–184 B.C.) and Publius Terentius Afer (195–160 B.C.) transact the ordinary business of social and economic life, rallying to the crises of individuals, not civilizations. The *fabulae* they adapted from the authors of Greek New Comedy portray typical people, the rich father, the son in love and in debt, clever slaves, nervous parasites, accomplished courtesans, vainglorious soldiers, well-dowered wives, free maidens whose identity and future is in doubt. On the surface they are a replica of Greek middle-class life. If Plautus was fourteen or so when Livius Andronicus first staged drama in Latin at Rome he would have long since heard how Rome had won out over Carthage. The battle cry "Stetson! You who were with me in the ships at Mylae!"[1] would have sounded old hat to him. Yet when he was producing his own first plays Plautus would hear of Hannibal on the mainland of Italy, a clear and present danger to Rome.[2] A dozen years later he would hear of Scipio Africanus' invasion of North Africa and his defeat of Hannibal at Zama in 202 B.C.

Terence was born in Carthage and brought to Rome for sale as a boy slave. A Roman named Terentius Lucanus bought him, brought him up in his own household, educated him, and set him free. Subsequently, Terence became a friend of Scipio the Younger, the adoptive grandson of Africanus, who was then beginning his career of combined brilliance in intellectual, military, and political life. In the company of Scipio the Younger and the friends gathered around him who shared his ardent interest in Greek culture and thought, Terence would become aware of the extension of Roman power to the mainland of Greece, registered by the impact of such battles as the defeat of the Macedonians under Philip V at Cynoscephalae in 197 B.C. and their final defeat under Philip's son Perseus at Pydna in 169 B.C. Such events meant another form of direct contact with Greek civilization, the acquisition of Greek works of art, and the subjection of the old world to the new.

After Pydna, one thousand eminent citizens of Aetolia were deported to Rome as hostages and kept in confinement for sixteen years without a trial or hearing, finally to be released only after seven hundred of them had died. Among them was the soldier-diplomat Polybius who had the good luck to be chosen as the tutor of the young Scipio. When writing his own great *Universal History* Polybius could not refrain from reflecting on his own role in the drama:

[1] Mylae, near the Straits of Messina, was the scene of the first great naval victory of Rome over Carthage in 260 B.C.

[2] Hannibal's defeat of the Roman armies at Cannae in 216 B.C. meant the loss of some 50,000 Roman lives.

There is this analogy between the plan of my history and the marvelous spirit of the age with which I have to deal. Just as Fortune
made almost all the affairs of the world incline in one direction, and
forced them to converge upon one and the same point; so it is my task
as a historian to put before my readers a compendious view of the
part played by Fortune in bringing about her general purpose. It was
this peculiarity which originally challenged my attention, and determined me on undertaking this work.

(Book I, Ch. 4)

Or again, standing beside Scipio the Younger at Carthage in the
spring of 146 B.C., Polybius shows a universal concern for the
world and its people:

At the sight of the city utterly perishing amidst the flames Scipio burst
into tears, and stood long reflecting on the inevitable change which
awaits cities, nations, dynasties, one and all, as it does every one of
us men . . . And unintentionally or purposely he quoted—the words
perhaps escaping him unconsciously—

"The day shall be when holy Troy shall fall
And Priam, lord of spears, and Priam's folk."
(*Iliad*, Bk. VI)

And on my asking him boldly (for I had been his tutor) what he
meant by these words, he did not name Rome distinctly, but was evidently fearing for her from this sight of the mutability of human
affairs.

(Book XXXIX, Ch. 5)

Like Polybius, Plautus and Terence were destined to play
some part of their own in that staggering world. The dramatic
tradition they were to figure in received its first strong impetus
from Southern Italy, whose cities, long since colonized by Greece,
were centers of Hellenistic culture. Livius Andronicus translated
the *Odyssey* into the native Latin Saturnian meter for use as a
schoolbook, in addition to adapting tragedies and comedies. The
next playwright in chronological order, Gnaeus Naevius (270–
201 B.C.) was a native Roman who had served in the First Punic
War and written an epic poem in Saturnians mentioning Aeneas,
Dido, and the Trojan origins of Rome. Some six tragedies and

thirty comedies are attributed to Naevius, who was an outspoken and free-thinking man.[3]

Slightly after Plautus in chronological order, the versatile Quintus Ennius from Rudiae (between Tarentum and Brindisi) claimed to have three souls because he spoke Latin, Greek, and Oscan! Ennius wrote "saturae" (miscellaneous works), a historical epic in dactylic hexameters, two comedies and some twenty tragedies. His work exerted a marked influence on such poets of a later age as Lucretius, Vergil, and Horace. Ennius' successor in tragic poetry was his nephew Pacuvius (220–130 B.C.). Rome's most prolific writer of tragedies, Lucius Accius (170–86 B.C.), to whom some forty-five plays are attributed, was known to Cicero when the latter was a young man. In comedy Caecilius Statius, a slave from the region of Gaul near Milan, won his laurels as a playwright at Rome, and is said to have first encouraged Terence.

Although only fragments of the work of the many writers in this evolving poetic tradition have survived by being quoted and referred to in the works of later writers, the twenty plays of Plautus and the six of Terence have come down to us in nearly complete form. And later Roman authors seem to be fully aware of the achievement of Plautus and Terence, alike in their common interest in the subjects of comedy, very different in their treatment of themes and characters, and both luckily swept into the current of Rome's first great literary tradition.

As the dramatic presentations, or *ludi scaenici,* became a more and more popular part of the games, races, and athletic contests offered in Rome at the various holiday festivals spaced throughout the year, the system of production took practical form. The chief city officials, the aediles, provided the money;

---

[3] Naevius was imprisoned for insulting the famous Metellus family, and Plautus refers to the incident in his *Miles Gloriosus,* as follows:

> *Nam os columnatum poetae esse inaudivi barbaro*
> *Quoi bini custodes semper totis horis occubant*

> I've heard that a certain barbarian poet has his
> Face behind bars and two guards watching over him
> all hours of the day

> (ll. 211–212)

A *barbarus poeta,* barbarian poet, is one who does not write in Greek.

the main actor and director of a troupe of players chose the play, probably reading the one he liked best to the aediles, who authorized him to pay the poet for the text and who subsidized the costs of production for the actor-director (such a man, for instance as Ambivius Turpio whom Terence introduces gratefully in his prologues) and his troupe.

There were no theatres as such, but in the Circus or some other open space where the play was to be shown an improvised stage, the *proscaenium,* was constructed on a raised platform, with a wood framework of high boards at the back, the *scaena,* on which were painted two or three adjoining housefronts. Doors in the houses of the backdrop could be used as entrances and exits as well as the sides, one of which led to the Forum, the other to the country. Across the long platform of the stage the actors could scamper or saunter, adapting its 180 feet of space to the purposes of a city street in front of the houses, deliver monologues and soliloquies, entering at one end without being immediately recognized by characters already on stage at the other.

The action all takes place out of doors, a not abnormal Mediterranean circumstance, and the plot, of course, depends to some extent on this physical fact. Interior scenes must always be described; lovemaking is not transacted in public. The plays are quite talky because so much has to be described, but Plautus makes the most of his opportunity to wield as many colorful words as the ear can accommodate. The players can run on stage or across it, slink back into concealment against the housefronts, stroll about in groups of two or three, or one set can play off against the other, with ample room for the gestures and the bodily caricature that comedy dotes on. They can exit meaningfully toward the center of town, or away from town, bent on additional business, which will then later be fed back into the plot.

Improvised and confined as this temporary wooden theatre was, it played to teeming audiences admitted free, seated on chairs temporarily installed, who saw a new play each time. A particularly popular comedy might be recalled by popular demand at a later festival, but the usual performance procedure was both competitive and novel. Each time the Roman poet-author-translator, combining and transforming materials from the texts of Greek New Comedy, can employ his tactics of invading the cultural possibilities of the situation. Working freely with their originals, Plautus and Terence both convert the polished Greek plots and nicely limned but typical characters into Roman worthies and unworthies equally characteristic of their own culture. The result is perfectly Roman but no less human than the precedent on which it is based. Plautus and Terence both promise their audiences something borrowed and something new.

Plautus clearly had a great capacity for producing poetry that says what it means about the way of his world. His hard and fast dialogue never flags, his songs never falter (except when they are about faltering), his plots may drive you mad but they don't make you mad. One important artistic element Plautus developed to its highest point, and one which Terence does not make use of, is that of song, the lyrical *canticum*. Many passages in his plays depart from the routine iambic and trochaic metres of dialogue into the different lyric metres for snatches of song or for whole monodies. The actor would render these in the style of an aria or long recitative, accompanied by a flute in the wings. A comedy by Plautus is thereby much more like a musical comedy than is a play by Terence which restricts itself to the sphere of conversational social comedy.

Terence was the literary personality, accepted for his gifted, modest intellectual sensitivity into the sophisticated circle of Scipio and his friends. The older playwright Caecilius is supposed to have discovered Terence's talents at the first reading of the *Andria* and from then on Terence wrote under the approving eyes of his patrons. He is said to have lost his life in his thirty-sixth year while on a voyage to Greece in search of additional plays of Menander. Again, the conjectural biographical fact confirms the implication most germane to Terence's genius. He was a "writer," rather than a performer, a poet of ideas rather than a man of action. So in his comedies the extravagant and burly style is entirely absent and replaced by a concentration on the psychological interaction of the characters. It is humanity that amuses Terence, in a thoughtful yet vivid way; it is the Romans and their Mediterranean counterparts that Plautus knows by heart.

The chronological order of Terence's plays is taken to be as follows:

166 B.C.	*Andria*	Ludi Megalenses (a festival in April)
165 B.C.	*Hecyra*	Ludi Megalenses (withdrawn as a failure)
163 B.C.	*Heautontimorumenos*	Ludi Megalenses
161 B.C.	*Eunouchus*	Ludi Megalenses
	Phormio	Ludi Romani (a festival in September)
160 B.C.	*Hecyra*	Ludi funebres (funeral festival) for L. Aemilius Paullus. Second failure.
	Adelphoe	Ludi funebres for L. Aemilius Paullus
	Hecyra	Ludi Romani (successful performance)

The happy reception finally accorded one of his earliest efforts no doubt pleased Terence as he left Italy for Greece in search of more Menander manuscripts. The literati had recognized and encouraged his talents early; now the unruly Roman populace had welcomed back a play it had twice refused to sit still for. Comedy, like life, had to take its chances.

In his short career Terence ably presided over the comic genre of Roman literature. He fashioned a precise, often lapidary style, and wrote fluent, idiomatic, graceful Latin. Respectful of tradition, he adhered closely to the Greek New Comedy stage world, much more strictly than Plautus could be bothered to. And yet, while creating the illusion of his prototypes, Terence saw his people and their predicaments in a new way. For all their common elements, each of these six comedies is entirely different from the other in manner, idea, logic of action, and psychology of character. There is something unclassifiable about Terence's dramatic poetry, as each time the audience is invited to witness a new spectacle on familiar grounds and each time the play moves in a new direction.

To Terence both thought and style were important. In the

prologue to the *Andria,* distinctions in thought and style are mentioned in connection with the two Menander plays on which Terence drew:

> *ita non sunt dissimili argumento sed tamen*
> *dissimili oratione sunt factae et stilo.*

> In plot they are not very different, yet they have
> been composed in a different thought and style.

Discussing his method further, Terence adds that the practice of combining elements from different Greek plays into one new Latin play was common. Naevius, Ennius, Plautus, did it and Terence approves of this method (called *contaminatio*), as offering better results than the dull and dingy lines of the Latin poet Lanuvinus, who has been taking Terence to task for combining various sources in his plays and thereby "contaminating" them.

> *quae convenere in Andriam ex Perinthia*
> *fatetur transtulisse atque usum pro suis.*
> *id isti vituperant factum atque in eo disputant*
> *contaminari non decere fabulas.*
> *faciuntne intellegendo ut nil intellegunt?*
> *qui cum hunc accusant, Naevium, Plautum, Ennium*
> *accusant, quos hic noster auctores habet,*
> *quorum aemulari exoptat neclegentiam*
> *potius quam istorum obscuram diligentiam.*
>
> (ll. 11–21)

> He admits that he transferred what suited from
> "the Perinthian" to "the Andrian," and used
> them as his own. These critics revile him for
> this and differ over the point that plays should
> not be mixed up together. But by being so knowl-
> edgeable, do they not show how little they under-
> stand? In accusing him they also accuse Naevius,
> Plautus, and Ennius, whom our poet takes as his
> precedents, and whose carelessness he would rather
> emulate than the mystifying carefulness of those critics.

In the prologue to the *Heautontimorumenos* Terence lets his spokesman, the great actor and entrepreneur delightfully named Ambivius, argue again on behalf of the poet's style and

thought. He wants me to plead a case for him, announces Ambivius, not speak a prologue, and I hope I can be persuasive in my
eloquence as I deliver these lines. After all, Terence, wrote them.
A critic says Terence is a mere newcomer to the ranks of com-
posers:

> *repente ad studium hunc se adplicasse musicum*   (1. 23)

He is a neophyte borrowing literary talent from his friends instead of deriving it from his own abilities:

> *amicum* [4] *ingenio fretum, haud natura sua*   (1. 24)

But, Ambivius says, only you, the audience, can judge what his
abilities are. In the play you are about to see, the stereotyped
roles are conspicuously absent, no "running slave," no "angry old
man," "hungry parasite," "self-serving confidence man." In this
play there is *not* a lot of racing around the stage and shouting at
the top of the lungs, fast action and clamor. Most modern playwrights keep asking me to do their loudest, fastest scripts. But
here I hope you will allow me the chance of performing in a quiet
play, in silence:

> *adeste aequo animo, date potestatem mihi*
> *statariam agere ut liceat per silentium.*
>   (ll. 35–36)

Ambivius is glad to perform at last in a *fabula stataria,* and ends
his prologue with a plea to the audience to give Terence a fair
hearing. For this is a play written in an honest style, in simple un-
affected speech:

> *in hac est pura oratio.*   (1. 46)

In the prologue to the *Eunuchus* Terence disarmingly under-
scores his critic's bad style. Terence's aim is simply to please as
many people as possible and to offend as few. He feels unfairly
treated by an abusive critic and fellow-poet whose main trouble
is that he cannot translate well and does not write good Latin:

> *qui bene vortendo et easdem scribendo male*
> *ex Graecis bonis Latinas fecit non bonas.*
>   (ll. 6–7)

---

[4] Equivalent to *amicorum* in Latin of this period.

. . . who, by translating literally [5] and writing plays
in bad Latin has made out of good Greek plays Latin
versions that are no good.

Terence then suggests a few criticisms of his own on Lanuvinus'
recent productions, and admits freely to deriving characters from
Menander but denies plagiarizing any Latin source:

> *Colax Menandrist: in east parasitus Colax*
> *et miles gloriosus: eas se hic non negat*
> *personas transtulisse in Eunuchum suam*
> *ex Graeca; sed ea ex fabula factas prius*
> *Latinas scisse sese, id vero pernegat.*
>
> (ll. 30–34)

> The Colax is a play of Menander's; in it
> there is Colax, a parasite, and a braggart
> warrior. Terence does not deny that he has
> transferred these characters into his
> *Eunuch* from the Greek. He assuredly
> does deny that he was aware that those
> parts had been already translated into
> Latin.

Where would a poet get his stock characters, Terence asks, running through a list of types (sometimes present, sometimes absent from his plays, but always in quite novel relationships)
unless he consulted the tradition? There's nothing one can say
which has not been said before:

> *nullumst iam dictum quod non sit dictum prius*   (l. 41)

The audience could have reserved judgment on this point, at least
until they heard *The Eunuch*. As Douglass Parker shows in his
introduction, later commentators have often been compromised
by their view that this is an atypical, un-Terentian comedy, un-
easy about how to classify its uncharacteristic quality. But perhaps true wit is indeed "nature to advantage dressed, what oft
was thought . . . ." and Terence didn't want to help his critics
by adding "but ne'er so well expressed."

---

[5] *bene vortendo* (equivalent to *vertendo*): Richard Bentley interpreted this
phrase to mean a literal translation, word for word, that neglects the Latin idiom.

The *Phormio*, like the *Eunuchus*, is a *fabula motoria* fraught with fast action and clamorous near-catastrophes. In the prologue Terence recurs briefly to the matter of style and thought. Citing Lanuvinus' deprecation of his dramatic poetry as

tenui oratione et scriptura levi

poor in language, meager in style   (1. 5)

Terence defends himself on the grounds that he sees little value in sensationalism and the melodramatic effects (closer to tragedy than comedy) which Lanuvinus featured. Also, the older poet's successes have been due more to the skill of the performers than the virtues of the poetry they had to work with. Later he adds that "the prize is open to all who apply to the dramatic art":

. . . *in medio omnibus*
palmam esse positam qui artem tractant musicam.
(ll. 16–17)

Surely here we are listening to the well-modulated resentment of an ambitious, sensitive young competitor in the ranks whose Latin style has been slighted, the order of his thought (*oratio*) brushed aside as *tenuis* ("skinny"), his "writing" (*scriptura*) as lightweight (*levis*). And finally, in the prologue to the *Adelphoe*, Terence meets the charge of collaboration with noble men (Scipio and the members of his circle) by admitting that there are none he would rather work with. He is complimented, not insulted, to think that he "pleases those who please you all and the public; the aid of whom in war, in peace, in private business, each one has availed himself of, on his own occasion, without any haughtiness on their part":

nam quod isti dicunt malivoli, homines nobilis
hunc adituare adsidueque una scribere:
quod illi maledictum vehemens esse existimant,
eam laudem hic ducit maximan, cum illis placet
qui vobis universis et populo placent,
quorum opera in bello, in otio, in negotio,
suo quisque tempore usust sine superbia.
(ll. 15–21)

The noble men Terence collaborated with need not be confined to the Scipionic circle. Why can it not include the characters he created? An authoritarian if somewhat uncomprehending father in *The Self-Tormentor* gave voice to what was to become Terence's most memorable line:

> *homo sum: humani nil a me alienum puto.*

> I am a man and nothing human is foreign to me.
>   (1. 77)

When Chremes said this he was excusing himself for poking his nose into his neighbor's business. It is in part a funny rationalization of his curiosity. But the Latin also carves into lapidary form the Stoic doctrine of the brotherhood of man. So it is both a funny attitude for Chremes to take, and the expression of a noble purpose. If our minds dwell on the thought—or later we match it with a son's expression of loving admiration for his adoptive father, who, the son declares, is more like a brother or a boon companion than a father—we may be stirred to reflect that a fundamental issue for mankind is not the conflict between father and son, but all men's potentiality as brothers. Of course it is dangerous to detach any one line or saying from its context, and rather imperils its aesthetic equilibrium.

Many would prefer among Terence's maxims:

> *quot homines, tot sententiae: suus cuique mos.*

> As many men, as many opinions; each to his own taste.
>   (*Phormio*, l. 453)

Actually Terence has introduced a proverbial saying, voiced by one of the three lawyers who arrive at three different opinions in the same case. It is sententious, rather pompously cited by one of the lawyers in defense of their common indecisiveness. There is also a cutting psychological edge to the remark, so well encased in its first four words that the last three are usually left out when this quotation in Terence is quoted. Uniformity of opinion signals the end of active thought. Relativity has a place.

A slave, bent on helping out his young master, but with no clear idea at all of what to do, proudly proclaims:

quod fors feret feremus aequo animo.

What fortune brings, we'll put up with,
with equanimity.

(*Phormio*, 1. 138)

An admirable expression of Stoic fortitude and unflappability,
neatly turning on the two meanings of *fero*, alliterative and asso-
nant in its stress on what the Stoics prized most, "equanimity."
But in context, the remark serves no practical purpose; the slave
never capitalizes on it. The fact is, he's so nervous that this is the
only way he can reassure himself as to his composure.

A brother envies his brother for being so well off in his love
affair—if only his brother could see it his way, and were in a state
of "mind capable of bearing all this with moderation." He goes
on to generalize:

ita plerique omnes sumus ingenio: nostri nosmet paenitet.

We are all like this by nature: we regret what we have.

(*Phormio*, 1. 173)

The truth tapped home by the concluding staccato of the last
three words is neatly converted when the supposedly well-off
brother replies that he only wishes he were in his brother's place.
So, anxiety is contagious and reciprocal.

In the range of behavior in Terence's comedies, fathers are
usually difficult and mothers understanding, but on occasion the
roles can be reversed. The two fathers in *The Self-Tormentor*
both create torments for themselves out of their imagination. By
the end of the play they seem to have exchanged roles, or char-
acteristics, as Menedemus pries into his neighbor Chremes' affairs, offering him advice on how to treat his son. But this is a
cheerful bluff on Menedemus' part; he ultimately reassumes his
role as the most self-critical, indulgent, loving, and altogether
sympathetic father even seen on any stage.

A courtesan like Bacchis in the *Hecyra* is hard-hearted,
clever, and affectionate enough to return a ring that discloses the
identity of her former admirer's next love. Thais in the *Eunuchus*
is unclassifiable, being protective, thoughtful, and tender while
also self-regarding, dominant, and much smarter than any of the

men. She is an economic pawn, to some extent, but in the long run a psychological queen. An expensive courtesan in *The Self-Tormentor* discusses the chances women take when they make a profession of love. The beauty that draws lovers to her is perishable, and when it wanes she'll be dropped. If she has not provided for her future, she's lost for the rest of her life.

The young men in love, intent on marrying their girls, or buying them with money they don't have, may seem like nervous wrecks, totally lacking in confidence. But they are just as much the aggressors, the idealists who set the action moving. Their passion makes fools of them. It also makes men of them, husbands and fathers (often on the same day). They are determined to grow into their man's estate. The fathers of such sons are more reluctant to indulge the desire to leap into maturity. Life as fathers has taken its toll of them. Their passions have been ravaged and they are left with only reason, whereas their sons have only ravished the objects of their passion, without taking much thought for the future.

The mother, often slighted in Roman literature as in Roman practical affairs, exerts herself manfully in several of Terence's comedies. The precarious fate of the *Hecyra* seems in fact to reflect Terence's unusual respect for and interest in this figure. Here he seems to be writing a deep poetry, making a serious study of womanhood. As for the servants, tutors, slaves, lawyers, dealers, middlemen, they are content to play both ends against the middle, or as the slave Geta said, after his remark about putting up with whatever fortune brought his way:

> *in me omnis spes mihist.*

> My only hope is centered in myself.
>
> (1. 139)

They all look after themselves while helping circumvent the oldsters as a way of encouraging the youngsters.

All these people experience emotional ordeals. They stumble upon themselves in the course of the comedy, and know more about themselves when it is over than they did when it began. We in the audience who share to some extent in their psychological trials also find ourselves afterwards in possession of some new knowledge drawn from the vast reservoir of traditional human behavior. Terence's genius lay in making sense of the complexities of human character, in fashioning this sense into honestly thought-out and well-spoken Latin poetry. *In hac est pura oratio.*

Palmer Bovie

NOTE TO THE READER

The line numbers throughout this volume are based on the original Latin text.

THE COMPLETE COMEDIES
OF TERENCE

THE GIRL
FROM ANDROS

(*ANDRIA*)

Translated by Palmer Bovie

INTRODUCTION

Terence's first play, *Andria,* or *The Girl from Andros,* is a relatively uncomplicated story of a young man named Pamphilus
who meets a young woman named Glycerium, makes love to her
and when she becomes pregnant promises to marry her. Pamphilus' father, Simo, intends for his son to marry the daughter
(named Philumena) of a rich friend, Chremes. Glycerium is a
statusless orphan who has come to Athens from the island of
Andros as the ward and virtually, if not legally, adopted daughter of a woman of Andros named Chrysis. Chrysis has earned her
living and amassed her property in a house next door to Simo's
by living as a hetaira, an agreeable companion to various younger
and older men who are free citizens of Athens. When Chrysis dies
she entrusts Glycerium to Pamphilus, who promises to care for
her and to acknowledge the paternity of their child. In the last
act of the play Crito, Chrysis' cousin, comes from Andros to
Athens to establish his legal claim, as next of kin, to Chrysis'
property.

A friend of Pamphilus, named Charinus, is in love with
Philumena and wants to marry her. He is of course disconcerted
by Simo's efforts to negotiate a marriage contract with Chremes
between Pamphilus and Philumena. At Chrysis' funeral Simo had
begun to suspect that his son was actually in love with Glycerium.
Soon afterwards Chremes learns that this is in fact the case and
promptly cancels the wedding bargain. But Simo continues to
pretend to Pamphilus that the wedding is on, to ascertain how
Pamphilus really feels toward his inamorata and how he will react
to his father's wishes and better judgment.

Davus, Simo's chief household slave and by extension the
mentor and guide for young Pamphilus, plans a series of moves

to help Pamphilus hang on to Glycerium, trying to thwart the schemes of Simo and to resolve Pamphilus' nervewracking dilemma. Glycerium gives birth to a baby boy. Davus is very hard put to it to maneuver around this mixed blessed event, but he keeps plotting. The action comes to a showdown between father and son. At this point Crito wanders in from Andros. Although he came to eye Chrysis' property, when he hears of the situation he looks sympathetically on the predicament. He of course knows the whole story of how Chrysis adopted Glycerium in the first place, and who Glycerium is. When these facts are brought out in a scene between Crito, Chremes, and Simo, they provide the means for moving Pamphilus from despair and anxiety into the sphere of contentment known to young people as love and marriage.

I said "relatively uncomplicated." We see in Terence's later plays, the *Phormio* and *The Brothers*, how much more intricately Terence can fashion his double plots. Here he writes of simpleminded true love and young passion, a trial for Pamphilus because the woman of his choice is not acceptable to his father. Even Simo had to admit that when he saw Glycerium at Chrysis' funeral she was a lovely person, "fair and noble":

> *erat forma praeter ceteras*
> *honesta ac liberali*

(ll. 122–23)

But a Roman father (in the convention of the play, Greek) could not tolerate his son's marrying a courtesan. Besides, Chremes' offer included a handsome dowry in the amount of something like $20,000. Simo cannot see that Pamphilus' love for Glycerium is the real thing. As for Pamphilus, this fact is nearly all he can see and it blinds him to almost everything else, so that he is very grateful to Davus for looking out for him. One unwavering element in Pamphilus' character is his love for Glycerium, and his sense of responsibility toward her. Another is his respect for his father and his sense of filial responsibility. He does not wish to defy his father's wishes. Simo, for his part, manifests a good share of respect and affection for his son.

How this plot, this play, this *fabula* can proceed to a happy ending remains to be seen. But that it might is contained as much in the character of father and son as it is in the deft, often impromptu action.

In 1930 Thornton Wilder wrote a novel called *The Woman of Andros,* a version and a transformation of this story. He changed many elements and ended by converting it into a tragedy. He suffused Terence's world with melancholy by adhering to the pastoral setting of the island of Andros, by altering the plot, and by envisaging the birth scene as a premonition of the Nativity. Well, why not? Terence is as much an *anima naturaliter Christiana* as Virgil was—he believed in faith, hope and love. But for Terence the greatest of these was hope. Wilder tinkered craftily with the plot, and as a young writer probably still remembered his brief days as a Latin teacher. In his novel Pamphilus and Glycerium are reconciled by Simo's purchase of Glycerium from a slave-dealer after Chrysis' death. Glycerium is brought to Pamphilus' home and looked after there; she dies in childbirth, as does the child. A little like the bridge of San Luis Rey, then, the affection of these people collapsed of its own weight and of the traffic of other people using it. Wilder's Simo tries to discuss the matter reasonably with Pamphilus:

Well, to begin with, it's only right to face the fact that there is no outward obligation to marry the girl. I've looked into the matter. She is not a Greek citizen. She happens to have been brought up in a sheltered manner, or so I take it. . . . Now, mind you, I can see that she is modest and well-mannered. . . . But she could never have hoped for anything above the situation she is now in. The world is full of just such likable stray girls as this Glycerium, but we cannot be expected to welcome them into the fabric of good Greek family life. You may be sure that Chrysis knew perfectly well that Glycerium must some day become a hetaira like herself, or a servant. [p. 120]

Pamphilus is not persuaded by Simo's practical remarks, so the father does decide to give Glycerium to Pamphilus on his own terms, rather capitalistic and mercenary, if I may say so. But the destined childbirth, in Wilder's version, results in death.

Terence meant for these young people to live.

PALMER BOVIE

THE GIRL FROM ANDROS

First Performance: The Games for the Great Mother (*ludi mega-lenses*, April 4–9); the third day of this festival was devoted to plays. Licensed by the curule aediles Marcus Fulvius and Manlius Glabrio.
Production: Lucius Ambivius Turpio and Lucius Hatilius of Prae-neste.
Music: Scored for equal flutes by Flaccus, freedman of Claudius.
Greek Original: Menander.
Written in 166 B.C., in the consulship of Marcus Marcellus and Gaius Sulpicius.

CHARACTERS

SIMO, father of Pamphilus
SOSIA, his freedman
DAVUS, his slave
PAMPHILUS, a young man, Simo's son
CHARINUS, a young man, in love with Chremes' daughter
CHREMES, a father
CRITO, an older man, from Andros
BYRRIA, a slave of Charinus
MYSIS, a slave girl in the service of Glycerium
GLYCERIUM, a young woman

CANTHARA, an older woman, a midwife from Lesbos
DROMO, a slave of Simo, a bodyguard

SCENE: *The entire action takes place on a street in Athens, in front of the houses of Simo and of Glycerium.*

PROLOGUE [1]

When your poet first put his mind to writing
He thought the only thing he had to do
Was please people with plays that he composed.
But now he sees it's a much different order.
He wastes a lot of time writing prologues,
Not to unfold the plot, but to reply
To jealous charges from an older poet.[2]
I ask you now to note what they impute
As his fault. Menander wrote two plays,
The Girl from Andros, and *The Girl from Perinthos.*
To know one of them is to know them both,   10
They are so alike in plot; and yet they vary
In thought and expression. Terence admits
He transferred from *The Girl from Perinthos*
What suited him, to his *The Girl from Andros,*
To use as his. The old poet and his clique
Abuse Terence for doing this, maintaining
It's improper to combine two different plays.
Does not their knowledge show plainly they know
Nothing? Accusing Terence, they also accuse
Naevius, Plautus, Ennius, our poet's models,
Whose negligence he'd rather imitate   20

---

[1] Spoken by L. Ambivius Turpio, the manager of the troupe and the most famous actor in Rome before Roscius. A man like Molière, or Louis Barrault, no doubt.

[2] The poet Lucius Lanuvinus, a detractor of Terence's work.

Than the musty accuracy of those critics.
I warn them to keep still from this time on,
And stop cursing him.
                             Keep silence now,
Good audience, and try the case before you
In a friendly and fair-minded attitude,
So you can judge what you have to expect
And if his future comedies will be
Ones you may want to watch the whole way through
Or drive off stage before they've been seen through.

ACT I

Scene 1

SIMO, SOSIA [3]

SIMO (*To servants*): Take these things inside. Get going. But,
    Sosia,
    Wait here a moment. I want a few words with you.   29
SOSIA: What's on your mind? You want things done up brown?
SIMO: In fact, it's something quite different from dinner.
SOSIA: What larger scope do you have for my skill?
SIMO: There's no need now for special cleverness
    In what I'm planning but those qualities
    I know you have, loyalty and discretion.
SOSIA: I'm eager to know what you wish.
SIMO: Sosia,
    You are well aware how fair and considerate

---

[3] A character invented by Terence, not taken from Menander, who appears
only here. As a "protatic figure" (the Greek term for this role), he is a person
outside the plot who has no further part in the action, used to explain the plot
through his dialogue with Simo as the play begins.

I've been to you from the time when I bought you
As a little boy. I made you my freedman
Because you always worked so generously.
I paid you with the best reward I had.

SOSIA: I bear that well in mind.

SIMO: I would not change it.   40

SOSIA: Thank goodness. I'm pleased if anything I have done,
Or am doing, pleases you. That it has
Already pleased you is sufficient thanks for me.
But I am bothered when you mention it:
You seem to be reproaching me somewhat
As if I had forgotten your kindness.
In one word, say what it is you want of me.

SIMO: I will. And first, I'll let you in on this,
What you think is a wedding is not real.

SOSIA: Then why pretend it is?

SIMO: You'll hear it all
From the beginning. And so you'll come to know
My son's manner of life, my plans for him,
And what I want you to do in this case.   50
After he was twenty and so could live
More freely on his own—up to that time,
While youth and shyness and a constant mentor
Kept him reined in, how could you really know
His character?

SOSIA: Quite so.

SIMO: He went about
His life the way most adolescents do
Who get wrapped up in some consuming interest:
They breed horses or hunting dogs, or go
To hear philosophers. He didn't work
At any one of these things harder than
At the others, but kept them all in hand
With average skill. Well, I was overjoyed.   60

SOSIA: And rightly so. For "nothing in excess"
Is, I think, a prime factor in our lives.

SIMO: His style of life was to fit neatly in
With others' style, and to comply with all.

Whoever he was with he gave in to
And followed their pursuits. He crossed no one
And never put himself ahead of them.
This is the simplest way to win regard
Without any envy and win yourself good friends.
SOSIA: He ordered his life wisely. For today
 Fawning makes friends, truth breeds hostility.
SIMO: Meanwhile, three years ago a certain woman
 From Andros moved into this neighborhood,   70
 A lovely woman, in the bloom of youth,
 Driven here by her relatives' neglect
 And her own poverty.
SOSIA: I fear the woman of Andros
 Imports some mischief.
SIMO: Modestly, at first,
 She lived a frugal and demanding life
 And earned her food by working at the loom.
 But after first one lover came to her,
 Promising a good price for her favors,
 And then another—quite in keeping with
 The human tendency to incline more
 Toward pleasure than labor—she gave in
 On their terms and made that her source of income.
 The men in love with her at that time chanced   80
 To take my son along to dinner there.
 I told myself, "Well, now he's hooked. He's had it."
 I'd watch out for their slaves in the morning,
 Running errands, and ask them, "Tell me, lad,
 If you don't mind, who had Chrysis yesterday?"
 That was the name of the woman of Andros.
SOSIA: I see.
SIMO: They'd name Phaedrus or Clinia,
 Or Niceratus, her three favorites at the time.
 "But what about Pamphilus?" I went on.
 "What about him? He just chipped in his share
 And dined with them. Well, I was overjoyed.
 Another day, I asked them the same thing
 And found out nothing that involved Pamphilus.   90

I thought my son was well enough tested,
A model specimen of self-control;
Since one exposed to characters like these
Whose own spirit is still not taken in
By such contact, is fully capable,
You know, of managing his own existence.
That pleased me, and all men with one voice said
All sorts of good things about him, and praised
My good luck in having a son endowed
With such a character. But why waste words?
Impressed by this good reputation, Chremes   100
Came to me unbidden and betrothed
His only daughter as wife to my son,
With a tremendous dowry. I agreed
And promised him in marriage. And today
Was picked for the wedding.

SOSIA: So what prevents
The rites from taking place?

SIMO: You'll hear what does.
A few days after this had all been done
Chrysis, our neighbor, died.

SOSIA: That turned out well.
You give me joy. I was afraid for him
Because of Chrysis.

SIMO: Thereupon, my son
Was often with those who had loved Chrysis,
And helped them with the funeral arrangements.
From time to time he was very depressed,
And shed tears bitterly from time to time.
But I thought well of that, for I kept musing:
"He takes so personally the death of someone   110
He knew but slightly. Just suppose he had
Loved her himself. How would he mourn for me,
His father?" I thought of it as the duty
Of a humane spirit and a tender heart.
But let me cut this short. I went along,
For his sake, to the funeral, still thinking
No mischief was afoot.

SOSIA: Could there have been?
SIMO: You'll hear. The body was borne out, we walked
  Along behind. Among the women there
  I happened to see one girl in particular
  Whose beauty . . .
SOSIA: . . . was, no doubt, dazzling.
SIMO: In appearance
  Demure and charming, quite beyond compare.
  Because she seemed to me to be mourning
  More than the other women, and surpassed them
  In the noble freedom of her figure, I went up   120
  To ask of her attendants who she was.
  They told me she was Chrysis' sister. Right there
  It struck me. Ah, that's it. This is the source
  Of all those tears of his.[4] She is the source
  Of sympathy.
SOSIA: I dread the way you're going.
SIMO: The procession moved on, and we followed it.
  We reached the burial site. Chrysis' body
  Was lifted to the pyre. The women wept.
  And then the sister I mentioned went up
  So closely to the flames she was in danger.   130
  And that was when Pamphilus, in alarm,
  Disclosed the passion he had kept concealed
  So far and well dissembled. He ran forward
  And put his arms around that woman's waist,
  Saying, "Glycerium, my own, what are you doing?
  Why are you trying to destroy yourself?"
  And she, so that you could see readily
  How mutual their passion was, fell back
  Against him, weeping most affectionately.
SOSIA: What's that you say!
SIMO: I came home sick at heart,
  Angry, but not with any good reason
  To reprove him. He might say, "What did I
  Do, father, to deserve reproach? Have I   140

  [4] *hinc illae lacrimae,* an expression that became proverbial and was quoted,
for instance, by Horace and Cicero.

Offended you? I kept back one who wished
To throw herself into the flames; I saved her."
A proper way to put it.
SOSIA: You're quite right.
If you blame one who helped to save a life,
What can you do to one who inflicts harm
Or loss?
SIMO: The next day, Chremes came to see me,
Shouting "foul play," and saying he'd found out
That Pamphilus had had this foreign girl
As his wife. I denied, scrupulously,
That such could be the case, but he insisted
It was a fact. And when at last I left him
The understanding was that he no longer
Was offering his daughter.
SOSIA: You took your son . . . ?
SIMO: In hand? No. This charge still did not seem strong
Enough to face him with.
SOSIA: Why not? Do tell.   150
SIMO: "But father, you yourself," he might well say,
"Have put an end to this sort of conduct.
The time draws near when I must learn to live
According to another person's humor.
So meanwhile let me live in my own way."
SOSIA: What place is left then for reproving him?
SIMO: If he will not marry, because of love,
That, first of all, is an offense for which
He may be censured. So I have set myself
The task of finding, by this feigned marriage,
Real grounds for blame, if he refuses it.
I also want to see that rascal Davus [5]
Try any schemes he has in mind right now,
While his deceptions cannot do me harm.   160
He'll strive with might and main, and hands and feet,
To pull off something, more to outwit me
Than to oblige my son.

[5] Davus, Simo's slave and by extension his son's slave and friend, is the typical
intelligent slave of Roman comedy, helpful and resourceful and often caught in
his own net.

SOSIA: But why will he?
SIMO: You ask? That's just the way his tricky mind
   Works, and his shifty heart. And if I catch him
   I won't have to go on describing him.
   If it turns out as I wish, and Pamphilus
   Does not want to put off the wedding day,
   I still will have to bring Chremes around.
   I hope it all works out. Now, your mission
   Is to pretend, and make it look convincing,
   That the wedding is on, to panic Davus,
   To watch my son and see what he's up to,
   What counsel he is taking with Davus.
SOSIA: I see my charge and I'll look after it.   170
SIMO: Let's go inside. You first. I'll be right there.
   (*Exit* SOSIA)

Scene 2

SIMO, DAVUS

SIMO: No doubt about my son's unwillingness
   To take a wife. I saw how Davus flinched
   When he heard that the wedding would be held.
   But here he comes.
DAVUS (*Not seeing* SIMO): I'm not sure now precisely
   How things stand. And this constant forbearance
   On master's part makes me rather suspicious
   Of where it is leading. After he heard
   That a wife would not be given to his son
   He never said a word to any of us;
   He took it calmly.
SIMO (*Aside*):   He may have words now
   For you, and they will cost you heavily.
DAVUS: He wanted us to be led on, unsuspecting,   180
   By pretense of pleasure, to keep hoping

That fear could now be laid aside. So then
He'd catch us napping and leave us no room
For thwarting the marriage. It's well thought out.
SIMO (*Aside*): What is that scoundrel saying?
DAVUS: There's the master,
I hadn't see him.
SIMO: Davus!
DAVUS: Uh, what is it?
SIMO: Come over here to me.
DAVUS (*Aside*):   What does he want?
SIMO: I say . . .
DAVUS: You were discussing what?
SIMO: You ask?
The rumor is my son's in love.
DAVUS: You know how people are,
Always taking in rumors.
SIMO: Please concentrate
On what I'm saying.
DAVUS: Concentrated, sir.
SIMO: It's not proper for a father to pry
Into his son's affairs. I let him act
In keeping with his age and to fulfill
His curiosity. But this day brings
Another life and calls for different habits.
I call on you, or better, ask of you,   190
Davus, that he return to the right road,
Right now. What road? A man in the middle of
A love affair reacts strongly against
Having a wife conferred on him.
DAVUS: So they say.
SIMO: If he has had an evil counselor
In this affair, the preceptor will guide
A mind already lovesick by itself
Into the worse direction, usually.
DAVUS: I don't quite follow you.
SIMO: You don't?
DAVUS: I don't.

I'm only David, I'm not Solomon.
These words would be complex for Oedipus.[6]
SIMO: Would you like me to come right out and say
What else I have in mind?
DAVUS: I would indeed.
SIMO: If I catch you playing any tricks today
To thwart the marriage, or just to show off
How very smart you are at things like this,
I'll hand you over, well flogged, to the mill
To grind flour until your dying day
On the sole condition and terms that if
I ever set you free, I'll grind for you.   200
Now do you follow me, or is that still
Not clear?
DAVUS: Perfectly clear. You came right out
With the plain truth, and did not circle around
The subject.
SIMO: I would rather be deceived
In anything than this.
DAVUS: Are your fingers crossed?
SIMO: Oh, making fun of me? You don't fool me.
I tell you: Don't do anything impulsive.
And don't say you weren't warned. You just watch out.
(*Exit* SIMO)

Scene 3

DAVUS

DAVUS: Well Davus, there's no time for hanging back
Or playing dumb, so far as I have grasped
The old man's sentiments about the wedding.
If that's not taken care of cleverly

---

[6] Davus merely says: *Davus sum, non Oedipus.* I have embroidered the
remark slightly.

It's bound to sink me or my young master.
I'm not sure what to do, help Pamphilus
Or heed the old man's words. If I fail him
I fear for his life, if I help him out
I fear his father's threats. He's not a man   210
To toy with. First, he's found out all about
This love affair, and then he watches me,
Ready to strike, if I try to devise
Some scheme to thwart the wedding. Should he find
Me out, I'm lost. He has a whim of iron.
He'll make the most of any opportunity
To clap me, right or wrong, into the mill.
Another matter complicates my troubles:
That woman of Andros, whether his wife
Or mistress, is most certainly pregnant
By Pamphilus. It's worth the price of admission
To hear of their intrepid course of action,
Decided on by lunatics, not lovers.
They have resolved to acknowledge the child,
Whatever it is. They are inventing   220
A story that the girl is an Athenian
Free citizen. "For once upon a time
There was an old merchant who came from here:
He was shipwrecked off the island of Andros,
And there he met his death. Then, after that,
Chrysis' father adopted this small child
An outcast orphan daughter." Pack of lies.
It doesn't seem to me even made up
To look like truth. But their fiction appeals
To them. Here comes Mysis, from the girl's house.
I'll head for the forum to meet Pamphilus,
So his father does not come across him
And catch him unaware of what's afoot.
(*Exit*)

Scene 4

MYSIS

MYSIS (*Calling back inside*): I heard you the first time, Archylis,
   You want the woman from Lesbos brought here.
   (*To herself*) That's some midwife! Sloppy drunken slut,
   Hardly the sort you'd care to trust a woman   230
   With for her first child. But still, shall I
   Go get her? See what nags old women are:
   Because she's her drinking companion! Ye gods,
   I pray you, grant an easy delivery
   To this girl, and assign to someone else
   The place where that midwife makes her mistakes.
   Is that Pamphilus, wild-eyed and breathless?
   I'm worried. Let me watch from over here
   (*She goes to one side*) To find out whether this wrought-up
     condition
   Brings us bad news.

Scene 5

PAMPHILUS, MYSIS

PAMPHILUS: Is it human to do
   Or think of a thing like this? Is this the role
   A father plays?
MYSIS (*Aside*):   What's that?
PAMPHILUS: By the gods' faith,
   What is this but an insult. He decided
   To give a wife to me today. Ought I not

To have known in advance, and shouldn't he
Have talked to me about it first?
MYSIS: Poor me,
What words I'm hearing!
PAMPHILUS: Why would Chremes, who   240
Had refused to make his daughter my wife,
Change that decision when he saw that I
Had not changed my position? Stubbornly bent
On taking luckless me from Glycerium?
If that happens, I'm done for totally.
Is any man so unlucky in love,
So unhappy as I am? Oh, faith of gods
And men! Is there for me no way out of
Attachment with Chremes? Despised and scorned
So many different ways. Arrangements made,
The whole thing settled. I, the once rejected,
Am in demand again. But why, unless
Because, as I suspect, they have brought up
Such a monster in their bosom she can't
Be fobbed off on a soul, she goes to me.   250
MYSIS (Aside): This lengthy speech makes poor me faint with
     fear.
PAMPHILUS: Ah, how can I describe my father, doing
So large a thing as this so casually?
Just now catching up with me in the forum,
He said, "Today you take a wife, Pamphilus.
Go home and get ready." Which seemed to me as good
As saying, "Go right now and hang yourself."
I was stunned. You think I could get a word out?
Make some excuse, however crude and foolish
And implausible? I didn't say a word.
If someone now asks me what I would do
If I had known before: I would do anything
To keep from doing this. But now, how first
Shall I proceed? My worries hem me in
And drag my mind in different directions.   260
My passion, my concern for this poor girl,
This pressing marriage, and the real respect

I have for my father. Up to this point
He has put up with me indulgently
And let me do just what I wanted to.
Could I defy him? Blast me! I don't know
What to do.

MYSIS: Oh dear, I'm fearful of
Where that "I don't know" may be coming out.
I really must say something to him now
About her, face to face, or he must talk
With her, while his mind is not yet made up
And can be turned in one way or the other
By a slight impulse.

PAMPHILUS: Who's talking over there?
Oh, Mysis, greetings.

MYSIS: Oh, Pamphilus, greetings.

PAMPHILUS: How is she?

MYSIS: You ask? Her labor pains
Have come on, and she is upset as well
Because your wedding was planned for today.
Then too, she is afraid you may leave her.   270

PAMPHILUS: Could I attempt a thing like that, could I
Let that poor girl be cheated for my sake,
Who trusted her whole life and soul to me, whom I
Have loved with a true husband's love,
As one especially dear to me? Would I
Let such a well and properly brought up
And educated mind be forced into
Changing its nature out of poverty?
I will not do that.

MYSIS: I would have no fears
If it rested with you alone. I do worry
If you can bear up under these pressures.

PAMPHILUS: You think me so lazy, so unfeeling,
Indeed inhuman or unnatural,
That neither our familiarity
Or mutual affection and respect
Will not impel me, will not tell me to
Keep faith with her?

MYSIS: I only know one thing,   280
  That she deserves that you remember her.
PAMPHILUS: Remember? Mysis, Mysis, even now
  The words Chrysis said to me about her
  Are written in my heart. As she lay dying
  She called me to her. I went in, while you
  Others withdrew, and when we were alone
  She began, "Dear Pamphilus, you see
  How young and beautiful Glycerium is.
  To you it's no secret how flimsy is
  The value of her charm and inexperience
  To her for safeguarding her reputation
  And her income. I beg of you, therefore,
  By this right hand, and by your better self,
  And ask you to swear, by your own good faith,   290
  And by her helpless, lonely state, that you
  Will not put her aside, abandon her.
  If I have loved you as my own brother,
  If she has always made you her one man
  Worth loving, and in every way has sought
  To please you, I confer you on her now,
  As husband, friend, adviser, and father.
  All I own I bestow on you, I commit
  This to your trust." And then she gave the girl
  Into my possession. And right away,
  Death came to Chrysis. I received this girl.
  I will protect what I received.
MYSIS: I hope so.
PAMPHILUS: But why are you away from her?
MYSIS: I'm going
  To bring the midwife.
PAMPHILUS: Hurry then. But listen:
  Don't breathe a word about the marriage, or,
  In her present condition . . .
MYSIS: I understand.   300

ACT II

Scene 1

CHARINUS, BYRRIA, PAMPHILUS

CHARINUS: What's that, Byrria? She'll be given today
  To Pamphilus in marriage?
BYRRIA: That's what it is
CHARINUS: How do you know?
BYRRIA: I heard it from Davus
  Just now in the forum.
PAMPHILUS: What a blow for me!
  My heart has been swaying in suspense so far,
  From hope to fear, but with that hope removed
  It's gone slack and feels dazed, worn out with worry.
  By Pollux, I tell you, Charinus, when
  What you want to happen cannot be
  You have to wish for something else that can.
CHARINUS: I want nothing except Philumena.[7]
BYRRIA: You'd be much better off to get her off
  Your mind than to remind yourself how much
  Your passion yearns for what is denied it.
CHARINUS: We all give good advice to sick people
  When we are well. Were you this fellow here,
  You'd feel quite different.
BYRRIA: Have it your way, then.   310
CHARINUS: I see Pamphilus. My mind's made up to try
  Everything before I sink.

[7] Chremes' daughter (his *other* daughter, as it turns out happily for both Charinus and Pamphilus).

BYRRIA (*Aside*):   What does he mean?

CHARINUS: I'll talk to him himself, I'll plead with him
  And tell him of my love. I may succeed
  In having the wedding put off, at least
  For a few days. Meanwhile something, I hope,
  May turn up.

BYRRIA (*Aside*): That "something" sounds like nothing.

CHARINUS: What do you think, Byrria? Shall I confront him?

BYRRIA: Why not? If you gain nothing else by it
  You'll let him know that if he marries her
  He has a ready-made adulterous rival.

CHARINUS: Go hang, and take your foul suggestion with you!

PAMPHILUS (*Approaching*): I see Charinus. Greetings.

CHARINUS: Oh, greetings,
  Pamphilus. I come to you in search
  Of hope, of help, of rescue, of advice.

PAMPHILUS: I have neither the time to counsel you
  Nor resources for help. But what's at stake?   320

CHARINUS: You take a wife today?

PAMPHILUS: That's what they say.

CHARINUS: If you do, Pamphilus, this is the last
  Day you see me.

PAMPHILUS: But why?

CHARINUS: Oh, lord, I wish
  I didn't have to say. You tell him, Byrria.

BYRRIA: I'll tell him.

PAMPHILUS: What is it?

BYRRIA: He loves your bride.

PAMPHILUS: He doesn't share my feelings, I assure you.
  But come on, tell me now, Charinus, has something
  More than mere affection been going on
  Between you two?

CHARINUS: Good lord, Pamphilus, nothing.

PAMPHILUS: Oh, how I wish it had!

CHARINUS: For our friendship,
  I beg you, first of all: Don't marry her.

PAMPHILUS: I'll do my best not to.

CHARINUS: And if you fail,
  Or find the marriage to your taste . . .
PAMPHILUS: My taste?
CHARINUS: Postpone it for a day or two, while I
  Set out for foreign parts, and can't see it.
PAMPHILUS: Listen to me, Charinus. I don't think   330
  A true man ought to count it as a favor
  If he does nothing that deserves credit.
  I want to get out of these wedding rites
  As much as you want to get into them.
CHARINUS: You've saved my life.
PAMPHILUS: If you can do something—
  Or Byrria here—well, do it. Make it up,
  Invent a plan, and bring it into play,
  Some means in which she can be given you.
  And I'll do what I can to see that she
  Is not conferred on me.
CHARINUS: I'm with you there.
PAMPHILUS: I see good old Davus. It's his advice
  I lean on hard.
CHARINUS (*To* BYRRIA):
                         But you're no help to me
  At all, except in what I know already.
  So won't you just take off?
BYRRIA: I'll be glad to.

Scene 2

DAVUS, CHARINUS, PAMPHILUS

DAVUS: Good gods! I've got good news. But where
  Will I find Pamphilus, to empty out
  The fear his heart now holds and fill it up
  With pleasure?
CHARINUS: For some reason, he's happy.   340

PAMPHILUS: No matter. He has not found out about
  Our troubles yet.
DAVUS: I'll bet that if he's heard
  About the marriage plans for him, right now . . .
CHARINUS: Do you hear him?
DAVUS: . . . he's searching the whole town
  For me, with his heart in his mouth. But where
  Shall I look for him? Where shall I start first?
CHARINUS: Why don't you speak to him?
DAVUS: Oh, I know where.
PAMPHILUS: Hey, Davus, wait! Come over here.
DAVUS: Who is that man
  Calling me? Pamphilus, I was looking
  For you. Charinus, too. Good show: both here
  At just the right time. I wanted you both.
PAMPHILUS: Davus, I'm done for.
DAVUS: Wait till you hear this.
PAMPHILUS: I'm ruined.
DAVUS: I know what makes you afraid.
CHARINUS: By Hercules, my life is also, doubtless,
  Doubtful.
DAVUS: I also know what's troubling you.
PAMPHILUS: This wedding of mine.
DAVUS: Although I know about it . . .
PAMPHILUS: Today.
DAVUS: You keep on harping on it, though
  I have the information? You're afraid
  You'll marry her; and you, that you will not.
CHARINUS: You sum it up.
PAMPHILUS: That's just the situation.   350
DAVUS: Yet, there's no danger in the situation.
  You can look to me for that.
PAMPHILUS: Oh, then, I beg you,
  Release poor anxious me from my worries.
DAVUS: All right. I set you free. Chremes is not
  About to give a wife to you.
PAMPHILUS: How so?
  How do you know?

DAVUS: I know. Just now, your father
  Took me aside to say he would today
  Give you a wife. He made some more remarks
  But there's not time to go into all that.
  I raced right off to the forum to catch you
  And relay this news. Not finding you there,
  I climbed up on a vantage point and looked
  Around, this way and that. You were nowhere.
  I met Charinus' slave Byrria there
  And asked if he had seen you. He said no.
  A bit baffled, I wondered what to do.
  And coming back, a phony element
  In the whole act came to my mind. "But wait,"
  I thought, "he hadn't bought much food; and he
  Seemed in a bad mood. Then, these wedding plans
  Were made so fast. It doesn't hold together."   360

PAMPHILUS: Where does that lead?

DAVUS: It led me straight to Chremes.
  I got to his door: all was quiet there.
  So I was very glad.

CHARINUS: That sounds hopeful.

PAMPHILUS: But go on.

DAVUS: I waited. I saw no one
  Go in; no one went out. No maid of honor
  In the house, no lavish decorations.
  No bustle. I went closer, looked inside.

PAMPHILUS: I know.

DAVUS: Do such conditions
  Signify a wedding?

PAMPHILUS: Perhaps not, Davus.

DAVUS: "Perhaps," he says. You just don't understand,
  It's absolutely sure. I also met
  Chremes' houseboy, as I was leaving there,
  Bringing some vegetables and a few cents worth of fish
  For the old man's dinner.

CHARINUS: Thanks to your work,
  Davus, I'm free today.

DAVUS: Oh, no, you're not.   370

CHARINUS: Why not? It's sure he won't give her to him.
DAVUS: Blockhead! As if it was a sure thing, then,
  That you will marry her if he does not
  Give her to him, without your looking sharp,
  Asking the old man's friends, and getting on
  Their good side.
CHARINUS: Good advice. I'll head off now
  And try that, even though my hopes that way
  Have been thwarted often already. Ciao.

Scene 3

PAMPHILUS, DAVUS

PAMPHILUS: What does father mean? Why does he pretend?
DAVUS: I'll tell you. If he now resents the fact
  That Chremes won't give you the wife before
  He's seen how you react to the marriage,
  He'll seem, in his eyes, wrong, and rightly so.
  But if you won't marry, he'll place the blame
  Squarely on you. And trouble will be made.   380
PAMPHILUS: I'll put up with anything.
DAVUS: He's your father,
  Pamphilus. That's the hard thing. And then, this woman
  Is quite defenseless. He'll find some reason,
  No sooner said than done, for getting rid
  Of her entirely.
PAMPHILUS: Getting rid?
DAVUS: And fast.
PAMPHILUS: What shall I do, Davus?
DAVUS: Say you'll marry her.
PAMPHILUS: Ouch.
DAVUS: What's up?
PAMPHILUS: Me say that?
DAVUS: And why not?

PAMPHILUS: I'll never do it.
DAVUS: Just don't say you won't.
PAMPHILUS: Don't urge me to.
DAVUS: But see what then results.
PAMPHILUS: I'll be excluded from Glycerium
　　And included with the girl in this house.
DAVUS: You won't. I think it goes like this. Your father
　　Will say, "I want you to marry, today,"
　　And you will say "I will marry." Now, tell
　　Me how he can hold anything against you.
　　You'll render his whole scheme, which now looks safe　　390
　　To him, unsafe, and not run any risk.
　　There can be no doubt that Chremes will not
　　Give you his daughter. But do not desist
　　From your present conduct, in case he does
　　Change his mind. Tell your father you're willing,
　　And even though he may want to, he can't
　　With justice show any anger at you.
　　If you entertain thoughts such as "Well, now,
　　With these habits I'll drive off any wife
　　Quite easily. No one will give me one"—
　　Your father will come with any sort
　　Of penniless prospect before he'll let
　　You throw yourself away on this stranger.
　　But if he thinks that you are bearing up
　　With equanimity, you will have made
　　Him careless and he'll go about his search
　　For another girl at his leisure. Meanwhile,
　　Some good may come of this.
PAMPHILUS: You think it will?
DAVUS: There's absolutely no doubt about that.
PAMPHILUS: See where you're leading me.
DAVUS: Won't you be still?
PAMPHILUS: I'll say I will. But do let's be careful
　　That he does not find out she has a child　　　　　　400
　　By me. I promised to acknowledge it.
DAVUS: What undivided gall!

PAMPHILUS: For Chrysis begged me
   To make her this promise, so she could know
   That Glycerium would never be abandoned.
DAVUS: We'll be careful. But here's your father now.
   Don't let him see that you are rather worried.

Scene 4

SIMO, DAVUS, PAMPHILUS

SIMO: I'm coming back to see what they are up to,
   What schemes they are hatching.
DAVUS (*To* PAMPHILUS):   He does not doubt
   That you'll refuse to marry. He's rehearsed
   His lines off somewhere by himself,
   And hopes he's found a way of putting it
   That will confuse you. Just make sure that you
   Have your wits about you.
PAMPHILUS (*To* DAVUS):   I only hope
   I have, Davus.
DAVUS (*To* PAMPHILUS):
          Trust me, Pamphilus. I say:
   Your father will not have a word to say   410
   To you today, if you agree to marry.

Scene 5

BYRRIA, SIMO, DAVUS, PAMPHILUS

BYRRIA (*Eavesdropping*): My master told me to drop everything
   And watch Pamphilus, so I might find out
   What he was doing with these wedding plans.

So here I come not to keep track of him.
There's my man with Davus. I'll listen in
On their conversation.
SIMO (*Approaching* DAVUS *and* PAMPHILUS): I see they're both
    here.
DAVUS (*To* PAMPHILUS): On guard.
SIMO: Pamphilus!
DAVUS (*To* PAMPHILUS):   Now look back
    As if you had just seen him.
PAMPHILUS: Oh, father!
DAVUS (*To* PAMPHILUS): Well said.
SIMO: As I told you, I want you to
    Take a wife today.
BYRRIA (*Aside*):   I'm worried, for our side,
    About his answer.
PAMPHILUS: You'll find no delay   420
    In me in that respect or any other.
BYRRIA (*Aside*): Good lord, what's this?
DAVUS (*To* PAMPHILUS):   You see, he's speechless.
BYRRIA (*Aside*): What did he say?
SIMO: You act becomingly,
    For I gain my request, and with good grace.
DAVUS (*To* PAMPHILUS): Was I not right?
BYRRIA (*Aside*):   From what I hear, my lord
    Has lost himself a wife.
SIMO: Go inside then,
    So when you are needed you will be ready.
PAMPHILUS: I'm going in.
BYRRIA (*Aside*):   Can no man be trusted
    For anything? But then, the common saying
    Is true that every man prefers his own
    Welfare to that of others. I've seen this girl.
    And I remember that she seemed to be
    A beautiful young girl. I'm on the side
    Of Pamphilus if he would rather he
    Held her in his dreams than have Charinus   430
    Do so. I will report so that Charinus
    Can give me a bad time for this bad news.

Scene 6

DAVUS, SIMO

DAVUS (*Aside*): This fellow thinks I'm bringing him some sort
   Of mischief, and stay here for that purpose.
SIMO: What does Davus have to say now? Something
   Along the same old lines? Or nothing? Hey?
DAVUS: Well, nothing much.
SIMO: But I was expecting as much.
DAVUS (*Aside*): It's come out rather beyond his expectations,
   I do believe, and this bothers the gentleman.
SIMO: Could you tell me the truth?
DAVUS: Nothing is simpler.
SIMO: The marriage doesn't bother him at all,
   In spite of his familiarity
   With this stranger, does it?
DAVUS: Not a bit—
   Or if it does still, slightly, his concern
   Will last two or three days, don't you know?
   Then he'll be over it. He has reconsidered   440
   In favor of the proper path.
SIMO: Good boy.
DAVUS: While he was entitled to it, and his youth
   Indicated, he had his love affair,
   And even that he conducted discreetly.
   He made sure the affair brought no gossip
   Down on him, as befits a gentleman.
   Now that a wife is called for, he has bent
   His mind on thoughts of marrying a wife.
SIMO: He seemed a bit on the sad side, to me.
DAVUS: But not because of the affair; rather,
   Because he's cross at you.
SIMO: Why should he be?

DAVUS: Oh, it's childish.

SIMO: What is it?

DAVUS: Oh, nothing.

SIMO: But won't you tell me?

DAVUS: He says you have spent

Too little on the feast.   450

SIMO: I have?

DAVUS: You have.

"He hardly laid out ten drachmas," he said.

"He doesn't look like he's giving his son

A wife. Which of my rich companions

Shall I invite to share this feast?" Between us,

I must say, you do look rather stingy.

SIMO: Oh, shut up.

DAVUS (*Aside*):   Ah, I got to him that time.

ACT III

Scene 1

MYSIS, SIMO, DAVUS, LESBIA,[8] (GLYCERIUM)

MYSIS: Well, then, of course it's just as you say, Lesbia,

You'll rarely find a man true to his woman.   460

SIMO (*Aside*): Isn't that the woman of Andros' servant?

DAVUS (*To* SIMO): I beg your pardon?

SIMO (*Aside*):   That's who it is.

MYSIS: But our Pamphilus . . .

SIMO (*Aside*):   What's she saying now?

MYSIS: Has made good on his word.

---

[8] Lesbia, i.e., a woman from the island of Lesbos. Her name is later given as Canthara, "Drinker."

SIMO (*Aside*):   Ugh!
DAVUS (*Aside*):   How I wish
That either she was mute, or he was deaf!
MYSIS: He ordered that the child she gave birth to
Was to be recognized as his.
SIMO (*Aside*):   Oh, Jupiter!
What am I listening to? The case is closed,
If what she says is true.
LESBIA: By your account
This is a young man of good character.
MYSIS: The very best. But come inside with me,
So you will be in time for her.
LESBIA: I'm coming.
DAVUS (*Aside*): What cure will I find now for this trouble?
SIMO (*Aside*): How can it be? Is he out of his mind?
A child by a foreign woman. Oh, wait . . .
Yes, that's it. I've just caught on, at last.   470
I was stupid.
DAVUS (*Aside*): What's he say he just caught on to?
SIMO (*Aside*): Here we have Davus' first clever maneuver:
They pretend she's giving birth, to scare off Chremes.
GLYCERIUM (*From inside the house*):
Juno Lucina! [9] Save me. Help, I pray.
SIMO (*Aside*): So sudden, eh? After she heard that I
Was here in front of her door, she
Got busy. (*To* DAVUS) Davus, your timing's way off.
DAVUS: *My* timing?
SIMO: Are your pupils so absent-minded?
DAVUS: I've no idea what you're talking about.
SIMO (*Aside*): Suppose he had attacked me by surprise
And the wedding was actually to be.
What fun he'd make of me. But as it is,
He's in deep water; I'm sailing around
Inside the harbor.   480

[9] From within, in childbirth, Glycerium calls on Juno in the goddess's aspect
as bringer of light and therefore patroness of childbirth.

Scene 2

LESBIA, SIMO, DAVUS

LESBIA (*Calling back inside*): Her symptoms, Archylis, as I see
   them
  Are all normal, and she's in good condition.
  Give her a bath, and see that she is given
  What I ordered to drink, and in the amount
  I mentioned. I'll be back here right away.
  (*To herself*) By Castor, that's a bouncing baby boy
  Born to Pamphilus. I only ask the gods
  To let him grow strong and well, since his father
  Is of good character, a man reluctant to
  Do any wrong to an excellent young woman.
SIMO (*To* DAVUS): And who would not believe, if he knew you,
  That this derived from you?
DAVUS: Now why is that?
SIMO: She didn't issue orders privately   490
  About what was to be done for the girl
  In childbirth, but after she came outside
  She shouted back to those inside the house.
  Davus, have you such low regard for me,
  Or do I seem to you so well suited
  To be your natural point of departure
  For such transparent tricks? You might at least
  Have had the subtlety to make it look
  As though I might cause fear if I found out.
DAVUS (*Aside*): By Hercules, it's truly he, not I
  Doing the deceiving now.
SIMO: I told you,
  I warned you, not to do it. But did you
  Respect my words? Did they do any good?
  Am I to trust you now in this affair
  Of that girl's bearing Pamphilus a child?

DAVUS (*Aside*): I see where he's gone wrong. I understand
 How I'm to handle it.
SIMO: Why not speak up?
DAVUS: Would you believe me? It's as if someone
 Told you about this trick ahead of time.
SIMO: Someone told me?
DAVUS: You mean, you figure out   500
 All by yourself, that this was just a ruse?
SIMO: You're mocking me.
DAVUS: Someone told you. How else
 Would that suspicion lodge in your mind?
SIMO: How?
 Because I know you.
DAVUS: But that's like saying
 It came from my prompting.
SIMO: I know it did.
DAVUS: You still don't know me well enough, Simo.
SIMO: I don't know you?
DAVUS: When I begin to tell
 You something, you begin to think, right off,
 I'm fooling you.
SIMO: And there's no grounds for that?
DAVUS: And so, by Hercules, I don't dare now
 Mutter one word.
SIMO: One thing I know for sure.
 No one gave birth in there.
DAVUS: You've found that out.
 So that's the way it is. Still, very soon,
 They'll leave a baby boy on your doorstep.
 I say to you, master, right now: they will,
 So you'll be in on it and not say later
 That this happened through Davus' plans and wiles.
 I'd like to see you rid of this idea.   510
SIMO: But how do you know this?
DAVUS: I heard it, and
 I believe it: many things fit in together
 That give grounds for my guess. The woman of Andros
 Said quite some time ago she was pregnant

By Pamphilus. That proved to be not true.
Now, after she sees a wedding is planned
At his home, she sends her maid right away
To get the midwife and to bring along
A baby boy. If it is not arranged
For you to see the child, the wedding plans
Are not going to change.

SIMO: But, look here, why
Did you not, when you learned what her plan was,
Tell Pamphilus about it right away?

DAVUS: Well, who got her away from him but me?
We all know well enough how desperately   520
He loved her. Now, he's looking for a wife.
So, let me wind up that business, and you
Keep right on working out the wedding plans
For your part, as you are doing. I hope
The gods will help you out with it.

SIMO: Not so fast:
You go inside the house and wait for me
In there, and see to what needs seeing to.
(*Exit* DAVUS)
He hasn't quite persuaded me as yet
To swallow this. And yet, perhaps it's true,
All that he said. I don't think much of it.
It means much more to me that my own son
Has given me his promise. I'll find Chremes,
And ask him for a wife for my son. Then,
If I prevail, what else could I wish for
Than have the marriage come about today?
The fact that my son promised me himself   530
Leaves no doubt that I can quite properly
Compel him to it, if he is unwilling.
Here's Chremes—right in time for our meeting.

Scene 3

SIMO, CHREMES

SIMO: Greetings, Chremes.
CHREMES: Oh, I was looking for you.
SIMO: And I for you. Lucky for me you're here.
CHREMES: Several people have come to me to say
  They heard from you that my daughter would marry
  Your son today. I'm back to see if you,
  Or they, are raving.
SIMO: Just listen a moment.
  You'll know what I wanted with you and what
  You came to find out.
CHREMES: I'm listening, so say
  What it is you want.
SIMO: I beg you, by the gods,
  Chremes, and in the name of our friendship
  That started in childhood and grew up with us,
  And in the name of your only daughter   540
  And of my son, whose fate lies in your hands,
  To help me in this matter and see that
  The wedding we had planned does come about.
CHREMES: Oh well now, don't implore me, as if you
  Could only win me over with your words.
  Do you think I'm a different person now
  From what I was when I offered my daughter
  To you just a short while ago? If this
  Will benefit them both, order the bride
  To be escorted here, but if it all
  Contains more harm than good for both of them
  I ask you to consult our common good,
  As if she were your daughter and I were
  Pamphilus' father.

SIMO: What I want, and ask,   550
Chremes, is for it to take place, and I
Would not ask that if the matter itself
Did not suggest it.
CHREMES: What is the matter?
SIMO: There's been a falling out between Glycerium
And my son.
CHREMES: So I hear.
SIMO: Severe enough
To make me hope that now he can be drawn
Away from her.
CHREMES: Nonsense!
SIMO: No: more like sense.
CHREMES: By Hercules, it's like this, I tell you:
Lovers' quarrels just make their love stronger.[10]
SIMO: Well, that's why I say let's go on ahead,
While we have time, while his passion is blocked
By spite, before these women's dirty tricks
And trumped-up tears lead back his lovesick heart
To pity them—let us give him a wife.   560
I hope that, with familiarity,
And bound to her in an honorable marriage,
Chremes, my son can extricate himself
From these troubles.
CHREMES: It may seem so to you,
But I don't think he can. And I don't think he can
Keep his mistress. I would not allow it.
SIMO: How can you know unless you try it out?
CHREMES: Trying that out with one's daughter is serious.
SIMO: The disadvantage, at the worst, comes down
To separation, if it should develop,
And may the gods prevent it. But again,
If my son learns to modify his ways,
See how many advantages there are.
Chiefly, you'll bring your friend's son back to him,   570
You'll gain a good son-in-law for yourself,
And a good husband for your daughter.

[10] *amantium irae amoris integratiost,* a typical Terentian maxim.

CHREMES: Well, then,
If you are really settled in your mind
That this is practical, I don't want you
Held up because of me.
SIMO: No wonder I
Have always thought the world of you, Chremes.
CHREMES: But here's a point.
SIMO: What's that?
CHREMES: How do you know
They've had a falling out?
SIMO: Davus himself
Told me, and he is in on all their plans.
He urged me to go through with the marriage
As soon as possible. He wouldn't do that,
Would he, unless he knew my son was after
The very same thing? But you'll hear it now
In his own words. Hey, inside there: tell Davus
To come out here. I see him coming out.   580

Scene 4

DAVUS, SIMO, CHREMES

DAVUS: I was coming to meet you.
SIMO: Why?
DAVUS: Well, why
Hasn't the bride been called? It's nearly evening.
SIMO (*To* CHREMES): You hear that now? (*To* DAVUS) I've been
    afraid of you
For some time now, Davus, worried that you,
Like any common slave, would play some trick
To fool me just because my son's in love.
DAVUS: I'd do a thing like that?
SIMO: I thought you might.
And fearing it, kept from you what I now
Will tell you.

DAVUS: Which is?

SIMO: You'll find out—for now
I almost have some confidence in you.

DAVUS: At last, you know what sort of man I am?

SIMO: This wedding was not to have taken place.

DAVUS: What's that? Why not?

SIMO: I only said it would,
To test your reactions.

DAVUS: Well, how about that!

SIMO: And that's a fact.

DAVUS: Just think. I never could
Have figured that all out. A crafty plan,
I must admit.

SIMO: But hear this: when I told
You to go in the house, my friend Chremes   590
Happened along at just the right time . . .

DAVUS (*Aside*): Oh, oh,
Are we in for it, after all?

SIMO: I told him
What you had just then reported to me . . .

DAVUS (*Aside*): Do I hear right?

SIMO: And asked him to confer
His daughter on my son, and managed to
Gain my request.

DAVUS (*Aside*): I'm dead. This is the end.

SIMO: I beg your pardon, what did you just say?

DAVUS: I said, a good deed, done by a good friend.

SIMO: And now he's ready to proceed.

CHREMES: I'll go
On home and tell them to get ready there,
And come back here and tell you when they are.
(*Exit* CHREMES)

SIMO: Now, Davus, I ask you, since you alone
Worked out this marriage for me . . .

DAVUS: Quite alone . . .

SIMO: Try next to get my son to mend his ways.

DAVUS: I'll do my best with that, by Hercules.

SIMO: And now you can, while he is still upset.

DAVUS: Well, rest assured.

SIMO: On with it, then. I wonder
   Where he is now?
DAVUS: Oh, probably at home.
SIMO: I'll go to him and tell him everything,
   Just as I told you it.
   (*Exit* SIMO)
DAVUS: I'm no one now.
   Why not take the shortest road to the mill?   600
   There's no way to beg off. I've wrecked it all,
   Misled my master, launched my master's son
   Into a marriage, made it all come out
   The way Pamphilus didn't want it to
   And Simo hardly dared to hope it would.
   That's ingenuity! If I'd kept quiet
   There would have been no trouble. Here's Pamphilus.
   I'm really done for now. I wish I had
   Some cliff handy to hurl myself over.

                            Scene 5

PAMPHILUS, DAVUS

PAMPHILUS: Where's that damned slave who ruined me?
DAVUS (*Aside*):   Done for.
PAMPHILUS: I must admit I deserved it, for being
   So dumb, so lacking in a plan as to
   Throw in my lot with a no-good slave. I'm paying
   For my foolishness, but he won't get off   610
   Unscarred.
DAVUS (*Aside*):
             If I get out of this tight spot,
   I know I'll never be in such danger
   Again.
PAMPHILUS:
         What can I say to my father?

That I'm unwilling to marry, when I
Just said I would? Have I the nerve
To try something like that? I don't know what
To do with myself.
DAVUS (*Aside*):   Even I don't know,
And I'm concentrating. I'll tell Pamphilus
I've hit on something, so as to fend off
Disaster for a while.
PAMPHILUS: Oh, there you are.
DAVUS (*Aside*): I've been spotted.
PAMPHILUS: Look here, my fine fellow,
You see how you've tied me up like a captive
With your advice?
DAVUS: But soon I'll get you out.
PAMPHILUS: You'll get me out?
DAVUS: Of course I will, Pamphilus.
PAMPHILUS: Of course: the way you got me in.
DAVUS: Oh, no,
Better, I hope.
PAMPHILUS: Can I trust you, you crook?
Can you set right what's gone wrong and trussed me
Up tight? Look at the man I leaned on hard.
Today you got me out of perfect peace   620
Into a marriage. Didn't I tell you
It would work out that way?
DAVUS: You did.
PAMPHILUS: So what
Do you deserve for that?
DAVUS: The cross, I guess.
But give me time to get my senses back;
I'll figure something out.
PAMPHILUS: I only wish
I had the time to take it out on you
The way I want. I only have the time
To take care of myself, and not of you.

ACT IV

Scene 1

CHARINUS, PAMPHILUS, DAVUS

CHARINUS: Incredible, isn't it?
Not fit to be mentioned, is it?
The heartlessness some people are born with!
They take delight in other peoples' troubles.
They revel in their fellow man's distress,
Compared to their good luck.
Can that be right?
No. They're the very worst sort of men
Who haven't got the candor, at the moment,   630
To say no. Then, when the time comes around
To make good on their word, inevitably
They are forced to show their true nature.
Some nerve, the way they talk:
"Just who are you, and what are you to me?
Why should I give my girl to you?
Can't you see I'm more interested in me?"
And if you ask, "But where is your good faith?"
They show no sense of shame when it's called for.
But when there's no need of it, they have it.[11]
What shall I do? Go up to him, and fling
The insult in his face? Pile on the abuse?   640
Someone may say, "You won't budge him a bit."

[11] Charinus' excited soliloquy is written in lyric meters quite different from
the standard long lines in strict iambics and trochaics Terence usually employs.
So I have rendered it as a recitativo.

I say, a lot. I'll give him lots of trouble
And satisfy my mind, to some extent.
PAMPHILUS (*Seeing* CHARINUS): Charinus, I was so impetuous
I've ruined you and me, unless the gods
Do us a favor.
CHARINUS: So impetuous?
So now at last you've found a good excuse?
You broke your word.
PAMPHILUS: So now at last?
CHARINUS: You still expect to lead me on again
With words of yours?
PAMPHILUS: Why say a thing like that?
CHARINUS: Because, after I said I loved the girl,
She started looking good to you. Dumb me!
I judged your attitude by my feelings.
PAMPHILUS: You're quite mistaken.
CHARINUS: Wasn't your pleasure
In getting her solid enough for you,
Without your getting around her lover,
Leading him on with false expectations?
Keep her.
PAMPHILUS: Keep her, you tell me? You don't know
How much trouble I'm caught up in and how
My tormentor adds on anxieties
With his advice.
CHARINUS: What's strange about that,   650
If you're his model?
PAMPHILUS: You wouldn't say that
If you knew me or knew my love.
CHARINUS: I know:
You've just now had a quarrel with your father.
He's angry with you and can't force you to
Marry today.
PAMPHILUS: But that's not it at all,
And shows how little you know of my woes.
There was no wedding planned for me at all.
No one expected to give me a wife.
CHARINUS: Oh, I know. You were forced to volunteer.

PAMPHILUS: Hold on, you don't know yet.

CHARINUS: What I do know
Is that you're going to marry that girl.

PAMPHILUS: Why rub it in? Listen. He never stopped   660
Urging me to tell my father I would;
He talked, and argued, until I gave in.

CHARINUS: Who did?

PAMPHILUS: Davus.

CHARINUS: Davus?

PAMPHILUS: Yes. He's the cause
Of all the confusion.

CHARINUS: Why?

PAMPHILUS: I don't know,
Unless the gods became angry at me
For listening to him.

CHARINUS: You did this, Davus?

DAVUS: Indeed I did.

CHARINUS: You, lowest of the low,
May the gods do you in, then, in a manner
In keeping with your deeds. Come on, tell me:
If all his enemies wanted him hurled
Into marriage, what else would they advise
If not precisely this?

DAVUS: I've been outsmarted,
But I'm not faint-hearted.

CHARINUS: I realize.

DAVUS: We didn't get there this way, so we'll take   670
A different path. Unless, of course, you think,
Because we made too little progress first,
This trouble can't be turned to our advantage.

PAMPHILUS: Oh, no! I'm sure, if you put your mind to it,
You'd contrive two weddings for me from one.

DAVUS: I owe it to you, in my slave status,
To strive both hand and foot and night and day,
To run the risk of death, provided that
I'm of some help to you. It's your duty,
If my hopes don't pan out, to pardon me.
What I'm up to has not had much success,

But I'm doing my best. Find something better
Yourself, if you like, and get rid of me.   680
PAMPHILUS: I want you. Get me back the situation
We started with
DAVUS: I'll do that.
PAMPHILUS: Do it now.
DAVUS: Well . . . wait: the door to Glycerium's house
Just creaked.
PAMPHILUS: That's nothing to you.
DAVUS: I'm thinking.
PAMPHILUS: Oh, finally you're thinking, now?
DAVUS: And soon
I'll give you the findings I've come up with.

Scene 2

MYSIS, PAMPHILUS, CHARINUS, DAVUS

MYSIS (*Calling back inside*): Wherever he is, I'll see that your
    Pamphilus
Is found and brought back home with me:
Don't you, my dear, keep tormenting yourself.
PAMPHILUS: Mysis!
MYSIS: Who is it? Oh there, Pamphilus.
You show up just at the right time.
PAMPHILUS: Why so?
MYSIS: My mistress said to ask you, if you love her,
To come to her. She says she's so eager
To see you.
PAMPHILUS: Lord! I'm finished. This trouble
Begins again. (*To* DAVUS) See what a sorry state
You've reduced her and me to by your work?
I'm called for now because she realizes
The wedding's being staged.   690
CHARINUS: A stage of things

That could have been avoided easily,
If he had kept quiet.

DAVUS: Go on, keep at it.
As if the man was not beside himself,
All by himself; keep goading him.

MYSIS: Well, gracious knows, that's just the way it is,
And why the poor girl is prostrate with grief.

PAMPHILUS: I swear to you by all the gods, Mysis,
I will never desert her, even if
I know that all mankind must be taken
As enemies of mine. I sought her out,
And fortune made her mine. We suit each other.
Farewell to those who would keep us apart.
No one but death will sever her from me.

MYSIS: I'm coming to my senses.

PAMPHILUS: Apollo's word
Is no truer than what I say to you.
If we can keep my father from thinking
The marriage was held up because of me,
All right. If not, I'll take the easy way   700
And let him know I was the obstacle.
How do I look to you?

CHARINUS: As sick as I do.

DAVUS: I'm searching for a plan.

PAMPHILUS: Well, good for you!
I know: something to take effect . . .

DAVUS: Effectively,
For you.

PAMPHILUS: I need it now.

DAVUS: But I've got it.

CHARINUS: Got what?

DAVUS: For him, not you. Don't get me wrong.

CHARINUS: All right. I'll wait.

PAMPHILUS: What will you do? Tell me.

DAVUS: I'm not even sure today is long enough
For me to do it. Don't think I have time
To discuss it. Clear off now, both of you.
You're only in my way.

PAMPHILUS: I'll go see her.
    (*Exit*)
DAVUS (*To* CHARINUS): And why are you hanging around?
CHARINUS: You really
    Want to know?
DAVUS: Sure. The first part of a speech
    Is heading my way.
CHARINUS: Well, what about me?
DAVUS: You're foolish, that's what. Isn't it enough   710
    That I give you a little extra time
    By putting off the wedding?
CHARINUS: Still, Davus . . .
DAVUS: Still what?
CHARINUS: What I want is for you to get
    Me married.
DAVUS: That's absurd.
CHARINUS: Come to my house,
    If you come up with something.
DAVUS: Me come there?
    I've come up with nothing.
CHARINUS: Still, if something . . .
DAVUS: All right, I'll come if I come up with something.
CHARINUS: I'll be at home.
    (*Exit*)
DAVUS: Now Mysis, while I'm out
    Wait here for me.
MYSIS: What for?
DAVUS: Because you must.
MYSIS: Hurry up, then.
DAVUS: I'll be back in a flash.

Scene 3

MYSIS, DAVUS

MYSIS: Heavens, you can't rely on anyone.
　I thought our man was just the greatest good
　For my mistress, a friend, lover, a man
　For all seasons. What trouble the poor girl   720
　Gets from him now! Surely there's more distress
　From him now than the good there was before.
　Here comes Davus. My dear man, heavens!
　What's up? Where are you taking that baby?
DAVUS: I need your cleverness right now, Mysis,
　Your quick thinking.
MYSIS:　　　　　　　　Why? What are you up to?
DAVUS: Take this baby boy from me—quickly now—
　And lay him at our doorstep.
MYSIS:　　　　　　　　　　Heavens! On the ground?
　Oh, get some myrtle branches from that altar,
　And put them under him.
MYSIS:　　　　　　　　But why don't you
　Do it yourself?
DAVUS:　　　　　Because if, for some reason,
　I have to swear an oath to my master
　That I did not put the child there, I can
　With a clear mind.
MYSIS:　　　　　　I see. You've just acquired
　Some scruples. Give him here.
DAVUS:　　　　　　　　　　Faster, can't you?   730
　Then you'll see what I do next. Jupiter!
MYSIS: What?
DAVUS:　　　Bride's father. Coming this way.
　I'll have to modify my plans somewhat.
MYSIS: But I don't know what you're talking about.

DAVUS: I'll vanish and then make it look as if
　I'm coming that way too. You play along
　When I talk to him. If you have to speak,
　Back up my words with yours.
MYSIS:　　　　　　　　　　　I don't get it,
　What you're up to, but if you all can use
　Some help from me, since you see it better,
　I'll stay and not be a hindrance to you.

Scene 4

CHREMES, MYSIS, DAVUS

CHREMES: Here I am, after making the arrangements　　　740
　For my daughter's wedding. Now I can call
　For her to be escorted here. What's this?
　A little boy, by Hercules. Say, woman,
　Did you put this child here?
MYSIS (Aside):　　　　　　　Oh, where's Davus?
CHREMES: Can't you answer me?
MYSIS (Aside):　　　　　　　Nowhere to be found.
　I'm out of luck. He went off and left me.
DAVUS (Sauntering in): Heavens, what a mob down at the forum!
　So many men, all suing each other.
　And prices are up. That's all I have to say.
MYSIS (To DAVUS): For heaven's sake, why leave me here alone?
DAVUS: Look here, what kind of comedy is this?
　Say, Mysis: where did the little boy come from?
　Who brought him here?
MYSIS:　　　　　　　　Are you in your right mind,
　To ask me that?
DAVUS:　　　　　Who should I ask, when I
　See no one else around?
CHREMES:　　　　　　　I wonder where.　　　750
DAVUS: Will you answer me what I'm asking you? (Grabs her arm)

MYSIS: Ouch! That hurt.

DAVUS (*To* MYSIS): Go over there, more to the right.

MYSIS: You're raving. Didn't you yourself . . .

DAVUS: If you
Say one word more than to answer
What I'm asking, look out! Raving, am I?
Where did that child come from? Loud and clear.

MYSIS: From our house.

DAVUS: Oh ho, so that's it, eh?
How strange for such a loose abandoned woman
To act so brazenly!

CHREMES: That servant-girl,
She's the woman of Andros' maid, I do believe.

DAVUS: We look like people you can make fools of?

CHREMES: I got here just in time.

DAVUS: Hurry up now,
And take that kid away from our front door.
(*Aside*) Hold it! Don't budge a step from where you are. 760

MYSIS: I wish the gods would tear you up by the roots,
You've got me terrified.

DAVUS: Am I speaking
To you, or not?

MYSIS: What do you want from me?

DAVUS: You ask? Whose child is this you put here? Tell me.

MYSIS: You don't know?

DAVUS: Never mind what I don't know.
Just answer the question.

MYSIS: Well, then, it's ours.

DAVUS: Ours whose?

MYSIS: Glycerium and Pamphilus.

CHREMES: Good lord!

DAVUS: Pamphilus?

MYSIS: Well yes. Isn't it?

CHREMES: Quite right of me to steer clear of that wedding.

DAVUS: Well, that's a dirty trick worth noticing.

MYSIS: Why shout so loud?

DAVUS: The child I saw you bring
Last night to your place?

MYSIS: Well, you've got some nerve!
DAVUS: No, truth. I saw Canthara padded out in front.   770
MYSIS: Well, I can thank the gods some freedwomen
  Were present at the lying-in.
DAVUS: Your woman
  Does not know our man here, if she starts off
  Her scheme along these lines. "If Chremes sees
  The child in front of their house, he won't give
  His daughter to him." Hercules! He will,
  All the more so.
CHREMES: He will not. Hercules!
DAVUS: And you'll find out right now, if you don't cart
  That kid away, I'll send him rolling down
  The middle of the street, and you'll be tumbling
  After him the same way, in the mud.
MYSIS: Heavens, you're drunk.
DAVUS: And now another trick
  Shoves the first one aside. I heard them whispering
  That Glycerium is a free citizen of Athens.   780
CHREMES: Narrow escape.
DAVUS: By law, then, Pamphilus
  Will have to marry her.
MYSIS: She is a citizen,
  Isn't she? for heaven's sake?
CHREMES: I almost fell
  For their little practical joke unawares.
DAVUS: Who's talking over there? Oh, Chremes. Good,
  You're just in time. Come and listen to this.
CHREMES: I overheard it all.
DAVUS: You did? All of it?
CHREMES: I'm telling you I heard the whole story
  Right from the start.
DAVUS: You did? For heaven's sake!
  Some mischief, eh? This woman ought to be
  Hauled off and put to torture. Here he is:
  Don't think it's only Davus you're fooling.
MYSIS: Oh, sir, mercy: I said nothing untrue.
CHREMES: I get the point. Is Simo inside there?

DAVUS: Yes, he's in there.

(*Exit* CHREMES)

MYSIS: Don't lay a finger on me,
You rat. If I don't tell Glycerium everything,   790
By heavens . . .

DAVUS: Stupid! Can't you see what's on?

MYSIS: How should I see it?

DAVUS: That was the bride's father.
There wasn't any other way for him
To know what we wanted him to believe.

MYSIS: You should have told me first.

DAVUS: So then, you think
It makes no difference whether you behave
Completely naturally, wholeheartedly,
Or whether you are putting on a show?

Scene 5

CRITO, MYSIS, DAVUS

CRITO: I was told Chrysis lived on this street.
She chose earning her money here at Athens,
Disgracefully, over living at Andros,
Her native land, a poor but honest woman.
By law her property reverts to me
At her death. I see some people there
I can inquire of. Greetings to you both.   800

MYSIS: Heavens! Do I see Chrysis' cousin, Crito?
That's who it is.

CRITO: Mysis! I hope you're well.

MYSIS: The same to you, Crito.

CRITO: Well now, Chrysis
Is really . . .

MYSIS: Yes, and her death has left us
In great distress.

CRITO: And you? How is it going?
  Are things all right?
MYSIS: With us? It goes like this:
  You know the saying, "Since we cannot do
  What we want to, we just do what we can."
CRITO: Has Glycerium found her parents here?
MYSIS: I wish she had.
CRITO: Not even by this time?
  My coming here is hardly opportune.
  If I'd known that, by Pollux, I would not
  Have set foot here. It was always said,
  And taken for granted, that Glycerium
  Was Chrysis' sister; so, she would inherit
  Whatever Chrysis owned. I, as a stranger,   810
  Stand warned by other cases how simple
  And straightforward it will not be for me
  To win a lawsuit. And I rather imagine
  She has some friend to look after her rights.
  She was quite grown up when she left Andros.
  They'll call me a cheap fraud, going to court
  For her inheritance. It bothers me,
  As well, to think of taking things from her.
MYSIS: Oh, best of visitors! Good heavens, Crito,
  You're still the same good man you always were.
CRITO: Take me to her, as long as I have come,
  So I can see her.
MYSIS: With the greatest pleasure.
DAVUS: I'll follow them. I would not like to have
  My master see me at a time like this.

ACT V

Scene 1

CHREMES: My friendship for you has been sorely tried,   820
　　Simo. I've run my share of risks. So, please
　　Stop coaxing me. While I was trying hard
　　To go along with you, I nearly played
　　The fool with my own daughter's life.
SIMO:　　　　　　　　　　　　　　Oh, no,
　　Chremes. For now I'm only asking you
　　And urging you to put into effect
　　The favor you assured me of in words
　　A while ago.
CHREMES:　　　　See how unfair you are,
　　From eagerness. Provided you can get
　　What you are after, you don't give a thought
　　To what you're asking of me, or what limits
　　There may be to my favor; for if you did,
　　You'd stop piling unjust requests on me.
SIMO: Such as?
CHREMES:　　　　You ask? Such as your urging me
　　To give my daughter to a youth engaged
　　In carrying on another love affair,
　　Quite loath to marry, to hand her over to
　　A wobbly marriage in a tense household.   830
　　So I can heal your son by the therapy
　　Of my daughter's distress, of her sorrow.
　　You won me over. And as things then stood,

I took you up. But things don't bear me out:
You'll have to bear with that. His girl, they say,
Is a citizen here. And they've had a son.
Let go of us.
SIMO: I ask you, by the gods,
Don't let yourself be persuaded by them
That Pamphilus is lowest of the low,
A thought that serves their purpose perfectly,
To cancel the marriage well on its way.
When their excuse for doing all these things
Is taken from them, they'll lay off.
CHREMES: You're wrong.
I saw Davus myself having a quarrel with
Her maid.
SIMO: Of course you did.
CHREMES: Quite openly.
Neither of them had any idea
I was present.
SIMO: Of course Davus told me,
A while ago, the women would do that.   840
Somehow or other I forgot to let
You in on that today, although I meant to.

Scene 2

DAVUS, CHREMES, SIMO, DROMO

DAVUS (*Coming from* GLYCERIUM'S *house*): I tell you now, don't
    worry . . .
CHREMES: That's your Davus.
SIMO: But why in there?
DAVUS: You're under my protection,
    And our visitor's.
SIMO: What trick's he up to?

DAVUS: I never saw a more convenient man,
    A more convenient time for his arrival.
SIMO: Confound him, who's he praising to the skies?
DAVUS: We're out of deep water.
SIMO: Why don't I call him?
DAVUS: Oh, there's the master. How do I handle him?
SIMO: Greetings, my fine fellow.
DAVUS: Simo; friend Chremes.
    It's all set inside now.
SIMO: You took good care
    Of that.
DAVUS: Summon the bride when you want to.
SIMO: So well expressed. But as a matter of fact,
    That's the one element lacking in the situation.
    Answer me this. What were you doing in there?
DAVUS: Me?
SIMO: You.
DAVUS: You mean me?
SIMO: I mean you.
DAVUS: Just now   850
    I went in there . . .
SIMO: As if I asked you when.
DAVUS: With your son.
SIMO: Is he in there? I feel sick.
    Didn't you say they've had a falling out?
    You crook. You did.
DAVUS: They have.
SIMO: So why is he
    In there?
CHREMES: Why do you think? He's quarreling
    With her.
DAVUS: Oh no, Chremes, it's worse than that.
    I'll let you in on some real dirty business.
    An older man arrived—he's in there now—
    Sure of himself, the clever type; you see
    His face, you see a man of utmost worth.
    His countenance reflects strict honesty,
    His words ring true.

SIMO: What are you dishing up?
DAVUS: Nothing for me: just what I heard him say.
SIMO: And he said what?
DAVUS: That he knew that Glycerium
  Was an Athenian citizen.
SIMO: Hey, Dromo,
  Dromo, Dromo!   860
DAVUS: What's up?
SIMO: Dromo!
DAVUS: Listen.
SIMO: If you say one more word . . . Dromo!
DROMO: You called?
SIMO: Lift this guy up and cart him off inside
  As fast as possible.
DROMO: Which guy?
SIMO: Davus.
DAVUS: But why?
SIMO: Because that's what I want, that's why.
  Take him away, I say.
DAVUS: What have I done?
SIMO: Cart him off.
DAVUS: Well, let him kill me dead
  If you find I've said anything untrue.
SIMO: I don't hear you. I'll have you back here soon,
  A bit worse for wear.
DAVUS: Even if this is true?
SIMO: Even if. Make sure he's tied up and guarded,
  You hear? I want him bound tight, hands and feet.
  Take that. I'll show you, as I live, today,
  What risks you take when you deceive your master,
  What risks he runs when he fools his father.
CHREMES: Oh come, don't get so worked up about it.
SIMO: Ah, Chremes, there's filial piety for you!
  Don't you feel sorry for me when I get
  So much trouble for such a sorry son?   870
  Come out here, Pamphilus! Oh, Pamphilus,
  Come on out! Aren't you the least bit ashamed?

Scene 3

PAMPHILUS, SIMO, CHREMES

PAMPHILUS: Who wants me? It's father. I'm done for.
SIMO: Tell me,
    You, of all the . . .
CHREMES: Come now, state the case:
    Don't bawl him out.
SIMO: As if something too harsh
    Could be stated against him. And you, too, say
    Glycerium is a citizen?
PAMPHILUS: That's what they claim.
SIMO: "They claim"? Some nerve he's got. Does he take thought
    For what he's saying, or express regret
    For what he's done? Is there a blush of shame
    Giving some sign somewhere? Just think of him,
    So self-willed that in spite of everything
    He yearns to have this girl, to his disgrace,
    Regardless of the rights of citizens,
    Propriety, and his own father's wish!   880
PAMPHILUS: Poor me!
SIMO: At last, you realize it now,
    Pamphilus? Long ago, when you first turned
    Your mind to getting what you wanted, then,
    No matter how, that was the day "poor you"
    Applied best to you. But why should I grieve,
    Torment myself, eat my heart out?, or why
    Tax my old age with his insanity?
    Am I the one to suffer for his sins?
    No. Let him have her, let him go away
    And live with her.
PAMPHILUS: Oh father, dear.
SIMO: "Dear father"? As if you needed this father.   890

A home, a wife, children: you've found them all
Against your father's will.[12] So bring on those
Who claim that she's a citizen. You win.
PAMPHILUS: Father, may I say something?
SIMO: What can you have
To say to me?
CHREMES: Still, Simo, listen to him.
SIMO: Listen to him? And what will I hear, Chremes?
CHREMES: Still, let him speak.
SIMO: All right. I let him speak.
PAMPHILUS: I readily admit I love this girl.
If that's a sin, I also admit that.
I surrender to you, father. Command me,
Set me what task you will. Is it your wish
That I marry a wife and lose this girl?
I'll bear that as I can. But this one thing
I beg of you: do not believe that I
Suborned this visitor. Let me clear myself   900
Of that charge by bringing him out here
Into the open.
SIMO: Let you bring him out here?
PAMPHILUS: Please do, father.
CHREMES: He's asking for justice.
Consent to it.
PAMPHILUS: Let me convince you.
SIMO: All right.
I welcome any measures, just so long
As I am not found falling for a trick,
Chremes.
CHREMES: A mild form of the penalty,
Your displeasure at his serious mistake,
Should be enough to satisfy a father.

---

[12] *domus, uxor, liberi inventi invito patre:* the son has become a father *against his father's will;* and Simo, the typical Roman father, is outraged.

Scene 4

CRITO, CHREMES, SIMO, PAMPHILUS

CRITO: Stop urging me. Any of these reasons
   Tells me how to proceed: the fact of you;
   The fact that it is true; the simple fact
   That I wish well to Glycerium.
CHREMES: Do I see Crito of Andros? That's who it is.
CRITO: Oh, greetings, Chremes.
CHREMES: What brings you to Athens,
   Rare visitor?
CRITO: Oh well, it just worked out.
   But isn't this Simo?
CHREMES: This is Simo.
CRITO: You wanted me?
SIMO: It's you, isn't it, claiming
   That Glycerium is a citizen of Athens?
CRITO: Do you say she is not?
SIMO: And you came here
   Primed for that very purpose?
CRITO: Why would I?
SIMO: You ask why? And you'll get away with it?   910
   Here, involving young men, still unaware
   Of worldly ways, brought up as gentlemen?
   You'll involve them in your own mischief making,
   Coaxing and hoaxing them, you turn their heads?
CRITO: Are you quite right in yours?
SIMO: False marriage vows
   Let you cement a prostitute's passions?
PAMPHILUS: I'm done. I fear the guest won't stand for this.
CHREMES: Simo, if you knew him you wouldn't think
   About him this way. He is an honorable man.
SIMO: He is an honorable man. It "worked out"

So neatly for him to arrive today
And not before? Chremes, truly a man
To be believed.
PAMPHILUS: If I were not afraid
Of father, I'd give him some good advice
On that subject.
SIMO: You fortune hunter!
CRITO: Oh, well . . .
CHREMES: That's just the way he is, Crito. Ignore him.
CRITO: He'd better watch the way he's acting. If
He insists on telling me what he wants,
He'll hear some things he doesn't plan to hear.   920
(*To* SIMO) What interests me in troubling your affairs?
They're no concern of mine. Can't you put up
With your distress with equanimity?
Whether they're true or false, the things I've heard
And say, you'll soon be able to work out.
Some time ago, an Athenian citizen
Was shipwrecked on Andros, and with him
That little girl in there. The needy man
Attached himself to Chrysis' father first,
As a client, for the little girl's protection.
SIMO: So this is how he starts his comedy! [13]
CHREMES: But let him finish.
CRITO: Is he just going
To keep interrupting?
CHREMES: No, go ahead.
CRITO: The man who took in the shipwrecked victim
Was my cousin. From him I heard that he
Was an Athenian citizen. Then he
Died on Andros.
CHREMES: What was his name?

---

[13] *fabulam inceptat:* Terence likes to use the term for comedy in different ways
in this play. In general, *fabula* means story or fiction in our sense of "what's the
story?" But it is the Roman word for play, a drama. Earlier, when Mysis brings
the baby out and leaves it at Simo's door, on Davus' instructions, Davus re-enters
and in Chremes' presence says, "What kind of comedy is this?" *quae haec est
fabula?* (l. 747, p. 52)

CRITO: His name?
  So soon?
PAMPHILUS: His name was Phania.
CHREMES: Oh my god!
CRITO: By Hercules, I think it was Phania. One thing
  I know for sure, he said he was from Rhamnus.
CHREMES: By Jupiter, my district!   930
CRITO: And many others, Chremes,
  Heard him state that in Andros.
CHREMES: How I hope
  It's how I hope it is! But tell me now
  About the girl. Did he say she was his?
CRITO: No. She was his brother's daughter.
CHREMES: That means
  She's my daughter.
CRITO: How's that?
SIMO: How's that? How's that?
PAMPHILUS: Perk up your ears, Pamphilus.
SIMO: What makes you think so?
CHREMES: That Phania was my brother.
SIMO: I knew him,
  So I'm aware of that.
CHREMES: To miss the war,
  He fled Athens and lit out for Asia
  Following me. He was afraid to leave
  The infant girl here. For the first time, since then,
  I hear what happened to him.
PAMPHILUS: I can't keep still.
  My heart trembles with fear, with hope, with joy,
  With wonder at such good in store so fast.
SIMO: In many ways I'm so happy your daughter
  Has been found.
PAMPHILUS: My feelings too, father.
CHREMES: One little doubt still nags at me.   940
PAMPHILUS (Aside):   Typical!
  With your scruples, you seem bent on finding
  A kink in a bulrush.
CRITO: What could it be?

CHREMES: Her name does not fit.
CRITO: Oh, when she was small,
   She used another name.
CHREMES: And what was it, Crito?
   Surely you remember.
CRITO: I'm trying to think.
PAMPHILUS: Can I allow his memory to block
   My happiness, when I am able to
   Prescribe my own cure for this little wound?
   Oh, Chremes, what you're after is PASIBULA.[14]
CHREMES: PASIBULA? That's it.
CRITO: That's it, all right.
PAMPHILUS: I heard it from herself a thousand times.
SIMO: I trust, Chremes, that you believe we all
   Delight in this.
CHREMES: So help me, gods, I do.
PAMPHILUS: And father, as to what remains to be . . .
SIMO: This fact has long since had my blessing on it.
PAMPHILUS: You're such a good father. As for the wife:
   Since I am in possession, does Chremes
   Alter his stand?
CHREMES: Your case is quite airtight,
   Unless your father states a different view.
PAMPHILUS: Oh, that's the way it is, is it?
SIMO: Of course.   950
CHREMES: The dowry, Pamphilus, is ten talents.[15]
PAMPHILUS: And I accept it.
CHREMES: Now I'll hurry off
   To my daughter. And come with me, Crito,
   I'm sure she won't know me.
   (CHREMES *and* CRITO *exit*)
SIMO: Why not order
   Her brought here to our house?

[14] Glycerium's original name. In establishing identity after many years have intervened, in Greek comedy, in Roman comedy, in the Greek Romances—not to mention as in life in general—old names are helpful, new names confusing.

[15] A good sum of money, roughly equivalent to $20,000.

PAMPHILUS: A wise suggestion.
I'll go assign the business to Davus.
SIMO: He can't do it.
PAMPHILUS: Why not?
SIMO: He's got something
Hanging heavier on his hands.
PAMPHILUS: What's that?
SIMO: He's bound in chains.
PAMPHILUS: Father, that was not right,
To tie him up.
SIMO: I didn't order "right,"
I ordered "tight."
PAMPHILUS: But order him untied,
I beg you.
SIMO: Oh, all right.
PAMPHILUS: And please hurry.
SIMO: I'm going inside now to see to it.
(*Exit*)
PAMPHILUS: Oh happy day that brings such luck to me!

Scene 5

CHARINUS, PAMPHILUS, DAVUS

CHARINUS: I thought I'd drift back and see what Pamphilus
Is up to. Why, there he is over there himself.
PAMPHILUS: Someone may think I don't think this is true,
But I take great joy in thinking it is so.
Really, right now. I also think, therefore,
That the life of the gods is everlasting,
Because their joy is constant. I have gained   960
Immortal life, if nothing intervenes
To vex my happiness. And who would I
Most want to see to tell my story to?
CHARINUS (*Aside*): Joy? Happiness?

PAMPHILUS: I see Davus. No one
   I'd rather see. I know how he alone
   Will genuinely join in in my rejoicing
   For my joys.
DAVUS: Where can Pamphilus be?
PAMPHILUS: Davus!
DAVUS: Who's that talking?
PAMPHILUS: Me.
DAVUS: Oh, Pamphilus.
PAMPHILUS: You don't know what hit me.
DAVUS: That's true enough.
   I know, though, what hit me.
PAMPHILUS: And so do I.
DAVUS: The usual course of human events:
   You know about the trouble I got into
   Before I knew what good thing came your way.
PAMPHILUS: My Glycerium has found her true parents.
DAVUS: I think that's pretty nice.
CHARINUS: And so do I.
PAMPHILUS: Her father is our closest friend.   970
DAVUS: Who's that?
PAMPHILUS: Chremes.
DAVUS: You're telling quite a story now.
PAMPHILUS: And now there's nothing standing in the way
   Of my marrying her.
CHARINUS (*Aside*):   Could he be dreaming
   Of what he wished for when he was awake?
PAMPHILUS: As for the child, Davus . . .
DAVUS: Oh stop it now.
   It's you alone the gods really do love.
CHARINUS: I'm rather well off too, if this is true.
   (*Louder*) I'll talk to them.
PAMPHILUS: Who's speaking over there?
   Charinus, you're here just at the right time,
   I'm so glad.
CHARINUS: Well, I think it's pretty nice.
PAMPHILUS: You heard it?

CHARINUS: All. Now please look out for me
   In your good fortune. Chremes is now yours,
   I know he'll do anything you ask him.
PAMPHILUS: I don't forget you. But it's much too long
   To wait for him to come out here. He's there,
   Inside, with his Glycerium. So come along
   With me, inside. And Davus, hurry home
   And summon the escort to bring her here
   Into our house. Don't just stand there.
   Do something.
   (*Exit* PAMPHILUS *and* CHARINUS)
DAVUS: I'm going.
   (*To the audience*) [16]   Don't you just sit there,
   Waiting for them to come out here again.
   The ceremonies all take place inside,   980
   And whatever little settlements are left
   To work out with the property.
   Well now, it's all worked out quite properly, don't you think?
   Let's see: two husbands, two wives, two fathers,
   Probably a little property clause
   For Crito. Makes you pause
   And think. I think it's pretty nice,
   Love and marriage in a good cause.
   And you might want to add to it the spice
   Of a good round of applause.

[16] Since there was no curtain, Davus must tell the audience that the play is over and let the voice of the Cantor be heard singing PLAUDITE! I have expanded Davus's concluding speech and let him make the last request.

THE SELF-TORMENTOR

(*HEAUTONTIMORUMENOS*)

Translated by Palmer Bovie

INTRODUCTION

Fathers hope their sons will stay on good terms with them and behave properly. Sons grow up to be young men who fall in love and begin to get ideas of their own. Mothers move about, rather unobtrusively, trying to bring reason to bear on the conflicts that develop. There can be a collision of wills, and a generous share of misunderstanding. Helped, often inspired and impelled by, the trusted family servant, the sons act out schemes for circumventing their fathers. The action does not save the sons, but can stave off the inevitable showdown when everyone gets caught up in the truth. Then the fathers discover things they didn't expect to, and the sons can be lured into conforming to their fathers' wishes. The servant is spared punishment, for another day, and cheerfully contemplates the wreckage of his improvised plans.

As one of the sons in *The Self-Tormentor* expresses the predicament: "Fathers are not good judges of young men. . . . They think we should be born old. . . . They govern as their passion now dictates, not as it was then."

CLITIPHO: *Quam iniqui sunt patres in omnis adulescentes iudices!*
Qui aequom esse censent nos a pueris ilico nasci senes. . . .
Lubidine ex sua moderantur nunc quae est non quae olim fuit.
(ll. 213–216)

On the spot Clitipho promises himself that if he ever has a son he will treat the young man indulgently, remember what it is to be young, and understand his son.

A bit later on in the play Clitipho's father is equally sure of himself and his insistence on strict control:

73

We are all made worse by self-indulgent freedom.
He'll want whatever pops into his mind
And won't stop to consider whether it
Is right or wrong, but just go after it.

CHREMES: *Nam deteriores omnes sumus licentia.*
Quod quoique quomque inciderit in mentem volet
Neque id putabit pravum an rectum sit: petet.
(ll. 483–485)

The difference between Chremes and his son Clitipho forms
the second plot of the play. Its first plot unfolds in the opening
scene on Menedemus' farm adjoining Chremes, a few miles outside of Athens. Menedemus had quarreled with his son Clinia
over Clinia's love affair with a young woman of unidentified origins, brought to Athens from Corinth by a woman supposed to
be her mother. The father scolded his son and pointed out that
when he was young he was poor and had no time or money for
such affairs. Instead, he had enlisted in the army as a mercenary
in the service of an Asian king, winning glory and wealth for his
efforts. As Menedemus continued to criticise him in this vein,
Clinia took the lesson to heart and left his home in Athens to
serve in an army in Asia Minor. Menedemus felt lost and guilty,
sold his house and possessions in Athens, and bought the farm-
house and land next to Chremes'. This all took place some three
months before the time of the play, which begins with Chremes
coming out to find Menedemus hard at work on his land, raking
and hoeing. Chremes cannot keep from asking Menedemus why
he torments himself with such hard work. Menedemus suggests
that this is none of Chremes' business but Chremes answers with
Terence's most often quoted line:

homo sum: nil humani alienum mihi puto

I am a man and I consider nothing human foreign to me.
(l. 77)

Chremes further argues that if Menedemus' course is the right
one he can learn a lesson from it; if not, Menedemus can learn
from him how a father ought to manage his life. Menedemus
consents to the conversation, during which the background story

of the separation of Menedemus and Clinia is told. Chremes ob-
serves that Clinia's instincts are good and indicate an underlying
regard for his father. But a good father, he insists, must show his
son that he trusts him. Chremes then invites Menedemus to join
in a dinner party at his house that day, the Feast of Dionysus,
but Menedemus declines, and continues with his self-inflicted
hard labor.

In the next scene Clitipho brings Chremes the surprising
news that Clinia has returned from abroad and is already at their
house. The two young men have long been friends and Clinia is
as yet unwilling to face Menedemus, being more than ever in
love with the mysterious young woman over whom they originally
quarreled. Clitipho tells his father how mean and strict Menedemus is, but Chremes does not trust his son far enough to reveal
what he has already learned of Menedemus' true character. He
seems to use the conflict as a kind of object lesson, and delivers
a short lecture on how sons should restrain themselves in deference to their fathers' wishes.

The second act opens with Clitipho's soliloquy on fathers'
unfair judgments of their sons and proceeds to a scene of dialogue
between him and Clinia, waiting for their young women to appear for the dinner party. Clinia's anxiety about his mistress'
behavior in his absence is put to rest by the servants' account of
arriving at her house unexpectedly and finding her to be a model
of decorum. The young woman, Antiphila, was overwhelmingly
happy to learn that Clinia had come back. Clitipho also has a
mistress, Bacchis—an affair his father does not know about—but
she is a hardened mercenary and has already cost Clitipho a good
deal of money to maintain. Currently he owes her an additional
sum that he and the family slave Syrus are trying to acquire by
some means without Chremes' knowing of it. In view of Clinia's
return, Syrus improvises a scheme for getting around Chremes
by passing off Bacchis as Clinia's mistress and sequestering Antiphila with Clitipho's mother in the women's quarters.

The two women make their appearance, Bacchis praising
Antiphila for her single-minded devotion to Clinia, and contrasting it with the unevenness of her own existence as a prey to the

transitory male. For a brief moment, Antiphila and Clinia are happily reunited.

The third act begins early in the morning after the dinner party. Chremes is on his way to bring Menedemus the news of Clinia's return. When Menedemus expresses unqualified joy Chremes again cautions restraint. Mistakenly supposing Bacchis to be Clinia's mistress, Chremes regales Menedemus with an account of her fastidious expensive tastes and demanding ways as displayed at the dinner party. Chremes envisages Menedemus' unguarded welcoming of Clinia and his alleged mistress as financially ruinous. He also suspects the young men and Syrus of being up to something and suggests that he and Menedemus play along with whatever develops. Even if it involves some cash, outwitting their outwitters might be a better investment than unguarded indulgence of Clinia's least desire. Menedemus consents, thinking that Chremes sees his situation more clearly than he himself can.

In the ensuing scenes of Act III Syrus allows Chremes to talk him into pursuing the schemes he has in mind; Clitipho almost gives the truth away by fondling Bacchis and being observed by Chremes; Syrus pretends to be outraged by Clitipho's behavior and sends him off on a long walk; Syrus devises a plan for getting the money promised to Bacchis. He tells Chremes that Antiphila was left as a pledge in security for a loan to Bacchis by the old woman supposed to be her mother. The old woman died and Bacchis now has Antiphila as a servant in exchange for the money. Furthermore, she is hounding Clinia for the money and will not give up Antiphila until she gets it. Syrus proposes that they offer Antiphila to Menedemus as a captive of war who could be sold back for a great profit. When Chremes opposes this move on the ground that Menedemus is not in the market for bargains, Syrus airily says that that is quite all right because Menedemus will not really need to buy her. Chremes is left in the dark about what Syrus actually means.

The fourth act brings a third plot into view when Sostrata, Chremes' wife, informs him that Antiphila wears the very ring she had left with their infant daughter, exposed soon after her birth. Prompted by superstition, Sostrata says, she had given the child to another woman to expose but had also taken the ring from her own finger, to be left with the child. This way, should the child chance to survive and grow up she would not have been totally disinherited. Antiphila is, of course, discovered to be the daughter of Chremes and Sostrata. Both parents are now happy to have back their lost child.

But Syrus is in a dither because now that Antiphila is recognized as a free-born Athenian citizen she cannot be held as the alleged security for a debt he claimed she was. Wondering how to keep Chremes from learning that Bacchis is in fact Clitipho's mistress and also how to lay hands on the money promised to her, Syrus invents a new plan of action. He is rather impatient with Clinia's rapture at the discovery of Antiphila's true status, and proudly advances his new scheme for outwitting both fathers by simply telling the truth. He wants Clinia to return to Menedemus and take Bacchis with him, and simply tell Menedemus that she is Clitipho's mistress. Clinia can also of course ask for Antiphila's hand in marriage. Syrus assures Clinia, over his protests that this will interfere with his marriage, that they only need to maneuver long enough to get the money in question, and he will be helping Clitipho momentarily, and Clinia finally consents. Bacchis also, after giving Syrus a·jolt by threatening to leave entirely, falls in with the new scheme for producing the money.

Chremes can only pity Menedemus for having Bacchis as well as Clinia move in. When Syrus tells Chremes that Clinia had told Menedemus that Bacchis was in fact Clitipho's mistress, Chremes nimbly concludes that Clinia has not only said this but also asked for Antiphila in marriage to raise the money (as expenses for the proposed wedding) promised to Bacchis. When Chremes refuses to be party to such a scheme Syrus suggests that he at least recompense Bacchis outright for the loss of her servant Antiphila and Chremes agrees. Clitipho returns from his long walk and is given the bag of money to take to Bacchis.

Now Menedemus appears on stage to ask formally for Antiphila's hand in marriage to his son and inform Chremes of the truth that Bacchis is actually Clitipho's mistress. Chremes' strong disbelief of this hard fact even dissuades Menedemus for the moment; he respects the force of Chremes' argument and ruefully admits to the possibility, but still asks for the betrothal of Antiphila to his son, to satisfy Clinia's ardent wishes. And Chremes consents on the grounds that only this way can Menedemus see the light and discover just what and just how much his son is demanding of him.

In the last act the truth comes out. Chremes is crestfallen when regaled by Menedemus with a description of the bedroom scene at his house enacted by Bacchis and Clitipho. He is furious and determined to read his son the riot act. Menedemus responds by urging Chremes to consider more suitable ways of managing his son:

> MENEDEMUS: Let your son realize
> That you're his father. Let him have the courage
> To trust you every way, to ask for things,
> To seek your help, and not go looking out
> For some other support, and desert you.
>
> (ll. 925–927)

But Chremes is bent on revenge, on knocking sense into Clitipho's head, and tells him that he has been disinherited in favor of his sister Antiphila. At this penultimate crisis Syrus makes Clitipho believe that it sounds as if he is not their son after all, and Clitipho confronts his parents with the question of whether he really is. Chremes now reads Clitipho the riot act, a simple bill of particulars on his recent behavior as an idler and a cheat. Clitipho is genuinely sorry when he sees himself in this light. As Menedemus appears to intercede for Clitipho and calm down Chremes' anger, Chremes agrees to forgive Clitipho on condition that he now take a wife. Clitipho is reluctant to accept the condition but gives in, strenuously refusing the red-head his mother first offers and substituting as his choice a young woman he's had his eye on for some time. Clitipho also asks that Syrus be pardoned, not punished, and Chremes lets the slave off. So both sons are launched on the path of marriage and parenthood.

From Menander's original single-plot version of the *Heautontimorumenos* Terence has fashioned an intricate story of emotional gambits and moral pressures, of fathers hoping in very different ways to make good men of their sons without losing their companionship and respect. In the young men infatuation and genuine affections struggle for recognition and survival. The two fathers well represent the permissive and authoritarian species of this genus. If Menedemus' winning desire to cherish and honor his son dominates the atmosphere of this play in a noble and affectionate spirit, Chremes' hard-fisted standards and correctives also succeed in transforming Clitipho's behavior from the acrobatics of anxiety into a straight walk along the road to responsibility. Bacchis is once more left to her own resources, but they seem to be ample. Antiphila and Clinia were right all along in their devotion to one another, not only a sound instinct, but now even socially respectable. The emotional and moral behavior of both parents and children is seen to have many overtones.

All of this Terence has converted to use in steady, simple Latin poetry, straightforward in diction, sparing in imagery. Hardly ever is the voice raised. The lines of action are as complex and at times mystifying as the words are simple and unadorned. But Terence's art, like all good poetry, is "the clear expression of mixed feelings."

PALMER BOVIE

THE SELF-TORMENTOR

CHARACTERS

CHREMES, an old Athenian
MENEDEMUS, an old man, neighbor of Chremes
CLITIPHO, son of Chremes
CLINIA, son of Menedemus
SYRUS, a slave of Chremes
DROMO, a slave of Menedemus
BACCHIS, a courtesan, mistress of Clitipho
ANTIPHILA, a girl, loved by Clinia
SOSTRATA, wife of Chremes
PHRYGIA, a servant of Bacchis
CANTHARA, a nurse, servant of Sostrata

SCENE: *The adjoining farms of Menedemus and Chremes, a few miles outside of Athens.*

PROLOGUE *

In case you may be wondering just why
The poet gave the Prologue to an old man
When a young man usually delivers it,
Let me tell you why I'm out here.

* Spoken by L. Ambivius Turpio.

Today
I do the comedy *The Self-Tormentor*,
With its double plot, fashioned by Terence
From the original single-plot version.
I've told you what it is, and that it's new.
I'd tell you, too, who wrote the Greek version,
But most of you, I know, already know.
    I'll tell you why I learned the Prologue's role.   10
Terence wanted me to plead a case for him,
Not speak a prologue. He leaves the verdict
Entirely in your hands. I hope that I,
The advocate, can happily devise
And fluently present the speech he wrote.
    Some ill-willed critics have been handing out
Rumors that Terence tacked together plays
From several Greek originals, and made
A few Latin plays from them. And he did!
He doesn't say he didn't. He's not sorry
For it. He means to go right on doing it.
He has good writers as his precedent   20
And thinks he's quite entitled to practise
Their methods. As for what a mean old poet
Keeps saying, that Terence is a parvenu
And got into dramatic poetry
With no formal training, by leaning on
The talents of such friends as Scipio,
Not on his own ability—only
Your judgment and decision can resolve.
I therefore want to appeal to all of you
So that the arguments of enemies
Are balanced by the arguments of friends.
Be fair to us, and let those have a chance
Who give you chances to witness new plays,   30
I mean good plays, of course,
                     not Luscius' recent effort
To thrill his audience by letting a slave run wild
In the street. Why should the populace
Be at a madman's mercy? Terence will tell
You more about old Luscius' aberrations

When he writes more new plays; UNLESS he makes
An end of pointing out the flaws in Terence.
  So, be at hand with equanimity,
And let me act a quiet play for you,
So that The Running Slave, or The Old Grouch,
Or Greedy Parasite, or Sharp Con Man,
Or Pimp, do not have to be played by me
At the top of my voice and height of energy.   40
For my sake, tell yourselves my case is just,
So that my work can be lightened somewhat.
The men who write new plays have no mercy
On an old man like me. They have a script
That calls for lots of action—right away,
They come to me with it. But if it's light
And frothy, they engage another troupe.
  In this play Terence has a good clean style.
So make a test of what my powers are
In both directions, the fast action play,
Or here, the quiet one. I never have
Set too greedy a price on my own skill.
I think that I derive the greatest gain
By bringing you pleasure. Let me stand for that.   50
And let young actors have it in their hearts
To please you, rather than indulge themselves.

ACT I

Scene 1

CHREMES, MENEDEMUS

CHREMES: Although our acquaintance is so recent,
  Dating from when you bought this land next door

To mine, and we have had little to do
With each other—still, your manliness,
Or your being my neighbor, which I regard
As bordering on friendship, makes me bold
To talk to you on familiar terms.
It seems to me that you are acting out
Of keeping with your years, and quite beyond　　　　60
What your status requires. By all the faith
Of men and gods, what do you want of yourself?
What are you after? Sixty years ago,
Or more than that, I'd say, was your birthday.
In these parts no one has a better piece
Of property or one worth more. You own
Some slaves. But you do all the work yourself
As if you hadn't one. I never leave
In the morning or come back home at night
Without seeing you digging in your land,
Or ploughing, or lugging something around.
You never take time off, or take it easy　　　　70
On yourself. I'm sure this is no pleasure
For you. "Well, I'm not satisfied at all
With the work being done here." Still, if you
Put in the time you spend doing the work
On making them do it, you'd get more done.

MENEDEMUS: Chremes, are you so much at your leisure
　　From your business that you can look after
　　Others' business, foreign to your interests?

CHREMES: I am a man: nothing that is human
　　Is foreign to my interests. So, suppose
　　I want to offer you advice, or be
　　Advised by you of what goes on. If what
　　You do is right, then I should do the same,
　　If not, I might persuade you to desist.

MENEDEMUS: I have to act this way. You go ahead　　　　80
　　And act as you have to.

CHREMES:　　　　　　　　But must a man
　　Torment himself?

MENEDEMUS:　　　　I must.

CHREMES: Well, if you have
Some troubles, I could wish you didn't have them.
But what is your distress? Tell me just what
Has made you feel so guilty?
MENEDEMUS: Oh lord, lord!
CHREMES: Don't cry, but let me in on what it is.
Don't keep silent; don't be afraid; trust me.
I'll help you out, with money, or advice,
Or sympathy.
MENEDEMUS: You really want to know?
CHREMES: But that's the reason I've spoken to you.
MENEDEMUS: Well, then, I'll tell you.
CHREMES: Meanwhile, as we talk,
Put those rakes down, won't you? Don't keep working.
MENEDEMUS: I will not.
CHREMES: Why won't you?
MENEDEMUS: Don't let me give
Myself a moment off. 90
CHREMES: I refuse you that.
MENEDEMUS: Ah, that's unfair of you.
CHREMES: With a rake like that?
God, it's heavy.
MENEDEMUS: And just what I deserve.
CHREMES: Now tell me about it.
MENEDEMUS: I have one son,
A young man. "I have?" I meant, "I had."
Whether I've still got him or not, Chremes,
I don't quite know.
CHREMES: Why don't you know?
MENEDEMUS: You'll know.
An elderly woman came here from Corinth,
In reduced circumstances, and my son
Began to love her daughter to distraction.
It was as if he had her for his wife.
And all this started up unknown to me.
When I found out about it, I began
To treat my ailing son quite unkindly 100
As ill suited his case, violently,

The way fathers will act. I railed at him
Day in, day out. "I suppose you hope
You'll be allowed to carry on like this,
With your father alive and well, and have
A mistress in the place of a real wife?
You're wrong if you think that and, Clinia,
You don't know me. I want you for a son
Only as long as you conduct yourself
In a worthy manner. If you don't do that,
I'll find some way of dealing with your case.
This sort of behavior could not exist
Except for too much leisure. Why, when I   110
Was your age, I did not invest my time
In love affairs. For I was poor. And so,
I left for Asia, and out there I found
Money and reputation in the army." [1]
So it came down to this: the young fellow
Was won over by hearing, so often,
The same remorseless speech. He thought that I,
Through age and wisdom, knew more than he did.
He left for Asia, for army service
Under some satrap,[2] Chremes.

CHREMES: Well, I must say!

MENEDEMUS: He went without my knowing it, and now
    It's been three months.

CHREMES: You're both at fault,
    But his initiative remains the sign
    Of a respectful, far from lazy spirit.   120

MENEDEMUS: When I found out about it from his friends
    I came back home depressed, nearly frantic
    And sick at heart, upset, and bewildered.
    I sat down, slaves ran in, took off my shoes.
    I saw others hurrying to set the table
    And get dinner ready, doing what each one could
    To lighten my sadness. When I saw that

---

[1] *in the army:* that is, as a mercenary in the army of a ruler of a kingdom in the Near East.

[2] *Under some satrap:* Clinia follows his father's example.

I started thinking, "So many of them,
Worried for me alone, all so concerned
To care for me alone? All these housemaids   130
To see to my clothing? Ought I alone
To lay out so much money on my house?
And my son, who could equally make use
Of these things, or enjoy them even more,
At whose age it is only right for things
Like this to be available, I sent
Away from here in an unhappy state.
A sheer injustice! I'd think myself willing
To do whatever evil you could name
If I went on living in luxury.
As long as he leads such a life of need
And lacks a native land, because of my
Wrongdoing, so long will I slave for him."
I went ahead, left nothing in the house,   140
No furniture, no finery: I swept
It all away, the maids, and all the slaves
But those who could repay their own expense
By working on the farmland readily.
I put them all together and sold them.
I advertised the house immediately
For sale, and got some fifteen thousand ³ for it,
With which I bought this piece of land, and here
Is where I work. I had concluded, Chremes,
That I would be that much less in the wrong
By being a poor man for my son's sake;
That it was not right for me to enjoy
Any pleasure unless he came back here,
Safe and sound, to share in it with me.   150
CHREMES: I think you have a kind heart for your child,
    And he is utterly agreeable
    If handled properly and sensibly.
    But you did not know your son well enough,
    And he did not know you. When this is so,

---

³ *fifteen thousand:* fifteen talents in Greek silver, equivalent to $30,000 or more.

It's hard to live aright. You never showed
How much you valued him; he didn't dare
Believe in you the way a son should trust
His father. But if that had been the case,
These things would never have happened to you.
MENEDEMUS: It's like that, I admit. But I'm the one
Who's most at fault.
CHREMES: Menedemus, I hope
That things will be all right. And I am sure
That he will be here, safe and sound, quite soon.   160
MENEDEMUS: Would god it were that way!
CHREMES: Well, it will be.
If it suits you, please be my dinner guest
This very day. It's Dionysus Day.
MENEDEMUS: I cannot.
CHREMES: Why not? Spare yourself a bit,
I beg you. And your absent son would want
The same for you.
MENEDEMUS: It's not fitting for me,
Who drove him out to work, to take myself
Away from hardship.
CHREMES: Your mind is made up?
MENEDEMUS: It is.
CHREMES: Farewell, then.
MENEDEMUS: And the same to you. (*Exit*)
CHREMES: He brings me to the verge of tears, I feel
So sorry for him. But it's time today,
Time to remind my next door neighbor here,
Phania, to be my guest at dinner. I'll go   170
See whether he's at home. (*Exits and returns immediately*)
                              I didn't need
To remind them. They say they've already gone
To my house. So I keep my guests waiting.
I'll go right in. But why, I wonder now,
Are my doors creaking open? Who's coming out?
I'll just step over here and listen in.

Scene 2

CLITIPHO, CHREMES

CLITIPHO (*Calling back inside*): No need to worry, Clinia. They
    won't be long.
  I know she'll be with you right here today
  As soon as she gets the message. Dismiss
  The needless worry that's tormenting you,
  Right now.
CHREMES (*Aside*): Who can my son be talking to?
CLITIPHO (*Seeing him*): Oh, there's my father. I wanted him.
    Father,
  You're here in the nick of time.
CHREMES: Why is that?   180
CLITIPHO: You know our neighbor here, Menedemus?
CHREMES: Rather.
CLITIPHO: You know he has a son?
CHREMES: I heard
  He had. In Asia.
CLITIPHO: No, he isn't, father.
  He's here, at our house.
CHREMES: Well, I declare.
CLITIPHO: I caught
  Him disembarking, brought him from the ship
  Right off to dinner here. He's always been
  One of my best friends, from our childhood days.
CHREMES: You bring me pleasant news. I only wish
  I'd urged Menedemus to be with us
  More strongly, so I could be the first one
  To spring this unexpected happiness
  On him in my own home. But there's still time.
CLITIPHO: No: don't do that. It wouldn't work, father.
CHREMES: Why not?

CLITIPHO: Because Clinia's not at all sure
What he might do. He's only just arrived,
Afraid of everything, his father's wrath,
The way he feels toward his girl. He loves
Her to distraction, and on her account
There was a row, and Clinia left.
CHREMES: I know. 190
CLITIPHO: He sent his slave to find her in the city,
I sent our Syrus too.
CHREMES: How does he feel?
CLITIPHO: Clinia? He says that he's upset.
CHREMES: Upset?
Could anyone be less so? What is lacking
For him to have but what are called good things
For a man to have? Parents, countryland,
Friends, family, relations, affluence, all
Intact? Such things, of course, depend upon
Their owner's state of mind. For him who knows
How to use them, they are good things; for him
Who misuses them, they're a disadvantage.
CLITIPHO: His father always was a mean old grouch
And I'm afraid now more than ever, father,
He'll be angry at him more than he ought.
CHREMES (Aside): That man? But I'll restrain myself. It helps
If Clinia is still a little fearful.
CLITIPHO: What's that you're saying to yourself?
CHREMES: I'll say. 200
However things were going, Clinia
Should have stayed at home. Perhaps his father
Was a bit too hard on him for his passion.
He should have put up with it. For who can he
Put up with if he can't bear his own father?
Was Clinia to live in his father's style,
Or his father in his? He says he's hard on him.
That's wrong. Fathers' anger is almost always
Uniform; fathers, I mean, who are
Reasonable men. They want their sons not to
Be always after women, out for parties,

And give them small allowances. It all
Makes for good conduct. Once the mind is trapped
In sinful appetites, it cannot help
Following in its misguided footsteps.
It's wise to learn from the trials of others.
What is of use to you.   210
CLITIPHO: I'm sure it is.
CHREMES: I'll go in now and see what's for dinner
    And seeing now what time of day it is,
    Be sure you don't go too far from the house.

ACT II

Scene 1

CLITIPHO

CLITIPHO: What unjust judges fathers are of all
    Young men! They think it only right that we
    Should be born old men, instantly, as boys,
    Not privy to what adolescence brings.
    They govern as their passion now dictates,
    Not as it used to be. If I ever do have
    A son, he'll have an easygoing father,
    I swear; allowance made for his straying,
    An understanding of it, and forgiveness.
    Not like my father, who points out to me
    His own views through another. And, oh my god,   220
    When he's had a little to drink, how he
    Goes on about his own goings-on! And now
    He says, "Take your example of what's useful
    From others' trials." Shrewd! He just has no

Notion how deaf an ear I give his story.
My mistress' words move me much more, when she
Says, "Give me this," or "Get me that," but I
Have nothing to reply. I can't. No one
Is worse off than I am. For even Clinia,
Who has enough to deal with on his own,
Still has a nice, well-educated girl,
Unconscious of the courtesan's merry tricks.
There's no controlling mine: lady loverly's chatter!
She's so stuck-up, expensive, proud, a show-off.
As to what I might give her, I can say
Only, "Oh, certainly." I haven't nerve
To tell her I have nothing to draw from.
I've just got into the mess recently
As yet my father doesn't know about it.

Scene 2

CLINIA, CLITIPHO

CLINIA: If my affair was in all that good shape   230
   I know they'd have arrived by now. I fear
   That in my absence my woman has been
   Corrupted here. And many things fit in
   To strengthen that opinion in my mind:
   The place, the opportunities; her age;
   Her being subject to a scheming mother,
   Whose sweetest thoughts are those that tell of cash.
CLITIPHO: Clinia!
CLINIA: I feel so sorry for myself!
CLITIPHO: Won't you be careful not to let someone
   From your father's house see you coming out here?
CLINIA: All right. It's just that I sense some trouble
   In store for me.

CLITIPHO: Won't you keep from predicting
  Before you know the truth?
CLINIA: If it weren't bad,
  They'd have been here long since.
CLITIPHO: They will be here
  Quite soon.
CLINIA: But when will that "quite soon" be "now"?
CLITIPHO: Didn't you think how far it is from here?
  And you know women. While they're getting ready,   240
  Fussing around and starting to start out,
  It takes a year.
CLINIA: Oh, Clitipho, I'm afraid.
CLITIPHO: Breathe in, breathe out. Oh look there's Dromo now
  And Syrus with him. They're here now, for you.

Scene 3

SYRUS, DROMO, CLINIA, CLITIPHO

SYRUS (*Enters from far right*): That's it?
DROMO: That's it. Meantime,
    while we carved out
  Our sentences, the women got lost in transit.
CLITIPHO (*Seeing them in the distance*): Your woman's here, you
    hear that, Clinia?
CLINIA: I hear, at last, I see; I feel quite well.
DROMO (*To* SYRUS): No wonder, they're so loaded down, bringing
  That flock of maids with them.
CLINIA: Her maids? From where?
CLITIPHO: You're asking me?
SYRUS: It was wrong to leave them.
  What stuff they're lugging with them!
CLINIA: Oh dear, oh dear!
SYRUS: Gold trinkets, clothes. And now it's getting dark
  And they don't know the way. Stupid of us

To go ahead. Go back to meet them, Dromo.
Get a move on, don't stand there.

CLINIA: Oh dear me!   250
What a let-down!

CLITIPHO: Why so? What is it now
What torments you?

CLINIA: You're asking me? that question?
The maids, the jewels, clothes. When I left here
She had one servant girl. Where do you think she got
The rest of that stuff?

CLITIPHO: Oh, at last I get it.

SYRUS: God, what a mob! I know this house of ours
Will hardly hold them all. And will they eat!
And will they drink! Could anything be worse
For our old man? But there come the young men.
I wanted to see them.

CLINIA: What of our trust?
Oh Jupiter! While I, because of you,
Strayed off, half-mad, in exile from my land
You made yourself well-off, Antiphila;
You left me in the lurch, in great distress,
For whose sake I incurred the greatest blame
And disobeyed my father. Now I'm sorry
For him. I feel guilty. He used to harp
On such women's habits, to warn me off   260
In vain; he never could drive me away
From this one. But I'll do it now. But when
It would have been gracious of me, I couldn't.
No one could be worse off than me.

SYRUS (*Aside*):   I see:
He went astray because of what he heard
Us saying over there. (*To* CLINIA) Clinia, your girl
Is quite different from what you are thinking.
Her life is the same, her idea of you
The same it was, as far as we can judge
From first-hand evidence.

CLINIA: And what is it?

I'd rather think, more than anything, that I
Suspected her wrongly.
SYRUS: So you can know
   Each point in turn: the old woman, alleged
   To be her mother formerly, was not.   270
   And she is dead. I heard Antiphila
   Telling the other girl so, on the way
   To our house, just by chance.
CLITIPHO: What other girl?
SYRUS: Wait, Clitipho. I'll get to that after
   I've finished telling what I started to.
CLITIPHO: Well, hurry up.
SYRUS: Well, when we first arrived
   At their house, Dromo knocked hard at the door.
   An old woman came up and opened it
   And he burst in. And I was right behind him.
   The old woman bolted the door again
   And went back to her wool. So, in this way,
   If in no other, Clinia, you'd know
   How carefully she looked after her life   280
   In your absence. When you suddenly break
   In on a woman who doesn't expect you
   You have a good chance then to estimate
   The way of life daily habit prescribes
   For almost everyone's behavior.
   We found her working hard at her weaving,
   Modestly clad in black, and I suppose
   That old woman's death was the reason:
   No jewels; gotten up in the manner
   One dresses for oneself, no fancy garb
   Of the sort women wear to lead you on,
   Her hair let down and tossed back carelessly   290
   Around her head. But that's enough of that
CLINIA: Syrus, go on. Don't leave me in suspense
   About my happiness.
SYRUS: Well, the old woman
   Was working at her loom. One servant girl

Was working there beside her, clothed in rags,
Untidy, unlooked after.

CLITIPHO: If all this
Is true, as I believe it is, Clinia,
Can anyone be luckier than you?
That girl, you know, he said was so untidy,
Unlooked after? That's a good indication
Of how beyond reproach your mistress is,
Whose go-betweens are handled carelessly.
The system is for those who would approach   300
The mistresses to pay out money first
To their attendants.

CLINIA: Go on, please. But don't
You try to get in good with me. What did
She say when you mentioned my name to her?

SYRUS: When we said you were back and wanted her
To come to you, your mistress stopped her weaving
At once, her face became flooded with tears.
It happened, rest assured, for love of you.

CLINIA: I'm so happy, I don't know where I am.
The gods love me. And I was so afraid.

CLITIPHO: I told you it was nothing, Clinia.
But now it's my turn, Syrus. What about
The other girl?

SYRUS: We've brought Bacchis along.   310

CLITIPHO: You have? Brought Bacchis? Brought her where,
You character?

SYRUS: Where else, but to our house?

CLITIPHO: My father's?

SYRUS: One and the same.

CLITIPHO: You've got some nerve.

SYRUS: Well, after all, no daring deed is done,
No great move made, without taking some risks.

CLITIPHO: But look here, you devil, are you looking
For fame by throwing my life in the balance?
You make the slightest slip, and I'm done for.
(To CLINIA) What would you do to him?

SYRUS: I meant . . .

CLITIPHO: Meant what?

SYRUS: I'll tell you if I get a chance.

CLINIA: Give him the chance.

CLITIPHO: All right, Syrus, go on.

SYRUS: As the situation now stands, it's rather as if . . .

CLITIPHO: What's this long story he's starting out now
To tell me? Hell with that.

CLINIA: He's right, Syrus.
Lay off. Get to the point.

SYRUS: But really, I   320
Can't keep quiet, you're so unfair to me,
Clitipho, in so many ways; you're hard
To get along with.

CLINIA (*To* CLITIPHO): We ought to hear him out,
By Hercules, so just be still a moment.

SYRUS: You want to be in love, you want to get
Your girl, you want the money you give her
To be made up. You don't want to take risks
To get her. You're not wise foolishly,
Of course, if it is wise to want something
That cannot be. You either take the risks
Along with the blessings, or let the blessings go,
And with them the pitfalls. So, take a look
At which of these alternatives you want.
But still, I know the plan I found is right,
And a safe one. For at your father's house
You have the chance to be with your mistress
Without worry. The money you promised her [4]
I'll find the same way I planned to at first.
You've made me deaf in both ears asking me   330
To bring it off. Can you want something else?

CLITIPHO: If only this works out.

SYRUS: "If only"? Try it:
Then you'll see.

___

[4] *The money you promised her:* Syrus keeps trying to find means of helping
Clitipho get this sum, equivalent to $1,000, to smooth the course of his relationship
with Bacchis. If Clitipho can't get the money he will lose her.

CLITIPHO: All right, now: let's have your plan
  What is it?
SYRUS: We pretend that your mistress
  Is Clinia's.
CLITIPHO: Oh, great! So what will he
  Do with his own? Will she be called his too,
  As if the one were not disgrace enough?
SYRUS: Oh no, she'll be whisked off to your mother.
CLITIPHO: Why there?
SYRUS: It's a long story, Clitipho,
  If I tell you why I want to do that.
  I have a good reason.
CLITIPHO: Oh, what nonsense!
  It's not solid enough for me to think
  I won't be nervous.
SYRUS: Wait. If you're nervous—
  I have another scheme you'll both admit
  Is not risky.
CLITIPHO: I wish you could hit on
  Something like that.
SYRUS: Exactly. I'll meet Bacchis
  And tell her to go right back home.   340
CLITIPHO: I meant . . .
  What did you say?
SYRUS: I'll see that your worries
  Are all removed and you can sleep soundly
  On either ear.
CLITIPHO: Let's see. What shall I do?
CLINIA: You do? When something good . . .
CLITIPHO: Syrus, just tell me . . .
SYRUS: Just do what I tell you, or you will wish
  You had, too late, today, and hopelessly.
CLINIA: . . . is offered, take the pleasure while you can.
  You can't tell . . .
CLITIPHO: Syrus, I mean . . .
SYRUS: You may mean,
  But I intend to do it.

CLINIA: . . . when a chance
Like this will come your way again, if ever.
CLITIPHO: By Hercules, you're right. Syrus! Hey, Syrus!
I mean, don't go.
SYRUS (*Aside*): He's warming up. (*To* CLITIPHO) Did you want
   something?
CLITIPHO: Want something? Hey! Syrus, come back, come back,
Come back!
SYRUS: I'm right here. Tell me what you want.
You'll soon say you don't like this plan, either.   350
CLITIPHO: Oh no, Syrus. I trust you with myself,
My love, and my good name. You be the judge.
But don't do something I will be blamed for.
SYRUS: It's foolish, Clitipho, to caution me
On that subject, as if my own interests
Were less at stake than yours. If things go wrong
Somehow, for you there are hard words in store,
But for this man, hard blows. So this affair
Is not one I intend to take lightly.
But ask him to pretend that she is his.
CLINIA: Of course I'll do that. What it comes down to
Is that we have to.
CLITIPHO: No wonder I like you,   360
Clinia.
CLINIA: But don't let her spill the beans.
SYRUS: She's too clever for that.
CLITIPHO: I'm quite amazed
At how you could get her to come along
With you so nicely. She handles her lovers
Firmly: what lovers, too.
SYRUS: I got to her
At the right time, which is of first importance.
I came across an army officer
There, begging her to spend the night with him,
Beside himself with longing. She was handling
The fellow skillfully, and put him off
To keep his eager heart flaming, and earn
Your thanks for her efforts. But watch it, you,

And don't do something rash. You know how quick
Your father is to catch on to these things.   370
And I know how impetuous you are.
Suppress those sighs, those looks over the shoulder,
Those double-meaning phrases, those throat-clearings
And come-on coughs, and those giveaway smiles.

CLITIPHO: You'll praise my conduct.

SYRUS: See that you deserve it.

CLITIPHO: You'll marvel at me, you yourself.

SYRUS: How fast
The women are in following us here.

CLITIPHO: Where are they! Why are you holding me back?

SYRUS: She's not yours any longer.

CLITIPHO: Yes, I know,
As soon as she is in my father's house,
But meanwhile, now . . .

SYRUS: And no more now.

CLITIPHO: Give in.

SYRUS: I won't give in.

CLITIPHO: A tiny bit.

SYRUS: I forbid it.

CLITIPHO: Oh, just to say hello.

SYRUS: If you're smart, you'll depart.

CLITIPHO: I'm off. But what
About him?

SYRUS: He'll stay.

CLITIPHO: Lucky man!

SYRUS: Start walking.   380

Scene 4

BACCHIS, ANTIPHILA, CLINIA, SYRUS

BACCHIS: My dear Antiphila, by Pollux, I
Can only praise you and find you well advised

To see that your good habits compare well
With your good looks. I'm not at all surprised,
As the gods love me, that every man in town
Wants you for his. Your character is shown
In what you were saying, and how you think.
When I reflect in my heart on your life,
And on all of you women who steer clear
Of taking on the common mob of lovers,
It's not so strange you are the way you are,
And we the way we are. It suits you right
To be upright. As circumstances are,
They don't give us that choice. Drawn by our looks,
Our lovers cultivate our company.
When beauty starts to fade, they turn their minds   390
To someone else. Unless, meanwhile, we have
Some further prospect, we live quite alone.
But for you, once you've chosen to go on
Living with some man whose conduct most suits
Your own, lovers like those will stick with you.
In this way, you are good for one another
And truly bound together by each other,
So no disaster can fall on your love.
ANTIPHILA: I don't know about other women, but
I do know that I've always tried to make
My own desires match his exclusively.
CLINIA (*Aside*): Oh my Antiphila, that's just the way
Only you bring me back to my country.
When I was not with you all my troubles
Were ones I took lightly except for one,
Having to be without you.
SYRUS (*Aside*):   I agree.   400
CLINIA: Syrus, I can hardly stand it, not being
Allowed to make the most of my treasure
In my own way.
SYRUS: But from what I have seen
Of your father's reputation, he'll give
You a hard role to play for some time still.
BACCHIS: Who's that young man watching us over there?

ANTIPHILA: Oh, catch me, please!
BACCHIS: What is it, darling?
ANTIPHILA: I'm dying, dying!
BACCHIS: What's come over you?
CLINIA: Antiphila!
ANTIPHILA: Do I see Clinia,
   Or don't I?
BACCHIS: Who is it you see?
CLINIA: Hello,
   Darling.
ANTIPHILA: My darling Clinia, hello.
CLINIA: How are you?
ANTIPHILA: Happy that you are back home safe.
CLINIA: May I hold you, Antiphila? Oh you,
   The one my heart most wanted!
SYRUS: Go in. Chremes
   Has been waiting for you for some time now.

ACT III
(*The next morning*)

Scene 1

CHREMES, MENEDEMUS

CHREMES: It's getting light already. Shall I knock   410
   On my neighbor's door to let him know, first
   From me, his son is back? I realize
   His son would rather I didn't. But when
   I see how much his poor father suffers
   Because he went away, can I conceal
   So unhoped for a joy? I can't do that.

I'll help the old man any way I can.
I see my son ready to serve a friend
Of the same age, and to be his ally
In his affairs. It's only right for us,
As older men, to be of service to
Our fellow older men.

MENEDEMUS (*Enters*):   Either by nature I   420
Was born with a gift for unhappiness
Or the remark I hear so often made
Is not true, that time takes away the pain
And sorrow men have felt. Mine keeps growing
Larger each day, my sorrow for my son.
The longer he's away, the more I want
Him back, the more I long for him.

CHREMES: Oh, there
He is, coming outdoors. I'll go and speak to him.
Menedemus, greetings. I bring you news
You most want to be in on.

MENEDEMUS: You haven't heard
Something about my son, Chremes, have you?

CHREMES: Alive and well he is.

MENEDEMUS: Where is he, though?   430

CHREMES: At my house.

MENEDEMUS: My son?

CHREMES: Yes.

MENEDEMUS: He has come back?

CHREMES: Indeed he has.

MENEDEMUS: My Clinia is back?

CHREMES: That's what I said.

MENEDEMUS: Let's go. Take me to him,
I beg you.

CHREMES: He doesn't want you to know, yet,
He's back here, wants to keep out of your sight.
He's still afraid because of his misconduct
That your former severity may have
Grown even worse.

MENEDEMUS: But didn't you tell him
How I felt?

CHREMES: No.
MENEDEMUS: Why didn't you, Chremes?
CHREMES: Because it would be the worst thing for you,
   And for him too, if you showed so contrite
   And soft a heart.
MENEDEMUS: I can't be unbending.
   I've had enough of being a strict father,
   Quite enough.
CHREMES: Oh there you go, Menedemus,
   Impulsive either way, too generous,   440
   Or too stingy. You'll let yourself in for
   The same mischief, the one way or the other.
   Before, you scared your son away from here
   Rather than let him traffic with a mistress
   Who was quite happy, then, with small favors,
   And pleased with anything. Soon afterwards,
   Forced into it against her will, she started
   Pursuing profits in the common way.
   And now, when she cannot be held on to
   Without a huge outlay, you're eager to
   Give anything. To give you some idea
   Of how nicely set up she is at present   450
   To make a killing, first: she brought with her
   More than ten maids, loaded with clothes and jewels.
   If she had some Persian prince as her lover
   He'd never manage to meet her expenses.
   Much less can you.
MENEDEMUS: Is she inside there now?
CHREMES: Is she, you ask? I've felt it, I tell you.
   I've given one dinner just now, for her
   And her companions. If I had to give
   Another, I'd be done. To skip the rest:
   The wine alone she ran through, tasting, sipping it!
   "Oh, father," she'd say, "this is just so-so.
   And this, a little on the bitter side.
   See if you haven't something a bit smoother."
   I unsealed all the jars, and all the flasks.   460
   She had us all worried, and, mind you, that

Was only one night's feast. How will it be
For you, do you suppose, when they devour
You day after day? So help me god if I
Don't pity you, Menedemus, for your
Good luck.
MENEDEMUS: He's free to do just as he wants.
Let him have, use up, and exhaust my resources.
I'm quite determined to put up with anything
So long as I can have him here with me.
CHREMES: If you're set on that course, I think it is
Important not to let him know that you
Are giving him the money for his needs.
MENEDEMUS: How can I manage that?
CHREMES: Oh, any way
Except the one you're thinking of. Make use
Of anyone else, even if it means   470
Being tricked by some slave's clever dodges.
I know they were up to something, from the way
They acted on the sly at dinner, whispering
Together, Syrus and that slave of yours,
Advising the young men. For you it's worth
Losing a talent this way,[5] rather than
A mina your way. It's not so much, now,
A question of money as one of how
We give it to a young man with the least
Risk all around. Once your son understands
Your willingness to give away your life
And all your money rather than lose him,   480
Well, lord, how large a window you've opened
On idleness! How unpleasant for you
It would be then to live. For, all of us
Are made much worse by self-indulgent freedom.
He'll want whatever pops into his mind,

[5] *a talent this way, rather than/A mina your way:* Chremes is more money-conscious than Menedemus, perhaps because Menedemus was originally more well off, or has come to see that the value of money is nothing when compared to having a son. The mina is equivalent to a sixtieth of a talent, i.e., somewhat more than $25.

And won't stop to consider whether it
Is right or wrong, but just go after it.
Then you will not be able to endure
Both your money and him going to ruin;
And so you'll say you won't provide. Then, the issue
Will come to what he knows you most value,
And he will threaten to leave you again.

MENEDEMUS: You see it truly, and state it as it is.   490

CHREMES: By Hercules, I didn't close my eyes
In sleep last night, searching for some idea
Of how best to hand back your son to you.

MENEDEMUS: Here's my right hand, Chremes, I hope that you
Will offer me the same.

CHREMES: I'm with you there.

MENEDEMUS: You know what I would like you to do now?

CHREMES: Tell me.

MENEDEMUS: Since you have realized the slaves
Are starting to trick me, see to it that
They speed it up. I'm eager to give him
What he desires, and eager to see him.

CHREMES: I'll take the job. I have a little business
On hand that interferes. Our neighbors here,
Simus and Crito, are having a dispute
Over their boundaries, and they've asked me
To judge the case. I'll go to them right now   500
And tell them I can't help them out today
As I had said I would. I'll be right back.

MENEDEMUS: Please do. (*Exit* CHREMES) Oh, I could swear it by
    the gods!
How much better prepared by nature are
All men to see another's situation
And judge it than they are to see their own!
Is this because in our affairs we are
Too much wrapped up in our own happiness
Or in our sorrow? How much more this man
Knows of my case than I know by myself!

CHREMES (*Returning*): I've begged off, so I'm free to lend you
    help.

I'll have to catch Syrus and talk to him.
Oh, someone's coming out of my house now.
Let's step over toward your house a bit   510
So they don't think we've put our heads together.

Scene 2

SYRUS, CHREMES

SYRUS: Let's go, this way and that: in spite of all,
    We'll have to find money, and set a trap
    For his father.
CHREMES (*Aside*): It wasn't me, was it
    That they were setting their trap for? I guess
    Clinia's slave was too late getting here,
    And so the job was given to our man.
SYRUS: Who's talking over there? I'm done for now:
    Suppose he heard me!
CHREMES: Syrus!
SYRUS: Oh . . . er . . . ah.
CHREMES: What are you up to?
SYRUS: Oh quite up to scratch,
    Thank you. But I'm amazed, Chremes, to see
    You out so early. You drank so late last night.
CHREMES: Oh, nothing in excess.
SYRUS: You call that "nothing"?   520
    To me you're like one who, as they say,
    Has the constitution of an old eagle.
CHREMES: Now, never mind.
SYRUS: That woman's awfully nice,
    His mistress, quite polite.
CHREMES: Yes, I suppose so.
    She's awfully good-looking; that's the main thing.
SYRUS: Well, not good-looking as women once were,
    But as the style is now, I guess she'll do.

I'm not at all surprised that Clinia
Is crazy over her. He's got some father,
A frightful miser, terribly stingy,
Our neighbor here. You know him? As if he
Weren't dripping with money, his son decamped
For lack of means. Did you know that happened
As I say?
CHREMES: Why should I not know of it?
The man deserves the mill!   530
SYRUS: What man?
CHREMES: I meant
The young man's slave . . .
SYRUS (*Aside*):   Syrus, I was afraid
For you, for a moment there.
CHREMES: . . . who let it happen.
SYRUS: What could he do?
CHREMES: You ask? Somehow, he'd find
The wherewithal, invent some strategy
By which the boy could be given his girl
And keep his harsh father, against his will.
SYRUS: You're joking.
CHREMES: Syrus, that's what he should do.
SYRUS: But you're not praising those who fool their masters?
CHREMES: At the right time, I praise them.
SYRUS: You're right there.
CHREMES: In the sense that such tactics often are
A cure for much distress. For instance, here:
His only son would have stayed right at home.   540
SYRUS (*Aside*): I can't tell whether he's saying these things
In earnest, or joking. I only know
He gives me heart to feel better about
My plan.
CHREMES: And what's he waiting for, Syrus?
The boy to go away again because
His father won't put up with his expenses?
Isn't he inventing some clever plan
Regarding the old man?
SYRUS: He's much too dumb.
CHREMES: You ought to help him out for the young man's sake.

SYRUS: Oh, I can do that easily, if you
  Tell me to. I'm in close touch with how
  Business like that gets done.
CHREMES: So much the better, then,
  By Hercules.
SYRUS: Of course, it's not like me
  To be telling lies.
CHREMES: But do it anyway.   550
SYRUS: And you might make a point of remembering,
  If something else like this happens by chance:
  It's only human, if your son should act
  Along these lines.
CHREMES: There'll be no need, I hope.
SYRUS: I hope so, too. But I did not say that
  Because I'd noticed him planning something
  Along those lines. It's just that, if he does,
  I hope you won't be hard on him. You see
  How young he is. Of course, I have no doubt
  That, should occasion call for it, I could
  Handle you nobly, Chremes.
CHREMES: Well, as to that,
  Should need arise, we'll see what's to be done.
  Now get busy. (*Exit* CHREMES)
SYRUS: I never, ever, heard
  My master speaking more to my advantage,
  Or heard him offer such an invitation
  To me to outwit him and run less risk.   560
  But who's this coming out from our place now?

Scene 3

CHREMES, CLITIPHO, SYRUS

CHREMES: How dare you? How can you behave like that,
  Clitipho? Is that any way to act?
CLITIPHO: What did I do?

CHREMES: I saw you put your hand
On that woman's breasts just now, didn't I,
That courtesan's?
SYRUS (*Aside*):   It's all over now. I'm done for.
CLITIPHO: Me?
CHREMES: With my own eyes, don't you dare deny it.
You offer such an insult to Clinia
If you don't keep your hands off her. Some gall,
You've got, to invite a friend home with you
And toy with his mistress. And last night, too,
Over the wine, you were so shameless.
SYRUS (*Aside*):   That's right.
CHREMES: So ill behaved! I worried endlessly
About what might happen, so help me god.
I know what lovers are. They take notice
Of things you wouldn't think they were observing.   570
CLITIPHO: Believe me, father, I would never do
A thing like that to Clinia.
CHREMES: May be.
But I suggest you come out here, at least,
Some distance off, not stick so close to them.
Their passion packs a punch, but your presence
Keeps them from doing what it tells them to.
I speak from experience. There's not a friend
Among those I call mine, in whose presence
I'd dare reveal my secret thoughts, Clitipho.
In another's presence, his rank deters me.
I feel ashamed, in front of someone else,
Of doing something that would make me look
Awkward or brash. And you can rest assured
This is the case with him. We, for our part,
Are to respect the other's attitude
And where and how we must fit in with it.
SYRUS (*Aside*): How he goes on!
CLITIPHO (*Aside*):   I'm done for.
SYRUS: Clitipho,
Is this how I instructed you? You play
The role of sensible and self-controlled . . .   580

CLITIPHO: Oh shut up.
SYRUS: . . . gentleman, to perfection.
CHREMES: Syrus, I'm ashamed of him.
SYRUS: I can believe it.
    You have good cause. It even worries me.
CLITIPHO: You're wrecking my chances.
SYRUS: I only speak
    The truth as I see it.
CLITIPHO: Then I'm not to
    Go near them?
CHREMES: I ask you, is there one way
    To go near them?
SYRUS (*Aside*): It's finished. Clitipho
    Will give himself away before I've managed
    To get the money. (*To* CHREMES) Chremes, would you care
    To listen to a dumb bunny like me?
CHREMES: What should I do?
SYRUS: Tell him to go away,
    Somewhere away from here.
CLITIPHO: Go away where?
SYRUS: Wherever you want. Make some room for them.
    Go take a walk.
CLITIPHO: A walk? A walk to where?
SYRUS: God, it's not as if there wasn't any place.
    Just go out there somewhere, anywhere you want.
CHREMES: He's talking sense, I think.
CLITIPHO: May the gods wreck you,
    Syrus, for pushing me away from here!
SYRUS: And after this, you keep your hands to yourself! 590
    (*Exit* CLITIPHO)
    You do think so? What do you think he'd do
    If you did not chastise, control, and warn him
    As much as the gods give you means to do so?
CHREMES: I mean to tend to that.
SYRUS: He must be, now,
    Controlled by you, master.
CHREMES: It will be done.

SYRUS: That's a wise course. For he listens to me
  These days, less and less.
CHREMES: Have you managed anything
  About what I was speaking to you of
  A while ago, Syrus? Hit on something
  You like, or not?
SYRUS: Some scheme, you mean? Oh yes,
  I've just come up with something.
CHREMES: Good fellow.
  Tell me, what is it?
SYRUS: I'll lay it out now,
  But logically, as one thing falls in place
  After another.
CHREMES: Why do it that way, Syrus?
SYRUS: The courtesan's a shrewd number.
CHREMES: It seems so.
SYRUS: Ah, if you only knew! God, look at how
  She starts her scheming. There was an old woman   600
  From Corinth here. Bacchis had given her
  A loan of one thousand silver drachmas.
CHREMES: What then?
SYRUS: The old woman died, and left
  Her young daughter to Bacchis as a pledge,
  In security for the debt.
CHREMES: Oh, now I see.
SYRUS: Bacchis brought that girl here, and she's the one
  Who's with your wife now.
CHREMES: What then?
SYRUS: And so, then,
  She now insists that Clinia pay over
  The money right away, and says she won't
  Give her to him until she does. Insists
  On getting one thousand nummi for the deal.
CHREMES: Insists, does she?
SYRUS: God yes, no doubt about it.
  I took it just that way.
CHREMES: What have you in mind
  To do now?

SYRUS: Me? I'll go to Menedemus
   And tell him she's a captive from Caria,
   A wealthy, well-born girl. If he buys her,
   There's plenty of profit in the bargain.
CHREMES: You're wrong there.
SYRUS: How so?
CHREMES: I now answer you   610
   As if I were Menedemus: "No sale.
   I'm not buying." How do you answer that?
SYRUS: Precisely what I wanted him to say.
CHREMES: How's that?
SYRUS: He need not buy her.
CHREMES: He need not?
SYRUS: Lord, no.
CHREMES: How's that, I wonder?
SYRUS: You'll find out soon enough.
   But wait a moment. Why is our door opening
   With such a noisy creaking of those hinges?

ACT IV

Scene 1

SOSTRATA, CHREMES, CANTHARA (Nurse), SYRUS

SOSTRATA: Unless my mind is fooling me, this ring
   Is the same one, I do believe I left
   Beside my daughter when she was exposed.
CHREMES (*Aside*): Now what's the drift of this announcement,
      Syrus?
SOSTRATA: What do you say? Does it look like it to you?

CANTHARA: I said as much myself, the very moment
    You showed me it. That's it.
SOSTRATA: But do make sure
    You've looked at it closely enough, my dear.
CANTHARA: I really have.
SOSTRATA: Then go back in and tell me
    When she's finished bathing. (*Exit* CANTHARA) I'll wait out here,
    Meanwhile, for my husband.
SYRUS (*To* CHREMES):   It's you she wants.
    See what she wants. She seems rather upset.   620
    And not for nothing. I'm a little worried.
CHREMES: She took great pains to speak a lot of nonsense.
SOSTRATA (*Seeing* CHREMES): Oh, there, my husband.
CHREMES: Oh yes,
    good wife.
SOSTRATA: You were
    The very one I wanted.
CHREMES: Do tell me
    What you wanted to say.
SOSTRATA: I ask you, first,
    Not to believe I dared do anything
    Against your strict instructions.
CHREMES: You want me
    To believe that of you, when there can be
    No shadow of a doubt? Well, I believe you.
SYRUS (*Aside*): An apology like this implies some guilt.
SOSTRATA: You will remember once when I was pregnant
    How strongly you insisted that if I
    Gave birth to a girl you were unwilling
    To acknowledge the child?
CHREMES: I know what you did:
    You had the child and raised her.
SYRUS (*Aside*):   So she did.
    I've gained a lady boss, he's gained a loss.
SOSTRATA: Oh, not at all. There was a woman here
    From Corinth, a trustworthy older woman.
    I gave the child to her to be exposed.
CHREMES: Dear god, how could you have been so naive?   630

SOSTRATA: Too bad for me! What did I do?
CHREMES: You ask?
SOSTRATA: If I did something wrong, Chremes, I did it
    Unintentionally. I'm sure of that.
CHREMES: What I'm sure of, even if you deny it,
    Is that you speak and act very unwisely
    In everything you do. Just look, for instance,
    At the great number of mistakes you made
    In this affair. First, had you wanted to
    Abide by my instructions, you should have
    Let the child die, not say that she was dead
    In words, but in reality extend
    Hope for her life. I won't dwell on that. Granted,
    There is mercy, there are maternal instincts.
    But think how little thought you put into
    The consequences! It's quite obvious
    Your daughter was entrusted to that woman,
    For all you cared, to make her life one day
    As a courtesan, or to be sold off   640
    As a slave on the market. And I suppose
    You thought to yourself, "What matter, so long
    As she is kept alive?" But, why have dealings
    With people who know nothing of the law
    And have no care for what is just and right?
    Whether it's better, worse, advantageous
    Or inexpedient, they have no regard
    For anything but their own interests.
SOSTRATA: Chremes, I did the wrong thing. I'm convinced.
    I now ask this of you, that in so far
    As your nature is more severe, you be
    The more forgiving. Then, your sense of justice
    Will give protection to my foolishness.
CHREMES: Of course I'll overlook what you have done.
    But, Sostrata, my quickness to comply
    Teaches you much that isn't really right.
    Now come, what started you talking to me
    About this matter?

SOSTRATA: Since we are all so prone
　To silly superstitions, when I gave
　Our daughter to that woman to expose
　I took a ring from my finger [6] and told   650
　Her to leave it beside the exposed child.
　If she had died she still would not have been
　Cut off from her inheritance by us.
CHREMES: That was well done. You saved yourself and her.
SOSTRATA: And here's the ring.
CHREMES: Where did you get it?
SOSTRATA: The young girl Bacchis brought along with her . . .
SYRUS (*Aside*): Good lord, what's she saying?
SOSTRATA: . . . went in to bathe
　And gave it to me for safekeeping. At first
　I didn't notice anything, but afterwards,
　As soon as I saw what it was, right then
　I ran to you.
CHREMES: What do you make of her,
　Or suppose, now?
SOSTRATA: I don't know what to think.
　You might ask her where she came by that ring,
　If that could be found out.
SYRUS (*Aside*):   That does me in.
　I see more hope than I want to. If she's   660
　The one, she's ours.
CHREMES: The woman's still alive
　You gave our daughter to?
SOSTRATA: I wouldn't know.
CHREMES: At the time, what did she say she'd done?
SOSTRATA: That she'd obeyed my orders.
CHREMES: Her name, then?
　So she can be looked for.
SOSTRATA: Her name? Philtera.
SYRUS (*Aside*): The very one. Antiphila is saved,
　And I'm destroyed. No doubt about that fact.

　　[6] *a ring from my finger:* the primarily Greek custom of exposing an unwanted
child is hedged about by scruples—in this case Sostrata did not want her daughter
to be thought of as disinherited, utterly without resources.

CHREMES: Come inside here with me now, Sostrata.
SOSTRATA: This has worked out beyond my wildest hopes.
   I was so terribly afraid, Chremes,
   That you would be as dead set in your mind
   Today, as when you acknowledged [7] the child.
CHREMES: A man often can't be the way he wants,
   If circumstance prevents. And at this point
   I want a daughter. Years ago, I didn't.

Scene 2

SYRUS

SYRUS: Unless my mind is fooling me a lot,
   Disaster is not very far from me:
   So hard pressed are my troops, entrapped
   In a narrow pass. If I don't see some way   670
   To keep the old man from discovering
   That she's his son's mistress. As for my hopes
   Of getting the money, or thinking that
   I could fool him, they've come down to nothing.
   If I can just get off, without exposing
   My flank, it's a triumph. And what a pain,
   To have so juicy a morsel snatched off
   So suddenly, when my mouth was watering.
   So what to do, to think up? My whole plan
   Will have to be replanned. Nothing's so hard
   It can't be worked out with a little planning.
   Shall I begin this way? No, not this way.
   Then this? It comes to the same thing.

[7] *acknowledged: tollere,* "to acknowledge." According to a custom prevalent among both Greeks and Romans, the father of a new-born infant was called upon to decide whether it should be raised or exposed to death. If he decided upon the former course he formally raised (*tollere*) the child from the ground or other place where it had been laid for the purpose. Hence the Latin expression *liberos tollere,* which means "to bring up." Otherwise the child was exposed.

Ah, here's one. No: that's just not possible.
Oh, wait. Here's a good one. Oh, excellent!
I've got it just right, now. By Hercules,
I think I'll drag that runaway money
Back here to my side, yet, and still and all.

Scene 3

CLINIA, SYRUS

CLINIA: After this nothing could happen to me
   That could bring sorrow. Untold happiness
   Has started up for me. I give in now   680
   To my father, a much more model son
   Than even he might want.
SYRUS (*Aside*):   I wasn't fooled:
   She has been recognized, from what I hear.
   (*To* CLINIA) I'm happy that this has happened to you
   Just as you might have wanted it.
CLINIA: Syrus,
   Old boy, you heard about it?
SYRUS: How could I
   Not have when I was present all the time?
CLINIA: Have you ever heard of something so perfect
   Happening to anyone?
SYRUS: No, I have not.
CLINIA: So help me god if I'm not more happy
   For her sake than for mine. She is well worth
   Whatever recognition there may be.
SYRUS: I think so too. But come now, Clinia,
   And take turns listening. We have to see
   That your friend's situation is secure
   And his father does not find out about
   His mistress.
CLINIA: Jupiter! What joy!
SYRUS: Quiet!   690

CLINIA: Antiphila, my girl, will marry me!
SYRUS: Will you keep on interrupting like this?
CLINIA: What can I do? Oh, Syrus, I'm so happy:
    Put up with me.
SYRUS: I'm putting up with you.
CLINIA: We've entered on a life of the gods.
SYRUS: I guess
    I'm just wasting my time.
CLINIA: Now speak to me:
    I'm listening.
SYRUS: But not paying attention.
CLINIA: I will.
SYRUS: I said that now we have to see
    That your friend's situation is secure.
    If you leave us now and leave Bacchis here
    Our old man will know she's his son's mistress.
    But if you take her with you, the secret
    Will be as well kept as it has been so far.
CLINIA: But, Syrus, nothing could work more against my marriage.
    What face can I put on before my father? You see   700
    What I'm saying?
SYRUS: Why not face up to him?
CLINIA: But what to say? What excuse can I make?
SYRUS: I don't want you to lie. Just tell it plain,
    The way things are.
CLINIA: What's this you say?
SYRUS: I tell you:
    Say that you love Antiphila, and want
    Her as your wife, and that the other girl
    Is Clitipho's.
CLINIA: A reasonable request,
    A just command, an easy thing to do!
    And I suppose you then want me to ask
    My father to keep this from your old man?
SYRUS: Oh no. He tells it straight the way it is.
CLINIA: Are you sober, or in your right senses?
    You're wrecking his chances, clearly. Tell me:
    How can his situation be secure?

SYRUS: I think my plan deserves to take first prize.
   I take great pride in my capacities,   710
   My mighty cleverness, to fool them both
   By telling them the truth. When your old man
   Tells ours that Bacchis is his son's mistress,
   He still will not believe him.
CLINIA: But in this way
   You once again deprive me of all hope
   For my marriage. So long as Chremes thinks
   She's my mistress he won't give me his daughter.
   Perhaps you don't care what happens to me,
   So long as you look out for Clitipho.
SYRUS: How long the hell of a time do you think
   I mean for you to keep up this pretense?
   One day: until I've gotten the money.
   Just keep quiet that long; that's all I ask.
CLINIA: Is that enough? But what if his father
   Finds out about it? What will we do then?
SYRUS: Suppose I mention those who say "Suppose
   The sky fell in?"
CLINIA: I'm scared to do it.
SYRUS: Scared?   720
   As if you didn't have it in your power
   To clear yourself whenever you want to
   And bring the whole thing out into the open.
CLINIA: All right. Have Bacchis move over to our place.
SYRUS: That's fine. Here she comes, out of our place.

Scene 4

BACCHIS, CLINIA, SYRUS, DROMO, PHRYGIA

BACCHIS (*Pretends not to see* SYRUS *and* CLINIA):
   How nice of Syrus, enticing me out here
   With promises to lend me ten minae.

But if he stands me up, he'll ask me out
Again as often as he wants to come
And not find me. Or, when I've said I will,
And fixed the time, and he's told Clitipho,
Who's dangling in suspense, I won't show up.
Syrus will get paid back with a bruised back.

CLINIA (*Aside*): That's quite a shrewd promise she's making you.

SYRUS (*Aside*): You think she's only joking? She'll make good
  On it, if I'm not careful.

BACCHIS (*Aside*):   Still asleep.   730
  I'll wake them up. (*Louder*) Oh, Phrygia, dear, you heard
  About the country villa of Charinus
  That man was pointing out to us just now?

PHRYGIA: Yes, I did hear.

BACCHIS: He said it was next door
  To Chremes' farm, on the right side?

PHRYGIA: Yes, I remember.

BACCHIS: Well, run right over there, fast as you can.
  An officer is helping him enjoy
  The Feast of Dionysus.

SYRUS (*Aside*):   What's she up to?

BACCHIS: Tell him I've been detained unwillingly
  And am still here. But I'll work out some way
  To give them all the slip and slip away
  To join him there.

SYRUS (*Aside*):   That does us in. (*Aloud*) Wait, Bacchis,
    wait.
  Where are you sending that girl, for heaven's sake?
  Tell her to wait.

BACCHIS (*To* PHRYGIA): You'd better keep going.

SYRUS: I say the money's here and waiting.

BACCHIS: Well, then,
  I'll wait.

SYRUS: And then, you'll have it very soon.

BACCHIS: When you please. I'm not rushing you, am I?

SYRUS: I want you to do something for me, first.

BACCHIS: What?

SYRUS: You must move to Menedemus' house
  And take your train of servants and baggage.   740
BACCHIS: What are you up to now, you poor excuse?
SYRUS: Me? Forging money to give you.
BACCHIS: Am I
  Someone you think worth playing your tricks on?
SYRUS: I have my reasons.
BACCHIS: What business have I
  With you in that house?
SYRUS: None at all.
  I'm only giving you back what is yours.
BACCHIS: Well, let's be on our way, then.
CLINIA: Follow me. (*They go
    into* MENEDEMUS' *house*)
SYRUS: Hey, Dromo!
DROMO (*Coming out of* MENEDEMUS' *house*): Who wants
    me?
SYRUS: Syrus.
DROMO: What's up now?
SYRUS: Take all of Bacchis's maids and all her stuff
  Over to your house, right away.
DROMO: Sure. Why?
SYRUS: Don't ask questions. Let them take along
  Whatever stuff they brought with them to our place.
  Our old man's going to hope his expenses
  Are going down when they all go away.
  He doesn't realize how great a loss
  This gain will net him. You'll be smart, Dromo,
  If you don't know a bit of what you know.
DROMO: You'll be saying I've lost the power of speech.

Scene 5

CHREMES, SYRUS

CHREMES: So help me if it isn't my turn now
   To pity Menedemus; so much trouble   750
   Has come his way. He has to play the host
   To that woman and all her retinue.
   Of course I know he won't feel anything
   For some days yet, it means so much to him
   To have his son back home. But when he sees
   How much it costs him every day at home,
   With no end to it, he'll wish that his son
   Would go away again. But here's Syrus:
   Just when I wanted him.
SYRUS (*Aside*):   Shall I go up
   To him?
CHREMES: Oh, Syrus!
SYRUS: Oh yes, there you are.
CHREMES: How are things?
SYRUS: I'd hoped I'd bump into you.
CHREMES: You seem to have transacted some business
   With old Menedemus.
SYRUS: What we talked of
   A while ago? No sooner said than done,   760
   That's my report.
CHREMES: You're sure?
SYRUS: Well sure, I'm sure.
CHREMES: I can't resist patting your head for that.
   So come here, Syrus. I'll do something for you
   For that good deed, and do it with pleasure.
SYRUS: If you knew how good a notion I had!
CHREMES: Oh come now, you're not boasting just because
   It came out as you wanted?

SYRUS: No, not boasting,
　Just telling you the truth.
CHREMES: Tell me what's up.
SYRUS: Well, Clinia told Menedemus that Bacchis
　Was the mistress of your son Clitipho,
　And he had only brought her to their house
　To keep you from finding out about it.
CHREMES: A smart move.
SYRUS: What's that? How do you like it?
CHREMES: Almost too good.
SYRUS: You ought to know how good.   770
　But listen to the next moves we must make.
　Clinia says that he has seen your daughter;
　Her beauty won him to her at first sight.
　He wants her as his wife.
CHREMES: You mean my girl
　Who's just been found?
SYRUS: The same. And he intends
　To ask that you be asked for her in marriage.
CHREMES: But why, Syrus? I don't quite follow that.
SYRUS: Oh, you're too slow.
CHREMES: May be.
SYRUS: He'll get money
　To use for expenses, for clothes and jewels . . .
　You follow that?
CHREMES: You mean, to buy things with?
SYRUS: Precisely.
CHREMES: But I won't give her to him.
　I don't promise her to him in marriage.
SYRUS: You don't? Why not?
CHREMES: Why not? You ask me that?   780
　To someone who . . .
SYRUS: As you please. I didn't mean
　You ought to give her up for once and all,
　But just pretend you would.
CHREMES: It's not my style,
　To make pretenses. Tangle up your schemes
　But don't entangle me in them. Would I

Promise my daughter to a man I don't
Intend to give her to?
SYRUS: I thought you might.
CHREMES: Not in the least.
SYRUS: It could have been worked out
Quite cleverly. I started this because,
Some time ago, you urged me to so much.
CHREMES: I know.
SYRUS: As to the rest of what you say,
Chremes, I acquiesce.
CHREMES: But still and all,
I very much want you to do your best
To bring it off, but in some other way.
SYRUS: It will get done. I'll find a way somehow.   790
As I told you, the money your daughter
Owes Bacchis will still have to be paid back.
And you of course won't try to get out of it
By saying, "What has that to do with me?
I didn't borrow it, did I? Did I
Issue orders? Did she have any right
To mortgage my daughter against my will?"
You know they say, "The letter of the law
Often obliterates the right decision."
CHREMES: I won't do that, of course.
SYRUS: Oh, others might,
But not you. They all think you're plenty rich,
And well set up.
CHREMES: I'll take her the money
Myself, in fact.
SYRUS: No. Better tell your son   800
To do it.
CHREMES: Why?
SYRUS: Because he's now the one
Suspected of being in love with her.
CHREMES: So what?
SYRUS: So: it will look more natural
For him to give it to her. I can get

What I want then that much more easily.
Oh, here he is. Bring the money.
CHREMES: I'll bring it.

Scene 6

CLITIPHO, SYRUS

CLITIPHO: There's nothing so easy it isn't hard
When you don't want to do it. This walk, now,
Was not tiring, but I got tired of it.
There's nothing I fear more than once again
Being pushed off somewhere away from here
And left without a chance of seeing Bacchis.
I hope the gods and goddesses, all of them,   810
Destroy you, Syrus, with that crackpot scheme
You hatched. You're always thinking something up
Like this, to use to put the screws on me.
SYRUS: Get out, won't you, and go where you belong?
Your charging in here almost ruined me.
CLITIPHO: I wish it had, by god. You deserve it.
SYRUS: Deserve it? Why? I'm glad I heard you say that
Before you got the money I was going
To give you.
CLITIPHO: But what would you have me say
To you? You pulled my leg. You brought my mistress
Here, but I can't lay my hands on her.
SYRUS: Well, I've cooled down a bit. But do you know   820
Where your Bacchis is now?
CLITIPHO: She's at our house.
SYRUS: No.
CLITIPHO: Where, then?
SYRUS: She's at Clinia's.
CLITIPHO: I'm done for.

SYRUS: Cheer up. You'll soon be taking
  Her the money that you had promised her.
CLITIPHO: You're kidding. Where from?
SYRUS: From your own father.
CLITIPHO: You wouldn't kid me, would you?
SYRUS: You'll find out,
  When it happens.
CLITIPHO: I'm such a lucky fellow!
  You're great, Syrus!
SYRUS: Your father's coming out.
  Don't act surprised by whatever he does.
  Just go along with him. Don't say too much.

Scene 7

CHREMES, CLITIPHO, SYRUS

CHREMES: Where's Clitipho?
SYRUS (*To* CLITIPHO):   Say "Here I am."
CLITIPHO: Oh, here
  He is, father.
CHREMES (*To* SYRUS): Have you told him what's on?
SYRUS: I told him nearly everything.   830
CHREMES (*To* CLITIPHO):   Take this money
  And carry it.
SYRUS (*To* CLITIPHO): Go on, blockhead. Don't stand there.
  Why don't you take it?
CLITIPHO: All right. Hand it over.
SYRUS: Come with me quickly, this way. (*To* CHREMES) You wait
    here
  Until we come out. We won't be there long. (*They go out*)
CHREMES: My daughter now has ten minae from me
  I think of as paid out for her support.
  Another ten will follow these for clothes;
  And then they ask two talents for the dowry.

Our customs cost us more than is quite fair.
And now I'll have to let my business go
And look for someone, like a son-in-law,   840
To give the property I worked to own.

Scene 8

MENEDEMUS, CHREMES

MENEDEMUS (*Calling back inside to* CLINIA):
  My son, I think I'm a very lucky man,
  Knowing that you've come back to your senses.
CHREMES (*Aside*): How wrong he is!
MENEDEMUS: Chremes, I wanted you.
  Help me hang on to my son and myself
  And family, in so far as you can.
CHREMES: Tell me, what is it you want me to do?
MENEDEMUS: Today you found a daughter.
CHREMES: What of it?
MENEDEMUS: Clinia wants her given as his wife.
CHREMES: What kind of person are you?
MENEDEMUS: Person? I?
CHREMES: Have you forgotten already what we
  Discussed about the scheme, the smart method
  They'd use to get some money out of you?   850
MENEDEMUS: I remember.
CHREMES: That's what they're up to now.
MENEDEMUS: What's your story, Chremes? There is no doubt
  That it's Clitipho's mistress at my house.
  They say so.
CHREMES: And what's more you believe it.
  They also say that your son wants a wife,
  So when I have consented you will give
  Money to buy clothes for her, and jewels,
  And other things needed.

MENEDEMUS: That's it, of course:
  The money's for the mistress.
CHREMES: She's the one
  Who'll get it.
MENEDEMUS: Poor me, then! It did no good
  Being happy. But I'd do anything
  To keep from losing him. What can I say
  You said, Chremes, to keep him from knowing
  I found out, and holding a grudge against me?   860
CHREMES: A grudge? You're too easy on him, Menedemus.
MENEDEMUS: Let me go on as I've begun, Chremes,
  And see me through it.
CHREMES: Say that we've conferred,
  And taken up the matter of the marriage.
MENEDEMUS: I'll say that. And then what?
CHREMES: That I'll do it,
  That I approve the choice of son-in-law;
  And even go so far, if you want to,
  As saying that I offer him her hand.
MENEDEMUS: Well now, I'd hoped for that.
CHREMES: Then he can ask
  For what he wants from you the more quickly
  And you give him what he wants even sooner.
MENEDEMUS: That's what I want.
CHREMES: It won't be long before,
  In my view, you'll have had enough of him.
  No matter what, though, if you have good sense,
  You'll give with care, a little at a time.   870
MENEDEMUS: I'll do that.
CHREMES: Go inside. See what he wants.
  I'll be at home if you want anything
  Of me.
MENEDEMUS: I will want you. I'll want to let
  You know whatever it is I've been doing.

ACT V

Scene 1

MENEDEMUS, CHREMES

MENEDEMUS: I know I'm not so shrewd, so perceptive;
   But this stage-manager, prompter, director,
   Chremes, outdoes me. Any name you want
   That fits a fool applies to me: jackass,
   Lead-head, blockhead, dead log. But there's no name
   For him. His density outdoes them all.
CHREMES (*Calling back inside to* SOSTRATA):
   Oh, do desist from deafening the gods,
   Dear wife, by thanking them because your daughter
   Has been discovered. Unless, of course, you judge
   Them by your own standards, and think that they   880
   Don't understand a thing until it's said
   A hundred times over. I wonder now
   Why my son's been in there so long with Syrus?
MENEDEMUS: Who are those men you say are lingering
   Inside there, Chremes?
CHREMES: Oh, Menedemus,
   You're here. Tell me: did you tell Clinia
   What I told you?
MENEDEMUS: Yes, all.
CHREMES: What did he say?
MENEDEMUS: He started acting happy, like people
   Who want to marry.
CHREMES: Ho, ho! That's a good one!
MENEDEMUS: What makes you laugh?

CHREMES: I was thinking of my slave,
 The so resourceful Syrus.
MENEDEMUS: Why think of him?
CHREMES: He even shapes the looks on men's faces,
 The fiend.
MENEDEMUS: You mean, my son was just pretending
 To be happy?
CHREMES: Quite so.
MENEDEMUS: The same idea
 Occurred to me.
CHREMES: He's an old hand.
MENEDEMUS: You'd think so
 All the more if you knew more about it.
CHREMES: Is that so?
MENEDEMUS: Would you like to hear the rest?   890
CHREMES: Wait. First I want to know how much you lost.
 For when you told your son the girl was his
 Dromo, of course, dropped hints about the need
 For clothes, jewels, and servants for the bride,
 So you'd give them the money.
MENEDEMUS: No.
CHREMES: What? No?
MENEDEMUS: Yes. No.
CHREMES: Your son didn't?
MENEDEMUS: No. Not at all,
 Chremes. He only pressed me more for one thing:
 To celebrate the wedding rites today.
CHREMES: You tell a strange story. And my Syrus,
 He did something?
MENEDEMUS: Nothing.
CHREMES: I can't see why.
MENEDEMUS: That's strange, when you see all the other things
 So clearly. But then, it's that same Syrus
 Who shaped your son's behavior so shrewdly
 As to leave not the slightest doubt that she
 Was Clinia's mistress.
CHREMES (*Aside*):   What's going on?   900

MENEDEMUS: I won't mention the kissing and hugging:
    That doesn't count.
CHREMES: What more could their pretense
    Call for?
MENEDEMUS: Oh, really!
CHREMES: What else? Oh, really?
MENEDEMUS: Just listen. There's a room way at the back
    Inside the house. A bed was put in there
    And made up.
CHREMES: Then what happened after that?
MENEDEMUS: No sooner said than done, your Clitipho
    Went right in there.
CHREMES: Alone?
MENEDEMUS: Yes, quite alone.
CHREMES: I'm worried now.
MENEDEMUS: And right away, Bacchis
    Followed him there.
CHREMES: Alone?
MENEDEMUS: Yes, all alone.
CHREMES: I'm done in now.
MENEDEMUS: When they were in the room
    They shut the door.
CHREMES: Did your Clinia see
    This going on?
MENEDEMUS: How could he not see it?
    He was right there with me.
CHREMES: So, Bacchis is
    My son's mistress. I'm ruined, Menedemus.
MENEDEMUS: How so?
CHREMES: I've hardly cash for ten more days.
MENEDEMUS: Not worried are you, just because your son
    Does a favor for his friend?
CHREMES: For his girl-friend.   910
MENEDEMUS: If he does favor her.
CHREMES: Can you doubt it?
    You don't think any man's so easygoing
    And docile as to let his own mistress,
    Before his eyes . . . ?

MENEDEMUS: Why not? That's how they might
  Put one over on me more easily.
CHREMES: You're justified in making fun of me.
  I'm vexed at myself now. So many things
  Gave hints I could have understood completely,
  Had I not been a blockhead. What I saw!
  I'm really in a mess. But, believe me,
  They won't get away with it unpunished,
  While I'm alive. Right now, I'm going to . . .
MENEDEMUS: Control yourself. Don't lose your self-respect.
  Am I not enough of a lesson to you?
CHREMES: For anger, Menedemus, I'm not myself,   920
MENEDEMUS: For you to talk like that! Isn't it shameful
  To give others advice, be wise in public,
  And yet not be able to help yourself?
CHREMES: What shall I do?
MENEDEMUS: What you told me I did
  Too little of. Let your son realize
  That you're his father. Let him have the courage
  To trust you every way, to ask for things,
  To seek your help, and not go looking out
  For some other support, and desert you.
CHREMES: Oh, no! I'd rather he went anywhere
  In the world than by self-indulgence here
  Drive his father to need. If I keep on
  Paying his costly bills, Menedemus,   930
  My resources will soon reach the level
  Of garden rakes.
MENEDEMUS: But then you'll just create
  More trouble for yourself, if you're not careful.
  You'll show how strict you are, but later on
  You'll still forgive him and get no thanks for it.
CHREMES: You don't know how upset I am.
MENEDEMUS: Oh, well,
  Have it your way. But what about my wish
  To have your daughter married to my son?
  Or do you have some other preference?
CHREMES: Oh no. The son-in-law and the connection
  Appeal to me.

MENEDEMUS: What dowry shall I tell
My son you offered? . . . Why are you so still?
CHREMES: Dowry?
MENEDEMUS: That's what I said.
CHREMES: Oh. I . . .
MENEDEMUS: Chremes, don't worry if it's less than usual.
CHREMES: The dowry doesn't bother me at all.
I thought two talents might do well enough,   940
In view of my income. But if you want
To safeguard me, my money, and my son,
You'll have to say that I've made over all
My property to set up that dowry.
MENEDEMUS: What are you up to there?
CHREMES: Pretend that you
Are taken by surprise. Ask Clitipho
The reason I'd do it.
MENEDEMUS: In fact, I can't
See the reason you should do such a thing.
CHREMES: Why do it? To make a dent in his mind
That's flowed over into extravagance
And self-indulgence: bring him to the point
Where he no longer knows which way to turn.
MENEDEMUS: What's on your mind?
CHREMES: Leave me with it. Let me
Behave the way I want in this affair.
MENEDEMUS: I won't press you. You do want it this way?
CHREMES: I do.
MENEDEMUS: It will be done.
CHREMES: Now, have your son
Prepare to have his bride summoned to him. (*Exit* MENEDEMUS)
My Clitipho will get his dressing down
In words, as suits children. But, as I live,
I'll dress up that Syrus with blows, not clothes.   950
And hand him over so well combed and groomed
He'll remember me all his life. He thinks
I'm someone to laugh at, to have fun with.
He wouldn't dare do what he's done to me
To a defenseless woman, so help me god.

Scene 2

CLITIPHO, MENEDEMUS, CHREMES, SYRUS

CLITIPHO: Can it be really so, Menedemus?
  In so short a time has he rid himself
  Of all his natural feelings as a father?
  For what misdeed? What horrible offense
  Have I committed, to my sorrow? Young men
  Normally act the way I did.
MENEDEMUS: I'm aware
  Of how this hurts more, is much harsher
  To, the person it lands on. But I too
  Take it as hard. I cannot understand
  How it can be. I don't grasp the reason.
  I only wish you well, with all my heart.
CLITIPHO: You said my father was waiting out here.
MENEDEMUS: And here he comes. (*Enter* CHREMES, *exit* MENE-
  DEMUS)
CHREMES: Why blame me, Clitipho?   960
  I took this action with a view to you
  And your shortsightedness. For when I saw
  How wrapped up in the pleasure of the present
  You were, with no thought for the length of time in store,
  I formed a plan so you would not be left
  In need, and yet could not waste all I have,
  This property. Then when your conduct made
  It wrong for me to hand it on to you,
  Who were entitled to first claim on it,
  I chose your nearest relative, and made
  It all over to him, to be his trust.
  There'll always be protection, Clitipho,
  For your folly with him, food and shelter,
  A roof over your head.

CLITIPHO: I'm out of luck!

CHREMES: This is much better than with you as heir
   For Bacchis to possess my property.

SYRUS (*Aside*): Well, I'm completely out of luck. Stupid!
   It's criminal the way I've messed it up
   For everyone, without intending to.   970

CLITIPHO: I might as well be dead.

CHREMES: You might as well
   Learn first what living means. When you know that,
   If life still leaves you cold, try the other.

SYRUS: Master, may I?

CHREMES: Speak up.

SYRUS: But in safety?

CHREMES: Speak up.

SYRUS: What sort of craziness is this?
   It makes no sense to take it out on him
   When all the fault is mine.

CHREMES: The meeting's over.
   No one's accusing you, Syrus. Don't you
   Get mixed up in it. You won't need an altar
   As a refuge, or some kind intercessor
   To speak for you.

SYRUS: But what are you up to?

CHREMES: I'm not angry, either at you, or you;
   And it's not right for you to be angry
   At me for what I do. (*Exit* CHREMES)

Scene 3

CLITIPHO, SYRUS

SYRUS: He's gone away?
   And I wanted to ask him . . .

CLITIPHO: What?

SYRUS: Where to look

For food. He's cut us off so completely.
I know there's some for you at your sister's.
CLITIPHO: It's come to such a pass, then, Syrus, has it,   980
   That I'm even in danger of starving?
SYRUS: As long as we're alive, there's still some hope . . .
CLITIPHO: Of what?
SYRUS: Of being hungry, both of us.
CLITIPHO: You laugh in this crisis, and don't help me
   One bit with your advice?
SYRUS: No, I was thinking
   About it while your father was talking,
   And I'm thinking right now. So far as I
   Can work it out . . .
CLITIPHO: What out?
SYRUS: Our plan.
   It's not far off.
CLITIPHO: What is it, then?
SYRUS: Just this:
   You're not their son at all. That's what I think.
CLITIPHO: How's that, Syrus? Are you in your right mind?
SYRUS: I'll tell you what's come to my mind, and you
   Decide that for yourself. So long as they
   Had only you and no other pleasure
   To bring them more delight, they fawned on you,
   They gave you everything. Now, a daughter
   Has been discovered, and a good excuse,
   In fact, for them to disinherit you.
CLITIPHO: That is quite probable.
SYRUS: You don't think he's   990
   Angry at you because you misbehaved?
CLITIPHO: I don't think so.
SYRUS: And look at something else.
   All mothers normally take the son's side
   To help him in trouble and lend support
   Against the father's strictness. That's not so
   For you.
CLITIPHO: You speak the truth. What shall I do
   Then, Syrus?

SYRUS: Raise this question with your parents;
   Bring it up openly. If it's not true,
   You'll soon evoke the sympathy of both,
   Or know whose son you are.
CLITIPHO: That's good advice.
   I'll take it. (*Exit* CLITIPHO)
SYRUS: I'm lucky this came to mind.
   The more he finds his suspicions groundless,
   The easier will he make peace with his father
   On his own terms. He just might take a wife.
   I can't tell yet. No thanks to Syrus, though.
   But what's this? Chremes coming out again.
   I'm taking off. For what I've done so far,   1000
   It's strange he hasn't ordered me hauled off.
   I'll take refuge in Menedemus' house
   And ask him to be my intercessor.
   I don't put any trust in our old man.

Scene 4

SOSTRATA, CHREMES

SOSTRATA: If you're not careful, my dear man, you'll do
   Our son real harm. I find it very strange
   That so foolish a notion could enter
   Your mind, my dear husband.
CHREMES: Will you persist
   In being a woman? Did I ever
   Want anything in my whole life, without
   Your contradicting me in it, Sostrata?
   But if I ask where I am in the wrong,
   Or why you act this way, you don't know why
   You take so strong a stand against me, foolish one.
SOSTRATA: I don't know why?
CHREMES: Well, yes. You do know why.

Let's not have the whole discussion once again. 1010
SOSTRATA: Oh, you're not reasonable to think that I'll
Keep still on a matter of this importance.
CHREMES: I don't ask that. Say what you want. But still,
I'll go ahead with it.
SOSTRATA: You'll go ahead?
CHREMES: I will.
SOSTRATA: Don't you see how much trouble you create
That way? He thinks he's a foundling.
CHREMES: Foundling,
You say?
SOSTRATA: It's so, and will be so, my husband.
CHREMES: Admit it, then.
SOSTRATA: Oh come now, I beg you.
That's something for our enemies to say.
Shall I say he's not my son, when he is?
CHREMES: You're not afraid, are you, that when you want
You can't prove he's your son?
SOSTRATA: You mean, because
Our daughter has been found?
CHREMES: I don't mean that.
I mean something that must win quick belief,
The fact that he behaves the way you do.
You'll prove he is your child quite easily: 1020
He's just like you. There's not a fault in him
That isn't matched in you. And furthermore,
No one but you could have a son like that.
Well, here he comes out, now. Ah, how straightfaced
He looks! So straightlaced, if you stop and think
Of what he's been up to, for some time now!

Scene 5

CLITIPHO, SOSTRATA, CHREMES

CLITIPHO: If there was ever any time, mother,
  When I gave you pleasure, was called your son,
  When both of you were willing to say so,
  I beg you to remember it and now
  Take pity on me in my time of need.
  I beg, implore you. Show me my parents.
SOSTRATA: Really, my son, you must think no such thought:
  You could not be another person's child.
CLITIPHO: I am.
SOSTRATA: Poor me! (*To* CHREMES) I suppose that this
  Is what you were after. (*To* CLITIPHO) I assure you,
  You are the son born to me and this man.   1030
  And please, if you love me, don't let me hear
  Such talk from you again.
CHREMES: And I tell you,
  If you fear me, don't let me see you acting
  The way you have been.
CLITIPHO: What way?
CHREMES: Well, if you want
  To know, I'll tell you: indulging yourself
  In guzzling, idling, wasting good money
  On parties, food and drink. Believe me, now?
  Believe, then, that you can be our true son.
CLITIPHO: Those aren't a parent's words.
CHREMES: Had you been born
  From my forehead, like Minerva from Jove's
  (They say), I would not let you, Clitipho,
  Any the more make me suffer disgrace
  Because of your contemptible behavior.
SOSTRATA: May all the gods prevent it!

CHREMES: I don't know
　　About the gods. I only know that I
　　Will do whatever I can to prevent it.
　　You're looking for what you possess: parents;
　　Not looking for what you don't have as yet:
　　A way to comply with your father's wishes
　　And look after what his hard work has earned.   1040
　　To fool me, and bring right before my eyes
　　That—I'm ashamed to use so vile a word
　　In this woman's presence; but you were not
　　At all ashamed to go ahead and do it.
CLITIPHO (*Aside*): Lord! How completely fed up with myself
　　I am right now! And how ashamed I am!
　　I don't know where to start to placate him.

Scene 6

MENEDEMUS, CHREMES, SOSTRATA, CLITIPHO

MENEDEMUS: Surely Chremes is tormenting the boy
　　Too harshly, too inhumanly. So I
　　Am coming out to make peace between them.
　　Oh, good! I see them there.
CHREMES: Menedemus,
　　Ah, why aren't you having my daughter called for
　　And coming to agreement on the sum
　　I offered for the dowry?
SOSTRATA: My dear husband,
　　I beg you, don't do it.
CLITIPHO: I ask forgiveness,
　　Father.
MENEDEMUS: Forgive him, Chremes. Let yourself
　　Be won over by them.
CHREMES: And consciously

Make a gift of my property to Bacchis?   1050
I won't do that.

MENEDEMUS: And we won't let you do it.

CLITIPHO: If you want me to go on living, father,
Forgive me.

SOSTRATA: Do, dear Chremes.

MENEDEMUS: Come, Chremes,
I beg you to: don't be so obstinate.

CHREMES: What to do now? I see I can't go on
As I began.

MENEDEMUS: That's much more like yourself.

CHREMES: I give in, then, but on this one condition:
He does what I think right for him to do.

CLITIPHO: Command me, father: I'll do anything.

CHREMES: You'll take a wife.

CLITIPHO: But, father . . .

CHREMES: I hear nothing.

SOSTRATA: I'll vouch for him: he'll do it.

CHREMES: I hear nothing
From him, as yet.

CLITIPHO (Aside):   Done for!

SOSTRATA: You hesitate,
Clitipho?

CHREMES: No. Let him choose for himself
Between the two.

SOSTRATA: He'll see it all right through.

MENEDEMUS (To CLITIPHO): At first, of course, it will seem hard
to you,
While you're still unfamiliar with it all,
But when you've gotten used to it, easy.

CLITIPHO: All right, father. I'll do as you command.

SOSTRATA: Oh, my dear son, I know a charming girl   1060
For you—you'll find her very nice—the daughter
Of our neighbor Phanocrates.

CLITIPHO: That redhead?
The girl with the cat's eyes? The freckle-face
With the turned-up nose? I can't do that, father.

CHREMES: He's so choosy! You'd think he'd thought and thought
  About it for some time.
SOSTRATA: I know another.
CLITIPHO: No, look: since I'm the one who's getting married,
  I know someone I might just like to have.
CHREMES: That's more like it. Good work, my son.
CLITIPHO: I mean
  The daughter of our friend Archonides.
SOSTRATA: She's a nice girl.
CLITIPHO: But father, there's one thing.
CHREMES: What is it?
CLITIPHO: I wish you'd excuse Syrus
  For what he did for me.
CHREMES: All right, I'll let him off.
(AMBIVIUS *reappears*)
  And we'll let you off now,
  Because,
  You see, that's how it was!
  Do we hear your applause?

THE EUNUCH

(*EUNOUCHUS*)

Translated by Douglass Parker

INTRODUCTION

Success dies hard. *The Eunuch* was Terence's most successful play during his lifetime, earning an immediate second production and a considerably increased royalty. It has yet to be forgiven this by critics who, equating excellence with unpopularity, prefer the *Hecyra's* double failure as an index of attainment. Since this is not a universal standard, they find themselves faced with a thorny problem: *The Eunuch* is fast and funny, and, in fact, an excellent case can be made for its being Terence's best play. How to dispose of it? The answer is simple and somewhat sinister: Call it "Plautine."

The precise meaning of this epithet is not so obvious as might at first appear, but its connotations are clear enough: When used by a pro-Terentian (or pro-Menandrean) critic, it implies that the play is a sort of regrettable mistake, an attempt at pit-pandering by a playwright who should have known better, and usually did. And, when picked up and employed by an anti-Terentian, it passes implicit judgment against his other five plays. Either way the poet loses.

And loses yet another way: In making *The Eunuch*, Terence modified Menander's *Eunouchus* considerably to admit two characters, the soldier Thraso and the parasite Gnatho, from another play by the same Greek author—the *Kolax* ("Toady" or "Yes-Man"). Unfortunately, literary politics compelled him to admit this in his prologue. I say "unfortunately," not because this defense of dramatic *contaminatio* failed (it did not), but because, by his rather detailed admission, he supplied critics of two millennia later with their most substantial handle for the reconstruction of lost Greek plays. Thus armed, they have prodded joyously

147

for a century or so, descrying the necessarily seamless excellence of the originals through the gaps they make in the Roman poet's necessarily shoddy composition.

The play, of course, however categorized or tortured, has not changed, and annoyance at its criticism may seem ill-taken. After all, "Plautine" can be a perfectly accurate and unexceptionable, if somewhat otiose, synonym for Donatus' *motoria:* it must be granted that fast and furious fun is not exactly a characteristic Terentian virtue (though the *Phormio* abounds in it). And there is certainly nothing wrong per se with the attempted recovery of Menandrean comedies. But, as it happens, the two practices described above have interacted to form a barrier to the proper understanding of just what Terence has done in this play, "Plautine" becoming a rug under which to sweep, unexamined, any difficulties in taste, *Quellenforschung* a sieve with which *The Eunuch* is axiomatically strained of any real dramatic unity.

To take the first point: Many critics who are not bothered by the hot-blooded rape of Pamphila become quite upset at the play's ending—the projected *ménage à trois* that involves the cold-blooded diddling of Thraso. If this does not signal a blast against the morality of the playwright, it is generally resolved by recourse to the adjective "Plautine." Such a situation obtains at the end of Plautus' *Asinaria* and *Bacchides* and unsettles no one; why should it here? But this begs the question; the unease remains undissolved. And that such a reaction from his audience might have been a reasoned dramatic aim of Terence is an observation that rarely occurs; the poet is evidently the prisoner of the style he has chosen.

Or the second point: Gnatho's bravura disquisition on his new method of coney-catching (Act II, Scene 2) is the longest and most memorable speech in the play; it should logically have something to do with the over-all action. But the seeker after Menander, anxious to pin something down for good, is all too ready to overstate his case for its derivation from the *Kolax* by declaring that the speech's only function is to delineate the character of the parasite.

These are not random points, but both are intimately bound

up with the meaning of *The Eunuch,* and the critic neglects them at his peril The play, whatever its genealogy, is more than farce, more than loose-knit romp; it is a serious dramatic exploration, all of a piece.

Returning to the ending, to call it "Plautine" merely intensifies the problem: Why should critics who are proof against anything written suddenly be found muttering about "the dubious morality of *The Eunuch*'s conclusion"? Why should otherwise hardheaded translators feel impelled to give their readers the perfectly gratuitous (and unfounded) intelligence that, when Gnatho proposes milking Thraso, Phaedria accepts the suggestion "reluctantly"? In sum, why should a phenomenon that passes without objection in a play by Plautus cause unease when it occurs in a play by Terence? Provisionally, the only possible answer would appear to be that Terence has somehow employed it in a different fashion. And he has; he has indulged in one of his most effective practices: Taking a comedic *datum* and, by a change in its context, pushing it beyond the bounds of comfortable acceptability, he has achieved that bite which is distinctly his own.

The change involved is one in "characterization"—a bad word for critics, but no matter. Terence has humanized and deepened the stock *personae* of New Comedy, not greatly, but enough to involve the audience with them at a different level, a level where hackneyed situations acquire a new and distressing reality through their participants. Upset at *The Eunuch*'s conclusion arises, not from abstract disapproval of confidence-games or *ménages à trois*, but from a directed feeling that *these* lovers ought not to be doing such a thing to *this* soldier. Therefore Phaedria must be "reluctant." Therefore at least one critic has suggested (I am not making this up) that Terence's ending must derive, not from Menander's, *Eunouchos*, but from his *Kolax*, since Thais, taken from the former play, is really too noble to be party to such an arrangement, even in prospect. Ridiculous remedies, arising from misreadings, but they locate the ailments: Phaedria, the lovestruck and ineffectual *adulescens* who possesses enough self-knowledge to see his weakness but not to avoid it;

Thais, the whore with, not a heart of gold, but an overlay of altruism [1]—they really should behave better.

For the object of the diddling is to be Thraso, and to dupe him is not to take a deserved revenge on a monster, but to shoot a very sorry fish in a very small barrel. In the abortive siege of Thais's house he has demonstrated his purely military futility, but other deficiencies have emerged as well. It is really ironic that this character should have supplied English with an adjective—*thrasonical*—to describe vaingloriousness; Thraso is the first *miles gloriosus* whose *words* completely fail him. He fumbles for quotations, relies on ludicrously inept repartee, goes gauche at the sight of Thais. He needs only poverty to match the most inept specimen of the breed, Armado in *Love's Labour's Lost*—like him, a would-be Hercules who cannot fight; like him, a hopeless lover who solicits instruction from an unqualified source; like him, total prisoner of a rhetoric that his opponents can use more effectively in fun than he can in earnest. Stupid and defenseless, a man rattling around in a monster's role, he resembles Armado in one more, one most important particular: Sincerely in love, he is the only person in the play actually willing to make a sacrifice for his love. And his sacrifice, to everyone else's profit, constitutes the ending of *The Eunuch*.

To return to the second point raised earlier—Gnatho's speech in Act II, Scene 2—it is certainly obvious that the ending proceeds, logically and inevitably, from the enlightened self-interest set forth in the parasite's *nouom aucupium*. It marks, in fact, the conversion of the principal members of the play's cast to Gnatho's way of life: Thraso, giving in to a hopeless love, will be gulled by almost everyone in sight.

This way of life is itself an answer to Parmeno's sarcastic comment on love's (and life's) vicissitudes in Act I, Scene 1:

[1] *an overlay of altruism:* Whores in comedy (to say nothing of tragedy) are always apt to be preyed upon by romantics in the audience, and Thais is no exception. She has even been compared to *La Dame aux Caméllias,* which is a rather hard price to pay merely for being a relatively sensitive and honest prostitute. Care should be taken to protect her bad name: Her real affection for Phaedria and Pamphila, an affection which she protests rather too much, should not be allowed to obscure the fact that it is ultimately subordinate to self-interest.

Incerta haec si tu postules
ratione certa facere, nihilo plus agas
quam si des operam ut cum ratione insanias.

No mind can reduce this mess
To any controllable order; you're better off
To spend your effort devising a plan to go mad on.

And a method for madness is what Gnatho supplies; more spe-
cifically, a blueprint for subservience. All of the principal characters in the play, one way or another, are in search of dependence
and its fruits: Chaerea, who puts on the weeds of slavery and
unmanliness to gain his beloved; [2] Thais, whose regard for her
"sister," however touching, is a means to patronage; Phaedria,
whose ideal love can always be altered by practical consideration.
Even Parmeno, whose moral disapproval is strongest, is not immune; he may think that the information he gives to Chaerea's
father is done in the boy's best interest, but his own admission
and Pythias' accusation show the truth. When the crunch comes,
try as he will, his guiding impulse is to save himself:

Huius quidquid factumst, culpa non factumst mea.

Whatever happened, it wasn't my fault that it happened.

In this play as elsewhere, comic characters are rarely to be taken
at their own evaluation.

The Eunuch, then, from Phaedria's initial whines to Thraso's
invitation to the slaughter, is a study of the workings of depend-
ency in which all noble motives, except for that of the play's
standard butt, shrink alarmingly to one ignoble motive—the one
unblushingly practiced and preached by that two-dimensional
caricature from the older style of comedy, Gnatho:

Me huius quidquid facio id facere maxumo causa mea.

Whatever I do, I do from pure self-interest.

[2] to gain his beloved: Chaerea is outgoing, frank, and hot-blooded if you will—
but whoever excuses (or praises) his actions as the instinctive, natural effects of
an unfettered, passionate soul should ponder two points: (1) the compulsive
gregariousness that renders him incapable of enjoying himself without an audience;
(2) the smarmy disingenuousness with which he reacts, in character, to Pythias'
accusation that he has raped a citizen: "conseruam esse credidi"—"I thought she
was one of us slaves."

A most unpleasant motif for a cynical sermon—but it is not offered as such. Its effect is to counterpoint and bind together the play's farcical fun, to weave its strands to a not-quite-happy end, to produce in the audience that reasoned confusion of viewpoints, that contradiction in attitudes, that mark the best comedy. And it is in this achievement, proceeding from the play's *Gestalt* rather than from any part of it, that we can see the playwright's excellence: The fun may be Plautine, the characters and plot may be Menandrean, but the totality is Terence's own.

DOUGLASS PARKER

THE EUNUCH

First Performance: The Games for the Great Mother, presented under the supervision of Lucius Postumius Albinus and Lucius Cornelius Merula, curule aediles.

Production: Lucius Ambivius Turpio and Lucius Hatilius of Praeneste.

Music: Scored for treble and bass flute [3] by Flaccus, freedman of Claudius.

Greek Original: Menander.

The author's second play. Third in order of production [4]—161 B.C., during the consulship of Gaius Fannius and Marcus Valerius.

CHARACTERS

PHAEDRIA, a young Athenian, elder son of Demea
PARMENO, slave to Demea
THAIS, a professional woman
GNATHO, a diner-out
* PAMPHILA, a virgin
* Her maid

[3] *for treble and bass flute:* So Donatus. The notice itself has, "for two treble flutes."

[4] *Third in order of production:* These words are added to make sense of a dating which clearly has something wrong with it.

* Denotes mute part.

153

CHAEREA, younger son of Demea
THRASO, a military man
* An Ethiopian girl slave
PYTHIAS, chief maid to Thais
DORIAS, maid to Thais
* WOMEN of Thais's household
CHREMES, a young country gentleman
ANTIPHO, friend to Chaerea
DORUS, a eunuch
* SIMALIO ⎤
* DONAX ⎬ household slaves to Thraso
* SYRISCUS ⎦
SANGA, cook to Thraso
SOPHRONA, an elderly nurse
DEMEA,[5] an elderly Athenian, father of Phaedria and Chaerea

SCENE: *Athens.*

PROLOGUE

Conceivably, playwrights exist who strive to supply
Maximum pleasure and minimum pain to people
Of taste. If so, our author declares himself their teammate.
Conceivably, someone exists[6] who may deduce

[5] DEMEA: This is the name given to the old man in the oldest extant manuscript of Terence, not at this point (none of the MSS presents a cast list), but in the scene-heading at Act V, Scene 5, where other MSS give the name Laches. Further, Donatus notes that the father in Menander's *Eunouchos* was named Simo. Inasmuch as the text proper finds no occasion to name the old man at all, my principal reason for sticking by Demea is a capricious neatness; I realize that it might have been supplied from the *Adelphoe*, even as Laches might have come from the *Hecyra*. Given the old man's somewhat uncharacteristic behavior, he might as well be named Cheeryble.

[6] *someone exists:* The someone is Terence's standing literary adversary, the elder playwright Luscius Lanuvinus.

* Denotes mute part.

That he is the object, in these remarks, of a harsh
Attack. If so, let's have this someone make
Another deduction: *These* words are defensive; the first,
Offensive attack was his.
                             After all, a man
Who phrases straight translations in such a tortured
Fashion that the best Greek plays are turned to Latin
Flops; a man who recently managed to murder
Menander's *Ghost;* a man whose *Contested Treasure*   10
(A gem of a play) contains a lawsuit in which
Defendant argues his right to the gold *before*
Plaintiff has brought that right into question—well, such
A man should scarcely presume that he is immune
To critics, or that he's silenced all fire from this quarter.
Fair warning: He really ought to give up war.
His shortcomings fill a long list; I'm glad to forget them—
But I'll publish them all unless he desists from this ceaseless
Sniping. Take today's play—Menander's *Eunuch.*   20
The authorities came, rehearsals began . . . and so
Did he:
        "A pirate did this, not a playwright.
    But he can't fool me. He lifted the leech and the major
    Straight from that antique farce by Naevius and Plautus,
    The Yes-Man."
                     If our author slipped, it was ignorance, void
Of any intent to steal. Here, judge for yourselves:
Menander wrote the original *Yes-Man,* containing   30
A leech (the title role) and a blowhard soldier.
Terence admits that he borrowed both from the Greek
For the cast of his *Eunuch,* but flatly denies any knowledge
Of their previous Latinization.
                                 If he's still enjoined from employing
This pair by virtue of their prior use . . . why, then,
All Comedy must be illegal: Running slaves,
Benevolent ladies, malevolent whores, the changeling
Routine, the stock deception of master by servant,   39
And love . . . and hate . . . and jealousy . . . come down to it,
There's nothing to say that hasn't been said before.

Therefore, please be fair. Face facts, and excuse
This new generation for doing once what the old did . . .
Over,
    And over,
        And over.
                —I now request
Your silence. Turn your minds to *The Eunuch*'s meaning.

    A street in Athens,[7] *on which front two houses: stage right, that of* DEMEA; *stage left, that of* THAIS. *The latter possesses an upper window which is, at the moment* (*and for most of the play*), *shuttered. In addition to the housedoors, there are also two wing exits: stage right, to the harbor and the country* (*and hence to the farms of* DEMEA *and* CHREMES, *as well as to* ANTIPHO's *house*); *stage left, to downtown Athens* (*and hence to* THRASO's *house*)

    [7] *A street in Athens:* The following frame for the play's presentation balances itself between the requisites of the text and such facts as we know about the Roman stage. It is a rationalization of the action, nothing more, and has two principal aims: (1) to establish with the audience, as the play unfolds, a knowledge of the pertinent offstage locations—put as simply as possible, the exit stage left leads to Thraso's house, while the exit stage right leads everywhere else; (2) to maintain aim while avoiding awkward meetings, at entrance and exit, by characters unaware of each other's presence. Such difficulties as arise will be dealt with as they occur. One other point: In common with most translators and commentators, I have opted here for a two-house set, though the presence of three doors on the Roman stage is undoubted. But the three need not always be used, and the physical representation of Thraso's house seems to contribute nothing but an onstage location for what is clearly conceived of as offstage action.

ACT I

Scene 1

PHAEDRIA *and* PARMENO *enter from* DEMEA'*s house.*

PHAEDRIA: . . . So what do I do *now?* She takes the trouble
To ask me over; do I go? Or make a resolution
To give up paying whores for nothing but insults?
Locks me out . . . summons me back . . .
                                                    Well, no.
She can go down on her knees; I'm not coming back.
PARMENO: The perfect approach. Has honor, quality . . . *but*   50
It needs ability. Once you start, you've got
To stay with it. Let *her* request a parley. Peace
On *your* terms. Don't weaken. Don't make the first move. If
   you do,
You might as well wear a sign: I LOVE YOU. CAN'T LIVE
WITHOUT YOU. And *that* is it, goodbye, you're dead. You lose
The war, and she knows it; she'll be one up for life.
Look, boss, you've got some time; give this some concerted
Thought: A state without reason or rules can*not*
Be ruled by reason. You're in that state—in Love,
A mixture of messy, uncivilized drives: Hurt,
Jealousy, Hatred, Forgiveness, Conflict . . . the Peace   60
Again . . . for a while. No mind can reduce this mess
To any controllable order; you're better off
To spend your effort devising a plan to go mad on.
As for your current private dialogue, this blend
Of pronouns and wounded pride—"Me to her
While she's with him? I used to be hers; now *he's* it.

I know; I'll die, and then she'll appreciate me"—
Just words. If she can manage to rub her eyes
And squeeze out a dribble of bogus moisture, their fire
Is quenched . . . and you'll be guilty because she says so,
And submit to torture because *you* say so.
PHAEDRIA: It isn't   70
Fair. I see it all now: She's a bitch
And I'm a wretch. It makes my gorge rise, and yet
The rest of me burns with love. With wisdom and forethought,
All faculties working, fully alive . . . I'm dying
And don't know how to stop.
PARMENO: I do. You're held
For ransom; buy your way out. As cheap as you can,
Of course, but hang the expense. Pay what you have to;
Don't worry about it.
PHAEDRIA: You think I should?
PARMENO: You know
You should. Love itself brings troubles enough;
Brace yourself and bear them—but don't go borrowing
More.
        —Oh-oh. Here comes the blight on the family
Farm. She gleams the profits before we can reap.   80

Scene 2

THAIS *enters from her house. She does not see* PHAEDRIA *and*
PARMENO:

THAIS: I'm worried sick about Phaedria. He's mad at me.
When I sent him away from the house yesterday, I'm afraid
He got the wrong impression.
PHAEDRIA: I'm shaking, Parmeno.
One look at her and I turn to gooseflesh.
PARMENO: Be brave.
    (*Pushing* PHAEDRIA *toward* THAIS)

Move up close to the fire. You'll thaw soon enough—
And more than enough.
THAIS: Who's this? Why, Phaedria, darling!
Have you been waiting out here—standing in the street?
Why didn't you come right in?
PARMENO (*Aside*):   She threw him out,
Of course—but why bring that up?
THAIS: Now, what's your reason?
PHAEDRIA (*Clenched teeth*): Because your door's never shut to
  me. Because
I'm always first in your affections.   90
THAIS: Let's forget that.
PHAEDRIA: *Forget?* Oh, Thais, why is our love so lopsided?
Why is our affair so unfair? Can't we adjust it—
Either you suffer the way I suffer . . . or else
I learn not to give a damn whatever you do?
THAIS: Phaedria, darling, please don't torture yourself.
I adore you. I swear that I didn't do what I did
Because I prefer someone else. It was just—circumstances.
I had to do it.
PARMENO: Happens all the time.
So much in love she had to lock you out.
THAIS: Is that the way you're playing it, Parmeno? My, my.
(*To* PHAEDRIA)
First, let me tell you why I had you come here.
PHAEDRIA: Please do.   100
THAIS (*Pointing to* PARMENO): But what about *him?* Is he discreet?
Can he keep a secret?
PARMENO: Nobody better. My tact,
However, has strings attached: I seal my lips
On principle. For truth, no trouble, my mouth stays shut.
But fibs, falsehoods, fabrications . . . right away, I shatter;
I'm a mass of cracks; I leak the secrets everywhere.
So, if you want integrity, tell the truth.
THAIS: My mother was born on Samos, but lived at Rhodes.
PARMENO: That secret I can keep.
THAIS: While we were there,
A businessman gave her a present—a little girl
Who'd been kidnapped from Attica.   110

PHAEDRIA: From here? A citizen?

THAIS: I think she is; we couldn't be sure. She could only
Tell us her parents' names, but not her country,
Or any other clues. Too tiny. Her buyer
Had one more report: The pirates who'd sold her to him
Said that they stole her from Sunium.
From the moment she
got her,
Mother trained her thoroughly, and brought her up
Like her very own daughter. In fact, most people thought
That she was my sister. But then the gentleman who kept me
Moved to Athens, and I came along. He was my only
Protector; he left me everything I own.   120

PARMENO: Two lies;
Two leaks.

THAIS: How so?

PARMENO: First, you weren't content
With one lone keeper; second, he wasn't your only
Source of funds. Phaedria's made considerable
Contributions.

THAIS: I agree; but do let me get to the point.
Later, I began an affair with a military man,
But he was transferred to Caria. Right after that
I met you, Phaedria. Since then, you know how close
You've been to me. I have no secrets from you.

PARMENO: Parmeno can't keep that one.

THAIS: Do you really doubt me?
Please pay attention.   130
Mother died at Rhodes
Just recently. Her brother, who tends, where money's con-
cerned,
To greed, took one look at the girl and saw
Her beauty and musical talent as potential profit.
He listed her right on the spot and sold her at auction.
By great good luck, the buyer was my former lover—
The military man. In complete and utter ignorance
Of all this business, he bought her for me as a present.

But now that he's back in Athens, darling, and knows
About us—about you and me—he works overtime
At inventing excuses to keep her.
$\qquad\qquad\qquad\qquad$ According to him,
It's a matter of trust: If he were completely certain
That I'd prefer him to you, if he weren't afraid
That I'd take the girl and drop him, he'd be quite happy $\quad$ 140
To hand her over. But he has his doubts.
$\qquad\qquad\qquad\qquad\qquad\qquad$ Or so
He says. I have my suspicions. I think he's fallen
For her himself.
PHAEDRIA: $\qquad$ Anything further than falling?
THAIS: Not yet. I asked her. But anyway, Phaedria poopsie,
I've got to wangle her out of his sweaty paws,
And fast. I have a whole raft of reasons.
$\qquad\qquad\qquad\qquad\qquad\qquad$ First,
She *is* my sister, so to speak.
$\qquad\qquad\qquad\qquad\qquad$ Then second,
I want to be the one who brings her back safe
To her family's bosom. I'm on my own in Athens;
I don't have powerful friends or family here.
But by that act of altruism, I can win
Myself an entry, some backing, and all through a labor
Of love. A labor that you can facilitate, Phaedria.
Be a dear and help me, please, by letting $\qquad\qquad$ 150
The Major head the cast with me for the next
Few days? (*A pause*)
$\qquad\qquad$ No answer at all?
PHAEDRIA: $\qquad\qquad\qquad\qquad$ Of all the unblushing
Tripe! How do I answer behavior like that?
PARMENO: Three cheers for our side, boss. It took long enough,
But she got your goat. Today you are a man.
PHAEDRIA: As if I didn't know what you're aiming at.
"Little girl kidnapped from Attica . . . Mother
Brought her up like her very own . . . my sister,
So to speak . . . I've got to wangle her away . . .
Bring her back to her family's bosom . . ."

                                    This whole damned
Prologue was programmed to arrive at the same old point:
He's a guest, and *I'm* dismissed!
                            And why?
There's only one reason: You love him more than me;   160
You're afraid this imported talent will purloin your military
Paragon—she'll steal your Major!
THAIS: I'm afraid of *that?*
PHAEDRIA: What other possible worries could you have?
  Gifts, for instance? Is he your only donor?
  Has my openhandedness ever been closed for repairs?
  You told me you were mad for an African maid—
  Remember? All my business went by the boards
  While I went shopping. You told me you wanted a eunuch,
  Because only queens have eunuchs.
                                    Well, yesterday
  I found both items. Twenty *minae* I paid
  For the set. Rebuffed as I was, did I forget?
  Not me. And what's my reward for such service? A snub!   170
THAIS: Such language, darling.
                            But look: I'm honestly
  Anxious to work her loose from him, and I really
  Believe that this is far and away the best,
  The only plan . . . but no. Forget it. Sooner
  Than lose your love, I'll do whatever you say.
PHAEDRIA: I wish you meant that. I wish those words were real.
  "Sooner than lose your love . . ." If I could believe
  You were telling the truth, no torture would be too much.
PARMENO (*Aside*): He's wobbling. Worsted by a word. So quickly,
    too.
THAIS: That hurts me, dear. Of course I'm telling the truth.
  Did you ever hint for anything, even in fun,
  That you didn't get from me? But all I want   180
  From you is two little days, and I can't get those.
PHAEDRIA: Well, if it's only two days . . . But don't let two
  Turn into twenty.
THAIS: I swear it. No more than two.
  Two or . . .

PHAEDRIA: Two or nothing.
THAIS: Two. At most.
  You've set the conditions. Now grant me my request.
PHAEDRIA: Absolutely. Milady's will must be fulfilled.
THAIS: Is it any wonder that I love you? You're such a help!
PHAEDRIA: I'll go to the country and waste away for the next
  Two days. It's settled. Thais must be humored.
  —Parmeno, see that that pair's delivered.
PARMENO: Assuredly.
  (*He exits into* DEMEA's *house*)
PHAEDRIA: Until we meet again, in two days' time,
  Thais, farewell.
THAIS: Goodbye, Phaedria dearest. (*A pause*)   190
  Will that be all?
PHAEDRIA: Just this. One last request:
  When you're with your Major, be without him.
  Fill your days and nights with loving *me:*
  Miss me, crave me, want me, ache and yearn for me,
  Think me, dream me, hope for bliss with me—
  To sum up, be my soul. As I am yours.
  (*He exits into* DEMEA's *house*)
THAIS: Oh, dear. He doesn't seem to trust me much.
  Basically, I'm afraid, he rates me the same
  As other girls. I'm not. My conscience is clear.
  I know I haven't told any lies; I know
  That I love Phaedria more than anyone else.   200
  Whatever I've done in this business, I've done to save
  My sister. And now I think (and I certainly hope)
  That I've discovered her brother. He's a young man
  Of the highest background. Comes of excellent family.
  He made an appointment to see me at home today;
  I'll go inside and wait there till he comes.
  (*She exits into her house*)

ACT II

Scene 1

PHAEDRIA *and* PARMENO *enter from* DEMEA'*s house.* PARMENO
stands by the door as PHAEDRIA *starts reluctantly off right.*

PHAEDRIA: You've got my directions. Have those two delivered.
PARMENO: Right.
  (*He turns to enter the house.* PHAEDRIA *turns back*)
PHAEDRIA: And don't bungle.
  (PARMENO *stops and turns back to him*)
PARMENO: All right.
  (*He turns back to the door.* PHAEDRIA *starts off right, quickly
  turns back*)
PHAEDRIA: And don't dawdle.
PARMENO (*As before*):   All right.
  (*He turns back to the door.* PHAEDRIA *starts; turns back again*)
PHAEDRIA: Are those instructions sufficient?
PARMENO (*Giving up any attempt at reentry*):
                                        All this asking. You'd
    think   210
  The job was a hard one. Throwing your money away, that's
    easy.
  I wish you could make it as simply.
PHAEDRIA: I'm throwing myself away,
    too,
  And I'm worth more to me than money. Don't be so stingy.
PARMENO: You're the boss. I'll see it's done.
                                        That's all, I hope.
PHAEDRIA: Gift-wrap the present in pretty words. Please do your
    best.

(He starts off, then stops)
And do your best at warding the enemy off.
PARMENO: Okay, but
I knew that already. No orders needed.
PHAEDRIA: And, as for me,
I'm going to the country.
                          What's more, I'm going to stay in the
    country.
(He starts off)
PARMENO: I heartily approve.
(He turns to the door. PHAEDRIA *stops)*
PHAEDRIA: Hold on.
PARMENO *(Turning back)*:   You called?
PHAEDRIA: Do you think
    I can do it?
Resist returning—stay holed up—holed out to the bitter
End?
PARMENO: Well, frankly, no. You'll return tonight, if not before—
Chased back by lack of sleep.   219
PHAEDRIA: I'll work in the fields till I drop.
I'll sleep in spite of myself.
PARMENO: You'll be a very fagged
Insomniac.
PHAEDRIA: Beat it. You're no help.
                             I must Take Steps
To stiffen up my willpower. I'm flabby, that's it, flabby.
But *I can do it.* Come right down to it, I can do
Without that girl, if duty demands, for as much as three days.
PARMENO: Three whole days? That's eternity. Don't make extrav-
    agant claims.
PHAEDRIA: My resolve is fixed.
(He stalks off right)
PARMENO: Pathological, god preserve us. A
    morbid
Infection, love. Induces complete dissolution of character.
There goes a boy once famous for standards, scruples, and
    brains.

(*Looking off left*)
Somebody's coming. Who is it?

                            Oh-oh. If it isn't Gnatho
The sponger, moocher-in-chief to Thais's Major. He's bringing
A virgin with him—Thais's present. She's gorgeous, too.   229
Worse luck. And here I am to present one ramshackle eunuch.
What a revolting contrast. This girl's more stunning than Thais.
(*He moves to* THAIS's *house, and takes up a position before her
door*)

Scene 2

GNATHO *enters left, followed by* PAMPHILA *and the maid who
attends her. Not perceiving* PARMENO, *he stops his procession and
addresses the audience.*

GNATHO: I shall never cease my amazement at the qualitative
    abyss
That yawns between man and man—the positive gulf that par-
    titions
Sage from clod.
                    This reflection was brought by a chance en-
    counter
Just now as I was en route. Fell in with a fellow whose birth
And status exactly parallel mine: A goodish background,
But gourmandized away the ancestral estates. A sight.
He'd let himself go rather sadly: Seedy, sick, shabby.
White at the temples, out at the heels. A mess.
                            "What means
This sad masquerade?" I asked.
                        "I'm broke. I've lost all I had,"
He replied. "I'm reduced to this. My friends, both casual and
    close,
Have left me flat."

                The contrast with me was too much. I couldn't
Conceal my contempt.
                      "You colossal ass," was the way I put it,
"Have you deliberately lost your hope as well? Did your brains
    go   240
The way of your fortune? We had the same origins, you and I,
But just take a look at me—my color, clothing, condition—
The picture of creature comfort. All possessions are mine,
Though I own nothing. My assets may be absolutely nil,
But I never suffer a shortage."
                              "I'm no good at that," he count-
    ered.
"I can't stand beatings; I won't be a butt."
                                 "Tut," I riposted.
"Do you really believe that's how it's done? You're utterly off.
I admit the profession proceeded by such outmoded methods
A century or so ago, but now we've changed all that.
There's a new system of swindling these days; a style, I might
    add,
That I pioneered. Attend:
                        There exists a subspecies of humans
Who lust to be first in all things, and aren't.
                                These are my game.
I dog their footsteps, ever ready to furnish laughter—
But not as a butt: *I* laugh at *them* . . . and show, of course,
My amazed amusement at their wit. Their least remark evokes
My praise; if they contradict it, well, I praise that, too.   251
I yea their yeas and nay their nays . . . in sum, I obey
A self-imposed command to reflect their smallest expression.
And such is the current procedure.
                            It simply brims with profit."
PARMENO (*Aside*): Talented fellow. Transforms idiots straight
    into madmen.
GNATHO: This exchange endured until we attained the market,
    where
An absolute mass of small tradesmen rose in joy and ran
To greet me. Dealers in candy, pastry, meat, and fish,

Sausage-stuffers and herring-hawkers—to whom I, flush
Or insolvent, have always been a constant source of profit.
They flooded me with welcomes, effusions of love, invitations
    to dinners.
Such an expression of status, such ease at winning a living
Was simply too much for my hapless companion's hunger to
    behold.   260
He beseeched me, then and there, to take him on as a pupil.
I told him to follow and observe.
                                I'm rather thinking of founding
A professional school of sponging. Named after me, of course—
Just like the philosophers:
                    Plato, Platonists.
                            Gnatho, Gnathonists.
It has a ring.
PARMENO (*Aside*): And that's what comes of free time and free
    meals.
GNATHO: To work: Presentation of girl to Thais, invitation of
    Thais
To lunch.
(*Aside*)—But who's this slouching in front of Thais's door?
Parmeno. The competition's slave. To judge from his gloom,
    the game
Is ours. I swear they're frozen out. My course is clear:
A little innocent fun at this clown's expense.
PARMENO (*Aside*):   How like them.
This gift, and they think they've taken a permanent lease on
    Thais.
GNATHO: Felicitous greetings from Gnatho to his most adored ac-
    quaintance,   270
Parmeno. How do things stand with us, eh?
PARMENO: Still.
GNATHO: I see.
Nothing here that upsets you, I trust?
PARMENO: Just you.
GNATHO: Indeed.
But nothing else?
PARMENO: Why should you ask?

GNATHO: You appear so sour.
PARMENO: Oh. Nothing.
  (*He makes an effort at smiling*)
GNATHO: Spare me.
  (*He indicates* PAMPHILA)
                              What's your impression of this
    little item,
    Fresh from the market?
PARMENO: Not absolutely disgusting.
GNATHO (*Aside*):   Got him
    Spitted and sizzling.
PARMENO (*Aside*):   But as it happens, our friend's all wet.
GNATHO: It's a present for Thais. Imagine her gratitude.
PARMENO: You mean
    to imply
    We've gotten the gate? Well, that's the way of the world. Now
    in,
    Now out.
GNATHO: Parmeno, I am about to make *you* a present:
    Six months of total vacation, an end to this jack-in-the-box
    Existence, these ceaseless sleepless nights. No more scurry,
    No more worry. Now, how does such generosity strike you?
PARMENO: Goody.
GNATHO: Merely the way I treat my friends.
PARMENO: Well, great.
GNATHO: I mustn't detain you. You were doubtless on your way
    somewhere?   280
PARMENO: Nowhere.
GNATHO: Then be a good fellow and do me a smallish
    service:
    Gain me admittance to Thais's presence.
PARMENO (*Moving out of the way*):   But go right in.
    You're bringing the girl; the door is open to you. For now.
GNATHO (*As he enters* THAIS's *house with* PAMPHILA *and her
    maid*): No messages, I imagine?
PARMENO (*To the closed door*): Just you wait for two days.
    Your luck's in now; you can open the door in my face with your
    little

Finger—but when I'm done, you'll have to kick it black
And blue to find out nobody's home.

GNATHO (*Emerging alone*):   Ah, steadfast Parmeno.
Still at your post? Have you been left behind on watch
To intercept secret messages between my Major and Thais?
(*He exits left*)

PARMENO: Witty as hell. Just what you'd expect from the Major's
   pet.
(*Looking off right*)
—Well, look at this. Here comes the old man's younger son.
Why'd he leave the Piraeus, I wonder? This is his day   290
For guard duty there.[8] Something's up, depend on that . . .
He's running fast enough. Seems to be searching for something.

Scene 3

CHAEREA *enters right, at a run, stops, and looks around. He does
not see* PARMENO.

CHAEREA: Oh, damn! Disappeared!
                         That girl—she's lost!
                                        And me—
   I'm lost!
Because I lost the girl!
                  Now what?
                         Where do I look?
Where should I hunt? Who can I ask? Which way do I go?
I don't have the slightest idea.
                         At least, there's one bit of hope:
No matter where she is, they can't keep her hidden for long—
Good god, what gorgeous, raving beauty!
                         From this day forward,

   [8] *For guard duty there:* This would be part of Chaerea's required service as
an Athenian *ephebos*.

I'm crossing the rest of the female sex right off my list.
Those garden-variety pretties turn my stomach.
PARMENO (*Aside*):   And here
We have the other brother. His topic is also Love.
Please shed a tear for their father: This one's a potential mad-
    man.
Once *he* gets started, you can file away the other affair   300
Under *Fun & Games.*
CHAEREA: Oh gods, please damn that doddering
    clod
For holding me up. And while you're at it, please damn me
For stopping, for giving a good goddamn about him.
                                                —Oh, look,
It's Parmeno.
                Hi.
PARMENO: What's the trouble? And why the hurry?
And where've you been?
CHAEREA: I'm damned if I know where I've been
Or where I'm going. I don't even know who I am.
PARMENO: Pardon
My asking, but why?
CHAEREA: I'm in love.
PARMENO: Uh-*huh!*
CHAEREA: Oh, Parmeno, now's
The time for you to show me how much of a man you are.
Remember your promise. You made it a thousand times:
    "Chaerea,
Just you find something to love," you'd say, "and then I'll make
You realize just how useful I am." That's what you'd tell me,
All those times when you were locked up in your little room,
And I'd raid Dad's private pantry, and sneak down to bring you
    food . . .   310
PARMENO: Stop it, stupid!
CHAEREA: Well, this is it—so please let me see
Those promises.
                Or take it as a challenge that's really worth
Your effort. This girl—she's not like your other girls. Their
    mothers

Make them sag their shoulders and strap their breasts to look
   skinny.
If one's a little bit pretty, up goes a chorus of "Heavyweight"
And slap she's put on a diet. Natural charm receives
The Treatment; it shrinks to a beanstalk.
                                        For most girls, that's
   the road
To Love.
PARMENO: But yours?
CHAEREA: A new departure in beauty.
PARMENO: Of course.
CHAEREA: Complexion, real; figure, not flabby but firm and plump
   And juicy.
PARMENO: Age?
CHAEREA: Her age? Sixteen.
PARMENO: Bursting into bloom.
CHAEREA: You've got to get her for me. Beg, borrow, or steal
   her . . .   320
The means don't matter, just so long as she's mine.
PARMENO: Now, wait—
   Whose *is* she?
CHAEREA: I don't have the slightest idea.
PARMENO: So where's she
   from?
CHAEREA: Ditto to that.
PARMENO: So where's she staying?
CHAEREA: Not even that.
PARMENO: So where'd you see her?
CHAEREA: Back there.
PARMENO: So how'd you
   manage to lose her?
CHAEREA: Exactly. That's what I got so mad at myself about
   Just now. I don't think there's another man alive
   Whose good luck's so damn bad.
PARMENO: And what went wrong?
CHAEREA: My life.
PARMENO: What happened?
CHAEREA: I'll tell you what happened. That
   crony of Dad's—a cousin

Or something; about the same age—Archidemides. Know
    him?
PARMENO: Oh boy.
CHAEREA: Guess who I met while I was trailing this girl?
PARMENO: That's pretty
    Distressing.
CHAEREA: Distressing, hell. Reserve "distressing" for trifles.
    Parmeno, this was disaster.   331
                        I can freely swear
That I hadn't seen him once in six, no, seven months
Before that moment, a moment when I had every motive
To miss him.
                    Does something up there hate me?
PARMENO: It looks that
    way.
CHAEREA: This old galoot was a good distance off, but he ran right
    up,
Bent double, loose-lipped, wobbly, and whinnying all the way:
"Whoa there! Whoa! I've got to talk to you, Chaerea!" So
I stopped. "You know what I wanted you for?"
                                    "Tell me."
                                        "My case
Comes up tomorrow."
                    "So what?"
                            "So be a good boy and remind
Your daddy to get to court early and give my plea some
    support."   340
To get this out, it took him an hour.
                        Would there be anything
Else, I asked.
            "That's all," he says.
                        And away I go.
I look back after the girl, and find she's just that minute
Turned up this way, into our street.
PARMENO (Aside):   I won't be surprised if he
    means
Thais's recent present.
CHAEREA: But when I got here, she was gone.
PARMENO: Point of information: Anyone with her?

CHAEREA: Oh, yes. A flunky
Of sorts, and a maid.
PARMENO: That's her.
                                              We can all go home.
Give up. The funeral's over.
CHAEREA: I don't understand what you mean.
PARMENO: I do. This business of yours.
CHAEREA: You know her, you mean,
or you saw her?
Which?
PARMENO: I saw her. I know her. I can even tell where they took
her.   350
CHAEREA: Parmeno—buddy—you know her? And you can tell me
where
She is?
PARMENO: They took her to Thais the whore. She went as a gift.
CHAEREA: What man has money enough to make a present like
that?
PARMENO: Major Thraso, Phaedria's rival.
CHAEREA: You're casting my brother
In a pretty tough part.
PARMENO: Tougher than you think. Just wait till
you see
The present *he's* got to match her.
CHAEREA: What in the world could it be?
PARMENO: A eunuch.
CHAEREA: Oh no. You couldn't mean that nauseating
thing
He bought yesterday, that antique freak?
PARMENO: The very same.
CHAEREA: With a gift like that she'll bounce him out of the
house.
            I didn't
Know Thais was living next door to us.
PARMENO: She just moved in.
CHAEREA: Damn. Just think, I've never met her. Tell me, is she
As pretty as everyone says?   361
PARMENO: Easily.

CHAEREA: Nothing compared
  To my girl, of course?
PARMENO: A different type.
CHAEREA: Oh, god, I implore you,
  Parmeno, get her for me!
PARMENO: All right, all right, I'll help you.
  Undivided attention.
  (*He starts for* DEMEA's *house*)
                 That all?
CHAEREA: Where are you going?
PARMENO: Home.
  I have to deliver those slaves to Thais. Your brother's orders.
CHAEREA: Delivered, inside this house! Oh, for the luck of that
    eunuch!
PARMENO (*Returning*): How so?
CHAEREA: Well, *think:* Within these walls, he'll have, as his
    constant
  Companion in slavery, that vision of total beauty. He'll see her,
  Talk to her, share the same house with her. Sometimes he'll eat
  The very food she eats. Or even sleep beside her.
PARMENO (*Offhand*): *You* could have that luck right now.
CHAEREA: I could?
  But how?
  Well, Parmeno, *how?*   370
PARMENO: Trade clothes with our eunuch.
CHAEREA: Trade clothes?
  Then what?
PARMENO: Then I'd deliver you instead of him . . .
CHAEREA: I see.
PARMENO: And say that you were the eunuch.
CHAEREA: Got you.
PARMENO: You could
  enjoy
  These bits of bliss you've been talking about: This eating
    together
  And sharing the house. This touching, playing, sleeping beside
    her.
  None of the women in here has any idea who you are.

And one thing more: You're a pretty boy, and just the right age;
You'd easily pass for a eunuch. A casual inspection, of course.
CHAEREA: Beautiful! I've never seen such advising!
(*Grabbing* PARMENO's *arm and setting off for* DEMEA's *house*)
                                        Well, let's go.
Into the house this minute. Wrap me up and send me.   381
Special delivery. Quick!
PARMENO: What do you think you're doing?
I'm only fooling.
CHAEREA: Baloney.
PARMENO: Dammit, what have I done
To myself?
              Now, quit this pushing. You'll knock me over.
                                                  I tell you,
  Stop!
CHAEREA: Let's go.
PARMENO: You mean it?
CHAEREA: I do.
PARMENO: It may be too hot
To handle.
CHAEREA: I can handle it. Please, just let me try.
PARMENO: But I'm the one who'll have to take the rap.
CHAEREA: No, no.
PARMENO: We are committing a crime.
CHAEREA: A crime?
                                        Parmeno, this
Is a whorehouse. It shelters tools of torture who take our youth
And fling it away, who torment us in every possible fashion.
Place me inside to pay them back, to victimize them
As they do us—is *this* a crime?
                            Would it be more just
To play their game and dupe my Dad? That would be con-
  demned,
And rightly so, if the world found out; but what we're doing
Can only bring us applause, and shouts of "Serves 'em Right."
PARMENO: So what's to reply?
                            If you mean business, I'll do it, but
  afterward,
Don't throw the blame on me.

CHAEREA: I won't.
PARMENO: Then this is an order?
CHAEREA: No, no order . . . it's a command, an ultimatum. I
    Shall never shirk a moral obligation.
PARMENO: God save us all.   390
    (*They exit into* DEMEA'*s house*)

ACT III

Scene 1

THRASO *and* GNATHO *enter left.*

THRASO: Really? Heartfelt thanks to me from Thais?
GNATHO: In thousands.
THRASO: Thrilled, you say?
GNATHO: And not so much
    By gift as by giver. Yourself. She's riding in triumph.
PARMENO (*Peering out of* DEMEA'*s house*): I'd better see if the
    coast is clear before
    I make delivery.
    (*Seeing* THRASO *and* GNATHO)
               Lo, the conq'ring hero.
    (*He watches unnoticed from the doorway*)
THRASO: Naturally endowed that way, you know. A sort
    Of innate grace enhancing all my actions.
GNATHO: Oh, yes. I've been quite struck by it.
THRASO: Likewise the King.
    My smallest service, he greeted with effusive thanks.
    Less to others, of course.
GNATHO: The victory won
    By the sweat of another man's brow is often preempted   400
    By the man of wit. As in your case.

THRASO: Exactly.

GNATHO: The King, I take it, only had eyes . . .

THRASO: Too true!

GNATHO: . . . For you?

THRASO: Precisely. Consigned his armies to me.
Made me privy to his Grand Designs.

GNATHO: I'm agog.

THRASO: There's more:

> When court and the affairs of state
> Had taken their exhausting toll,
> Had forced him to evacuate
> His . . . His . . .

                                        You know the line?

GNATHO: Like this,
I think:

> Had forced him to evacuate
> His throne and purge his griping soul.

THRASO: That's it.
On such occasions, he'd withdraw with a single
Guest—myself.

GNATHO: Imagine. A king with taste.

THRASO: Earned me no end of envy, of course. Backbiting   410
Behind my back. Couldn't have bothered me less.
Everyone sick with jealousy. One poor chap
In particular. Fellow in charge of the Indian elephants.
One day, was more of a screaming bore than usual.
Fixed his wagon. "Tell me, Strato," I said,
"Are your manners so monstrous because you manage monsters?"

GNATHO: You certainly had him there. Phrasing, point—
Right between the eyes. And what did he say?

THRASO: What *could* he say? Dead silence.

GNATHO: The only reply.

PARMENO (*Aside*): The gods are just. A fathead paired with a
fraud.

THRASO: Got in a neat stroke under the guard of a fellow
From Rhodes at a dinner once. I ever tell you
About it, Gnatho?   420

GNATHO: Never. I'd love to hear it.
(*Aside*)
The thousand-and-first performance.
THRASO: At a dinner once.
This fellow from Rhodes I mentioned. Young whippersnapper.
Had a camp follower with me, that started him off.
Innuendoes at her expense. Cheap cracks at mine.
Let him have it: "Show a little respect,
Sonny," I said. "The hare doesn't run with the hounds."
(*Hysterical laughter from Gnatho*)
What's all this?
GNATHO: It's witty, whimsical, droll,
An A-number-one retort. Original with you?
I thought it was old.
THRASO: What? Heard it before?
GNATHO: Again
And again. It's known as a real crusher.
THRASO: It's mine.
GNATHO: It pains me to think of its use on a thoughtless boy.   430
PARMENO (*Aside*): Damn you to hell.
GNATHO: Could he make a reply?
THRASO: Wiped out.
Rest of the party died with laughter. Then panicked.
Paled at the sight of me.
GNATHO: And well they might.
THRASO: Hold on. About Thais. She thinks I fancy that girl.
Best to relieve her suspicions?
GNATHO: Just the reverse.
Do your best to increase them.
THRASO: Why?
GNATHO: It's simple.
You know the effect any mention or praise of Phaedria
On Thais's part produces in you—that sudden
Heartburn?
THRASO: Feel it now.
GNATHO: There's only one cure,
And that's this: Whenever she says "Phaedria," you   440

Cut in with "Pamphila." Counter her "Let's have Phaedria
Over for dinner" with "Let's have Pamphila sing."
Whenever she praises his looks, extol the girl's.
Match her, tit for tat. Hit her where she lives.
THRASO: Might help, Gnatho. Provided she really loves me.
GNATHO: She's eager to get your presents, correct? Therefore
She loves them. Therefore, *she loves you,* too. And therefore,
It's easily in your power to cause her pain.
She lives in fear of your anger. You just might take
The harvest she reaps and sow it somewhere else.   450
THRASO: Beautifully put. But should have hit it myself.
GNATHO: You're joking. You simply chose to expend your mental
Energies elsewhere. Otherwise, you'd have leaped
To the same conclusion in a much more brilliant fashion.

Scene 2

THAIS *enters from her house.*

THAIS: Who's here? I thought I heard my Major's voice.
And so I did. Oh, Thraso darling, hello!
THRASO: Ah, Thais, you luscious morsel. Love me a little
For that girl guitarist?
PARMENO (*Aside*):   Now, there is finesse. The perfect
Amatory preamble.
THAIS: A lot, and you deserve it,
Every last bit.
GNATHO: And so to lunch.
(*To* THAIS)   Why aren't you
Ready?
PARMENO (*Aside*): The other master of tact. Can this one   460
Really be human?
THAIS: I'm ready whenever you are.

PARMENO (*Aside*): Time for my entrance. I'd better pretend I've been

Inside.

(*He moves from* DEMEA's *doorway to the group*)
Oh, Thais. Going for a walk?

THAIS: Er—Parmeno?

(*Improvising*)

I won't need you any more today. I was just

Going out . . .

PARMENO: Out where?

THAIS (*Aside to* PARMENO): Stop it! You see who's here?

PARMENO (*Aside to* THAIS): I do, and it makes me sick.

(*Loudly*) —Phaedria's presents

Are ready whenever you want them.

THRASO (*To* THAIS): No point in standing
Around here. Ought to be leaving.

PARMENO (*To* THRASO): Sir, by your leave,
Request permission for truce and parley with lady.
Object: Gifts, Presentation of.

THRASO: Hmmm. Gifts.
Magnificent items, no doubt. Equaling ours.

PARMENO: Learn first-hand. 470
(*He moves nearer* DEMEA's *door and calls*) Ahoy in there!
Send that pair

Out, on the double!
(*The African maid appears at the door*)
You first. Right this way.

(*She moves to him*)
—Direct from darkest Ethiopia!

THRASO: Three *minae*.

GNATHO: At most.
Pure schlock.

PARMENO (*Calling to the door again*):
Hey, Dorus! Where are you?
(CHAEREA *appears at the door, dressed as a eunuch*)

Over here.

(CHAEREA *moves to him*)

—Now there, I submit, is a eunuch! Kindly note
The thoroughbred features, the flawless freshness . . .

THRASO: Damnation.

Handsome beast.

PARMENO: Well, Gnatho, any observations?

No faults to pick at?

—Thraso, how about you?

—The ultimate accolade: Silence.

(*To* THAIS) Inspect him, please.

Examine his Literature. Music. Athletics. Guaranteed
Performance in all the pursuits deemed fit and proper
For a well-brought-up young gentleman.

THRASO: Know a pursuit

I wouldn't mind trying with him. If forced, of course.
Or even sober . . .

(GNATHO *jabs him in the ribs*)

PARMENO: The man who presents these gifts

Sets no conditions upon you. He does not demand   481
That you exclude your other friends and surrender
Yourself completely to him. He recites no battles,
He shows no scars, he sets no ambushes for you
On the street—like a certain party who shall be nameless.
He rests content if, on such rare occasions
As time, inclination, and circumstance may permit,
You will condescend to receive him.

THRASO: Owner of a slave

Like that—must be insolvent. Back to the wall.

GNATHO: I couldn't agree with you more. No man would struggle
Along with that if he could afford another.

PARMENO (*To* GNATHO): Shut up, vulture. You've dropped to the
     lowest rung

On Humanity's ladder by bowing and scraping to *that*   490
(*Pointing to* THRASO)

In cold blood. You'd scavenge your food from a funeral pyre.

THRASO: Time to be leaving.

THAIS: Just let me take them inside

And give the necessary orders. I'll be right out.
(*She conducts the maid and* CHAEREA *into her house*)
THRASO (*Highly offended, to* GNATHO): Departing. You wait for
  her highness here.
PARMENO: It figures.
The General Staff cannot be seen in public
With its Great and Good Friend. Has a bad effect on the troops.
THRASO: Er—pointless talking to you. Just like your master.
(*Again hysterical laughter from* GNATHO, *as* PARMENO *exits into*
DEMEA's *house*)
What's so funny?
GNATHO: Your witty comeback. A winner.
And then I remembered your slash at that boy from Rhodes.
—But here comes Thais.
(THAIS *enters from her house, followed by* PYTHIAS, DORIAS, *and
other women*)
THRASO: Run on ahead. Reconnoiter.
See that lunch is ready.
GNATHO: Aye, aye.
(*He exits left*)
THAIS: Now, Pythias,
Be very careful. If that man Chremes comes   500
While I'm out, first try to get him to wait. If that
Won't work, then ask him to come back later. If *that's*
Impossible, well, you bring him along to me.
PYTHIAS: All right.
THAIS: Now, what else was it I wanted to say?
(*To* PYTHIAS *and* DORIAS)
Oh, yes—be sure that the girl is properly cared for.
Don't leave the house.
THRASO: Forward!
THAIS (*To the other women*):   You come with me.
General exit: PYTHIAS *and* DORIAS *into* THAIS's *house;* THRASO,
THAIS, *and the other women left*)

Scene 3

CHREMES *stumbles on right and makes his way to* THAIS'S *door,
then stops and addresses the audience.*

CHREMES: I'm in danger.
                         No doubt about it. I try
To figure this out, and always get the same answer:
This Thais is fixing trouble for me. Big trouble.
Slick as she is, I see what she's doing to me.
Fattening me up for the kill. It started the very
First time she had me over.   510
                         I know what you're thinking:
"What was between you two?" Search me; I didn't
Know who she was. But I went, and had to wait.
Her excuse was, she had some serious business
To discuss with me, but was busy saying her prayers.
Well, now. Right then, I began to be suspicious;
All this was a trap. She sat down to dinner with me,
And pushed herself at me, sort of, and tried to start
A conversation. It died. She changed the subject: How long
Had my mother and father been dead? A long time, I told her.
Did I have a farm at Sunium? How far from the sea?
(She likes my farm, I bet. She probably wants   520
To steal it.) Finally, did I have a little sister
Who drowned down there, and was anyone with her when she
    died,
And what was she wearing, and who could identify her?
—Now, why would she ask all that, unless she was planning
To pass herself off as my sister, back from the dead?
Of all the nerve!
                         If my sister's still alive,
She's only sixteen; this Thais she's older than I am.
Not much, but older.
                         And now she's sent me another

Invitation. Serious business again. But this time
It's put up or shut up: She tells me what she's after,
Or gives up pestering me. I won't come see her
Again, and, that's for sure.   530
(*He knocks at* THAIS's *door*)
                              —Hey, anybody home?
Chremes is here!
(PYTHIAS *and* DORIAS *spring out*)
PYTHIAS: Lover, how divine to see you!
CHREMES (*Aside*): I told you. An ambush, yet.
PYTHIAS: Thais is out.
She left you an urgent message: Please come back
Tomorrow.
CHREMES: I'm going to the farm.
PYTHIAS: Oh, do it for me.
CHREMES: I tell you I can't.
PYTHIAS: Then wait inside—with us—
Till she comes home, hmmm?
CHREMES: Not on your life.
PYTHIAS: Why not,
Lover?
CHREMES: You go to hell.
PYTHIAS: You seem determined.
Then please go see her now?
(*Pointing off left*)   That way.
CHREMES: I'll go.
PYTHIAS: Dorias, take him right on over to the Major's.
(DORIAS *leads* CHREMES *off left.* PYTHIAS *exits into the house*)

Scene 4

ANTIPHO *enters right and stops in front of* DEMEA's *house.*

ANTIPHO: Yesterday, down at the harbor, a bunch of the boys got
together

And planned a party for today. We left the arrangements to
   Chaerea,   540
Gave him our IOU's, and agreed on a time and a place.
The time's gone by. The place is still there, but nothing's ready.
And Chaerea's nowhere. I don't have the slightest idea what
   happened.
The rest of the group's given me the job of finding him.
And so I'll see if he's home.
(THAIS's *door opens and* CHAEREA *emerges beatific, still in the
eunuch's clothes*)
                        —Who's this leaving Thais's?
Is it him or not?
           It's him.
                    But who's he supposed to be?
Why the disguise? What's wrong?
                     I'm floored. I can't even guess.
Unless, of course, I hide over here and find out what's up.
(*He conceals himself from* CHAEREA *in the space between the
house*)

Scene 5

CHAEREA: Anybody out here?
              Nobody.
                    Anybody follow me?
                            Nobody!
Is this the moment to let my rapture erupt?   550
                    O Jupiter,
My time has come. I'm ready and willing to meet my death,
Before life's little messes debase this total bliss.
—No interruptions?
             Nobody around to poke and pry,
To dog me, hound me, quiz me, pump me to death?
                      No questions?
Like, why am I shaking, or why am I happy, or where am I
   going,

Or where have I been, or where did I get this silly costume,
Or what am I leading up to, or am I sane or crazy?
ANTIPHO (*Aside*): He seems disappointed. I'll go and do him the
  favor he wants.
(*Moving to* CHAEREA)
—Hi, Chaerea. Why are you shaking like this? What's this
  costume
Leading up to? Why so happy? What does this mean?
Have you gone crazy?
                        Well, why are you looking at me like
  that?
Why the silence?
CHAEREA: Antipho, hello! My day is perfect.   560
There's nobody living I'd rather share this moment with.
ANTIPHO: I'd like it if you'd explain this.
CHAEREA: I'd love it if you'd listen.
You know my brother's mistress?
ANTIPHO: I know her. Thais, isn't it?
CHAEREA: That's her.
ANTIPHO: I thought it was.
CHAEREA: Today she received a
  present—
A virgin. I don't have to list the fine points of her beauty to you;
You know my standing as a qualified virgin-watcher. Just say
She knocked me out.
ANTIPHO: You mean it?
CHAEREA: The living end. One look'll
Convince you. I fell in love, that's enough. And was awfully
  lucky:
We had a eunuch at home. My brother had bought it for Thais
But hadn't delivered it yet. Well, Parmeno—he's our slave—
Suggested a plan. I snapped it up . . .   571
ANTIPHO: What sort of a plan?
CHAEREA: The stiller you are, the quicker you learn.
                                        —For me to
  trade clothes
With him and go in his place.
ANTIPHO: The eunuch's place?

CHAEREA: That's it.
ANTIPHO: What fun could you get out of that?
CHAEREA: Oh, really. The sight,
  the sound,
  The physical presence of a girl that I was mad for—is that
  A measly motive, Antipho, a shoddy stimulus?
                                                                —Thais
  Was thrilled when they put me into her hands. She hustled
  me in
  And put the girl straight into mine.
ANTIPHO: Your hands?
CHAEREA: My hands.
ANTIPHO: Well,
  safety
  First.
CHAEREA: She spelled out my orders: No man was allowed to
  visit.
  I wasn't allowed to leave the women's quarters. Compelled
  To stay by the girl at all times.
                              I lowered my eyes and nodded
  Assent.
ANTIPHO: Poor boy.
CHAEREA: "I'm going out to lunch," she said,   580
  And took her maids along. She left a couple behind
  To tend to the girl . . . but they were young ones, new at the
  job.
  They start to prepare her for the bath; I urge them to show
  some speed;
  She sits in her room, in the middle of all this bustle, inspecting
  A picture on the wall. A famous subject: Jupiter launching
  A shower of gold into Danaë's lap. I began to inspect it
  Myself. It repaid attention. Encouraging: Here was a god
  Long ago, who'd played almost the same game—disguised him-
  self
  (As a man) sneaked under another's roof (right down the
  chimney)
  And seduced a woman. And not just any god, but the one

Who makes the heights of heaven bound
And flounder at his thunder's sound.[9]   590
I might be only human, but couldn't I do the same?
And so I decided to do it.
                              During my internal debate,
They took the girl to the bath. She went, she bathed, she
    returned.
Lastly, they put her in bed. I stood there, waiting for orders.
"Hey, Dorus," says one of them, coming up, "you take this fan
And refresh her while we take our baths. Then, when we're
    done,
Take yours, if you want." I grumble a little, but take the fan.

ANTIPHO: I'd love to have seen you standing there—the look on
    your face.
A great big donkey like you waggling you itty-bitty fan.

CHAEREA: The words weren't out of her mouth before they ran out
    of the room,
Off to the bath with a whoop—when the cat's away, and all
    that.   600
Meantime, the girl fell asleep. I sneaked a sideways peek
Through the fan, like this. I took a careful look around.
The coast was clear. I locked the door.
    (*A pause*)

ANTIPHO: Then what?

CHAEREA: *Then what,*
You moron?

ANTIPHO: That's me.

CHAEREA: A chance like this, no matter how short—
Do you think I'd miss it? Temptation, aspiration, surprise, and
    passion
All mixed in one?
                    Just what do you think I am—a eunuch?

ANTIPHO: Enough. I'm convinced.
                              But meanwhile, what about our
    party?

CHAEREA: All ready.

---

[9] *at his thunder's sound:* According to Donatus, a parody of the Latin poet
Ennius.

ANTIPHO: Good boy. Your house?

CHAEREA: The freedman Discus's
    place.

ANTIPHO: That's quite a ways. Oh, well, so we hurry faster. Better
    Change those clothes.   609

CHAEREA: Okay, but oh hell, where? I'm banished
    From home, for now; my brother might be inside. Or, what's
    worse,
    Dad might be back from the farm already.

ANTIPHO: Come to my house.
    The nearest place where you can change.

CHAEREA: A good idea.
    Let's go. On the way, I'd like your advice about the girl:
    How do you think I can make her my own for good?

ANTIPHO: We'll see.
    (*They exit right*)

ACT IV

Scene 1

DORIAS *enters from the left.*

DORIAS: God almighty, after what I've seen, I'm nearly scared sick:
    The Major's lost his mind; he's liable to start a riot
    Or make an attack on Thais today.
                                        It happened at lunch
    Because of that fellow Chremes, our virgin's brother:
    When I brought him over, she pestered the Major to ask him in.
    The Major blew up, but didn't dare risk a flat refusal.
    Thais kept digging away: Invite him in. (And I know
    Why she did it—to keep him around till she could tell him

All she wanted to about his sister. This wasn't the time.)   620
With a very sour face, he invited him in. So Chremes stayed.
And oh, what table talk. The Major thought he'd seen
A rival installed there right before his eyes. Decided
He'd like to get some of his own back.

                                        "Boy," he said to a slave,
"Go bring Pamphila here to give us some entertainment."
"Pamphila here to lunch? Certainly not!" said Thais.
The Major insisted. From this, it was only a step to a fight.
Meanwhile, she slipped her jewelry off and gave it to me
To bring home. I know that sign: She'll slip out as soon as she
    can.

(*She enters* THAIS's *house*)

Scene 2

PHAEDRIA *enters right.*

PHAEDRIA: I was making my way along the road to the farm
    And started thinking. It's a habit I have when upset.   630
    One worry after another, each worse than the last . . .
    To put it briefly, I sank so deep in my thoughts
    I missed the house. I blundered a good way beyond it
    Before I noticed, then came on back, disgusted.
    I reached the turnoff, stopped . . . and started thinking
    Again:
            "Now, look—do you really have to stay
    Down here for two whole days? Alone? Without her?
    And afterward—what happens then?"
                                        "No worry there."
    "No worry, hell. The policy's 'Hands Off' now;
    You think it won't be 'Eyes Off'?"
                                        "So touching's out;
    At least they'll let me look."

                              "Well, long-range love   640
Is better than nothing."
                    —This time, I missed the house
On purpose.
(*Looking off left*)
                    —Here's Pythias. What's got her so flustered?

Scene 3

PYTHIAS *enters from* THAIS'S *house, followed shortly by an uncomprehending* DORIAS,[10] *who still carries the jewelry box. They
do not see* PHAEDRIA.

PYTHIAS: Where can I find that savage? Where do I look for that
    thug?
Disaster, catastrophe—how could he have the gall to *do*
A thing like that?
PHAEDRIA (*Aside*): Whatever this is, I'm scared of it.
PYTHIAS: When he'd had his fun with the girl, he did stop? Oh,
    no—atrocity
Wasn't enough for him; he shredded her dress and ripped out
Her hair in handfuls!
PHAEDRIA (*Aside*): He what?
PYTHIAS: Just let me at him—I'll take
    These nails and scoop his eyeballs out, that . . . ooh, that
    poisoner!
PHAEDRIA (*Aside*): It's not too clear, but I'd say there'd been a
    disturbance in there
While I was away. I'll go see.   650
                    —What's up, Pythias? Why this
Rushing around? And who are you hunting?

----

        [10] *an uncomprehending Dorias:* That is, Dorias has been greeted, upon enter-
ing the house, with an uproar; she knows that something is wrong, but doesn't
know *what*. Another solution is for her to knock at Thais's door at the end of Act
IV, Scene 1, wait patiently (and unperceivingly) for admittance throughout
Phaedria's soliloquy, and finally receive an answer when Pythias bursts forth.

PYTHIAS: Well, well—
   Phaedria.
Will you kindly take your pretty present and go to hell?
Or anyplace else that'll take you?
PHAEDRIA: What do you mean?
PYTHIAS: You know
   What I mean! You and your eunuch—you didn't bring us a gift,
   You brought us to rack and ruin! You know that girl from the
      Major?
   Your eunuch raped our virgin!
PHAEDRIA: He which? You must be drunk.
PYTHIAS: Whatever I am at the moment, I wish it on all my
     enemies.
DORIAS: Pythias, please! This thing you said—it's just not natural!
PHAEDRIA: I say you're crazy. He was a eunuch; how could he
     rape?
PYTHIAS: I don't know what he *was;* but, as to what he *did,*
   The evidence speaks for itself. The girl can't speak for hers;
   She's crying, too shaken to talk when you ask her what hap-
     pened.   660
   And Nature's Nobleman's nowhere around to be found. Which
     makes
   Another worry: It's likely he lifted some little items
   On his way out of the house.
PHAEDRIA: I'd be surprised if he got
   Very far away. A pretty sad specimen. Probably came back
   Home to us.
PYTHIAS: Please do me a favor. Go see if he's there.
PHAEDRIA: I'll let you know in a minute.
   (*He exits into* DEMEA's *house*)
DORIAS: But darling, this is awful.
   I never even heard of such an unspeakable act!
PYTHIAS: I have to admit I'd heard that, where women are con-
     cerned,
   Eunuchs are very lecherous types, but completely . . . unable.
   I never gave it the slightest thought. If I had, I wouldn't
   Have put him in charge of the girl; I'd have locked him up
     somewhere.

Scene 4

PHAEDRIA *enters from* DEMEA's *house, dragging after him the
frightened and confused eunuch* DORUS, *who is dressed, quite
badly, in* CHAEREA's *clothes.*

PHAEDRIA: Outside, goon! Stop dragging your heels and move,
    You rotten runaway! Forward, you waste of money,
    March!
DORUS: Mercy!
PHAEDRIA: Eccch, what a face he's making.   670
    Scare you to death.
    (*To* DORUS)   —Why the return to our house?
    Why the change of clothes? Let me have the story.
    —If I'd been just a little later, Pythias,
    I wouldn't have caught him inside. He'd already put on
    A disguise to escape in.
PYTHIAS: Oh please, have you got the man?
PHAEDRIA: Of course I've got him.
PYTHIAS: Wonderful!
DORIAS: I'll say it is!
PYTHIAS: Where is he?
PHAEDRIA: Where *is* he? Don't you see him?
PYTHIAS: See him?
    See who?
PHAEDRIA: This fellow here.
PYTHIAS: What fellow is that?
PHAEDRIA: The one they delivered to you today.
PYTHIAS: Oh, no,
    Phaedria. None of our girls has ever laid eyes
    On this one.
PHAEDRIA: They haven't?
PYTHIAS: Honestly, did you believe   680
    They delivered *this* to us?

PHAEDRIA: It's the only eunuch
  I had.
PYTHIAS: Oh, dear. There's no comparison here
  With the one we received. He was very handsome. Distin-
    guished.
PHAEDRIA: He only appeared that way because he was wearing
  Those gorgeous clothes. Now that he's changed, he looks
  Disgusting.
PYTHIAS: Please stop this nonsense. You talk
  As though the difference were tiny; it's not. The gift
  Delivered to us today was a boy. Youngish.
  And handsome?—You'd be happy to see him, Phaedria.
  This one's decrepit, dilapidated, desiccated—and *old*.
  His skin looks like a weasel's.
PHAEDRIA: Dammit, what sort
  Of a fairy tale is this? You trying to reduce me   690
  To confusion? I know what I bought.
  (*To* DORUS)   —Did I buy you?
DORUS: You did.
PYTHIAS: My turn. Have him answer one for me.
PHAEDRIA: Ask it.
PYTHIAS (*To* DORUS): Were you at our house today?
  (DORUS *shakes his head. She turns to* PHAEDRIA)
                                 —Negative.
  The other one came. A boy of about sixteen.
  Parmeno brought him over.
PHAEDRIA (*To* DORUS):   Come on, you. Give me
  Some answers. First, those clothes you're wearing: Where
  Did you get them?
           Well?
                 Look here, you freak, are you going
  To tell me or not?
DORUS: Uh . . . Chaerea came . . .
PHAEDRIA: My brother?
DORUS: Yup.
PHAEDRIA: Well, when?
DORUS: Today.
PHAEDRIA: How long ago?

DORUS: A little.

PHAEDRIA: Who with?

DORUS: Parmeno.

PHAEDRIA: You knew him before?

DORUS: Nope. I'd never even heard of him.

PHAEDRIA: Then how did you know that he was my brother? 700

DORUS: Parmeno

Said so. Your brother gave me these clothes.

PHAEDRIA: Oh, hell.

DORUS: He put mine on. And then they both went out.

PYTHIAS: I hope you're satisfied. Now was I drunk? Now was I
lying?

Now do you believe what happened to the girl?

                                        Rape!

PHAEDRIA: Calm down, now; don't go wild. Would you take the
word of *this?*

PYTHIAS: What's with taking words? The evidence speaks for itself.

PHAEDRIA (*Aside to* DORUS): Come over this way a little. Got me?
And just a bit more . . .

That's good.

(*The two converse privately, out of range of* PYTHIAS *and*
DORUS)

                 Now, let's go through these answers once again:

Chaerea stripped your clothes off?

DORUS: Yup.

PHAEDRIA: And put them on

Himself?

DORUS: Yup.

PHAEDRIA: And got delivered in your place?

DORUS: Yup.

PHAEDRIA (*Loudly*): Oh, god, of all the harebrained delinquents! [11]

---

[11] *of all the harebrained delinquents:* The motivation here adopted for this
line, and Pythias's reaction, is this: Phaedria has quizzed Dorus privately in the
hope of establishing Chaerea's innocence; when that hope is firmly defeated, he
shouts in annoyance at his younger brother's stupidity. Pythias, hearing the shout,
interprets it as directed against Dorus, an attempt to impugn his testimony.

PYTHIAS: Oh, no, not again!

  We were the victims of a sneak attack—won't you believe
      it?   710

PHAEDRIA: I know that you'll believe whatever this cretin says.

  (*Aside*)

  I don't know what to do.

  (*Aside to* DORUS)   —Now, get this: This time, answer

  No.

  (*Loudly*)

      —I'll tear the truth out of you if it takes me all day.

  Did you or did you not see my brother Chaerea?

DORUS: Nope.

PHAEDRIA (*To* PYTHIAS): See? Need torture to make him
      confess.

  (*Aside to* DORUS) —Stick right with me.

  (*To* PYTHIAS) —First it's Yup and then it's Nope.

  (*Aside to* DORUS)   —Now beg for
      mercy.

  (*He hits* DORUS)

DORUS: Phaedria! Mercy!

                    I mean it!

PHAEDRIA (*Loudly, as he kicks* DORUS): Get back in there, and
      hurry!

DORUS: Ouch!

  (*He exits into* DEMEA's *house*)

PHAEDRIA (*Aside*): It's the only way I can see to get out of this

  And save my standing.

  (*Loudly, after* DORUS)

                    —All right, you hoodlum, any more fooling

  Around with me and you have had it!

  (*He exits into* DEMEA's *house*)

PYTHIAS: As sure as I'm living,

  I know that this was one of Parmeno's tricks.

DORIAS: You're right.

PYTHIAS: I swear I'll find some way to pay him back. Today.

  An equal favor.

                    What do we do now, Dorias?

DORIAS: You mean   720
    About our virgin?
PYTHIAS: Yes. Do I tell Thais or keep it quiet?
DORIAS: Good lord, if you've got any sense, you don't know a
    thing.
    The eunuch, the rape, nothing. That way, you're out of this mess
    And build up thanks with *him*.[12]
    (*Indicating* DEMEA's *house, home of* PHAEDRIA)
                            Just say that Dorus has disappeared.
PYTHIAS: That's what I'll do.
DORIAS (*Looking off left*): Oh, look. It's Chremes. Thais'll be back
    Any minute.
PYTHIAS: How do you know?
DORIAS: She'd already started
    A fight with the Major before I left.
PYTHIAS: Well, take that jewelry
    Back in the house. I'll find out how things stand from Chremes.
    (DORIAS *exits into* THAIS's *house*)

Scene 5

CHREMES *enters left, very drunk.*

CHREMES: Behold the victim of a wicked trick. Undermined by
    wine—
I'm blind.
            'S odd. At table I seemed to be able to stay
Impossibly sober. But when I got up to go, my feet
Defected. My brain refrained from performing its usual func-
    tion.

---

[12] *build up thanks with him:* Or possibly with *her;* the Latin *illi* is ambiguous.
The possible candidates and reasons: Thanks would be due from (1) Phaedria, for
protecting his brother; (2) Thais, for concealing the somewhat shopworn condition of a counter which she hopes to trade for patronage and protection; (3)
Pamphila, for hiding her shame. (1) and (3) seem more likely than (2), and (1)
more likely than (3).

PYTHIAS: Chremes?   730
CHREMES: Who's there?
                                    If it isn't Pythias. What a quick
change.
Yum. How lovely you've gotten.
(*He embraces her. She works loose*)
PYTHIAS: God. How lively you've gotten.
CHREMES: I exemplify the proverb:
Without Demeter and Dionysus
Aphrodite a lump of ice is.[13]
                                        —Did Thais beat me
Back by much?
PYTHIAS: Has she already left the Major's?
CHREMES: Long since.
Years. There arose a rift. A rupture. A ruckus. A rhubarb.
PYTHIAS: Didn't she tell you to follow her?
CHREMES: Not in the least. The
merest
Hint of a nod as she left.
PYTHIAS: What size of a sign do you need?
CHREMES: I protest. I hadn't the least idea of her meaning. The
Major,
However, rectified my regrettable lack of experience.
                                                      He threw
Me out.
(*Looking off left*)
          —Oh, here she comes. How did I beat her back?

---

[13] *Aphrodite a lump of ice is:* Apologies are due somewhere for this doggerel,
as well as for the retranslation of Latin divinities into Greek that makes it possible.
Its only excuse is that it contributes to the general rhetorical inflation marking
Chremes' drunkenness—a drunkenness that lasts, incidentally, through all the oscil-
lations of his Dutch courage, until he has departed to get the nurse.

Scene 6

THAIS *enters right and addresses the audience.*

THAIS: He'll turn up here to reclaim her in a minute. I know he
  will.
Just let him try! If he so much as touches that girl
With his little finger, I'll rip his eyes out, right on the spot. 740
Stupidity I can endure, conceit I can stand—but only
As long as he sticks to words. If he translates his shortcomings
Into action, he'll pay with his skin.
CHREMES: Thais, I've been here for
  hours.
THAIS: —Chremes, darling, just the person I wanted to see.
  Do you know that you were the cause of that fight? that you're
    the focus
  Of this whole affair?
CHREMES: Who, me? Impossible. How?
THAIS: Because
  Of your sister. My attempts to return her to you safe and sound
  Involved me in this mess, and lots of others like it.
CHREMES: Where is she?
THAIS: There, in my house.
CHREMES: In *there*?
THAIS: Don't be
  worried;
  She's a decent girl. Quite worthy of you.
CHREMES: How do you mean?
THAIS: These are the facts: Your sister's my present to you,
    Chremes;
  I ask no payment in return.   749
CHREMES: I thank you, Thais. I assure you
  That you shall receive suitable expression of my appreciation.
THAIS: Good, but you'd better watch out: You may lose my gift
    before

You get it. She's the girl the Major's coming to abduct.
—Pythias, go get the evidence. The box of things that prove
Her identity.
CHREMES (*Looking off left*):
        Thais, look! Here comes . . .
PYTHIAS (*To* THAIS):   Where *is* the box?
THAIS: It's in the chest. Please hurry!
  (*Exit* PYTHIAS *into* THAIS's *house*)
CHREMES: . . . the Major! He's brought
  an army
Along. An attack—help!
THAIS: Now don't tell me you're scared.
CHREMES: Perish the thought—me scared? Don't know the mean-
  ing of fear.
THAIS: Just what we need.
CHREMES: I'm afraid . . . that you don't know
  the sort
Of man I am.
THAIS: But I do, I do. Now, think this over: 760
Remember that you're an Athenian citizen dealing with an
  alien.
You've got influence, reputation, friends. He hasn't. He's weak.
CHREMES: I know all that. But isn't it stupid to borrow trouble
When you can avoid it? Prevention is better than vengeance,
Isn't it? Why get hurt?
             Look here, you go on inside
And bar the door, while I take a quickish run downtown.
(*He points off left to downtown, checks, and points off right* [14]
to the harbor and the country)
We require reinforcements to fight this battle.
(*He starts off right.* THAIS *grabs his arm*)
THAIS: Stay here.

[14] *checks, and points off right:* This overfull blocking is necessary to reconcile
mise-en-scène with text, but I believe it has some additional warrant, thus: The
conventional downtown exit, stage left, has already been established as the way to
Thraso's house, and hence the route by which the army is approaching. Chremes
grabs at the first possible excuse to leave the field of honor, does a double take
when he sees that it would lead him into collision with the oncoming enemy, and
changes to a direction completely at variance with his suggestion.

CHREMES: My plan is better.

THAIS: *Stay here.*

CHREMES: Leggo. Be back in a minute.

THAIS: Chremes, we don't need help. Just tell him that she's your
sister.

You lost her when she was little, and today you identified her.

And then you show him the evidence.

PYTHIAS (*Entering from the house with a box*): And here's the
evidence.

THAIS (*Taking the box from* PYTHIAS *and thrusting it on* CHREMES):
Keep this.

Oh. If the Major resorts to force, just take him to court.

Have you got all this?

CHREMES: Oh, perfectly.

THAIS: When you say your piece,
Don't be nervous.

CHREMES: Depend on me.

THAIS: Let's gird up those loins!   769
(*Aside*)

Oh dear. Where can I find a defender to protect my champion?
(*Exeunt into* THAIS's *house*)

Scene 7

THRASO *and* GNATHO *enter left, followed by the motley army of*
DONAX, SIMALIO, *and* SYRISCUS. *They bear an assortment of household tools.*

THRASO: Flagrant dishonor, Gnatho. Escutcheon grossly be-
smirched.

Accept it? Never. Death were better.
                                —Forward, men!

Simalio, Donax, Syriscus—this way!
(*The group shambles to a stop in front of* THAIS's *house*)

                              Now, strategy: First—
House, Assault on.
GNATHO: Brilliant.
THRASO: Virgin, Plunder of.
GNATHO: Breathtaking.
THRASO: Thais, Reprisals Against.
GNATHO: A positive master-stroke.
THRASO: —Donax, you and your crowbar form the center, here.
    —Simalio, take the left wing.
                              —Syriscus, take the right.
—The rest of you men . . .
(*He realizes that there is nobody left*)
                              Where's Sergeant Sanga and his
    thieves' platoon?
(SANGA, THRASO's *cook, runs on bearing a dishmop*)
SANGA: All present and accounted for, sir.
THRASO: You goldbrick, why
    aren't you armed
With regulation gear? You thought that battles were fought
    with mops?
SANGA: No, sir. I knew my general's valor and the might of his
    men:
    I figured there'd have to be blood. So this is to swab out the
    wounds, sir.
THRASO: Where are the others?
SANGA: The others? Just what the hell do
    you mean, sir?
There's only Sannio left, and he's looking after the house.   780
THRASO: Draw up the troops. Posting myself in the second rank.
    Spot where I can command the entire field of battle.
(*The slaves, under* SANGA's *direction, move toward the house.*
    THRASO *moves away from it, followed by* GNATHO)
GNATHO: Tactical genius!
    (*Aside*)   A formation which keeps him safe in
    reserve.
THRASO: A maneuver made famous by General Pyrrhus.
    (THAIS *and* CHREMES, *unseen by the others, appear at* THAIS's
    upper window)

CHREMES: You see
    what's happening,
Thais? That was an excellent plan, barricading the house.
THAIS: One thing's certain: That may look like a hero to you,
    But it's just a fraud. Don't worry.
THRASO (*To* GNATHO):   Any suggestions?
GNATHO: I wish
    That you had a sling. It's time for long-range fire from cover.
    You'd cut them to pieces. The rout would be on.
THRASO: There's Thais.
    In person.
GNATHO: How soon do we sound the attack?
THRASO: Not yet. Exhaust all
    other
    Avenues before resorting to passage of arms. The mark
    Of a wise commander. Conditions gained without the use
    Of force, if possible.
GNATHO: Heaven preserve us, what a blessing   790
    Is wisdom! I never come near you without departing improved.
THRASO: —A question, Thais, before we begin: On receipt of that
    girl,
    You promised me your complete attention through tomorrow—
    yes?
THAIS: So what if I did?
THRASO: So what? Introducing your lover inside
    My house right under my nose . . .
THAIS: What business is it of yours?
THRASO: . . . Sneaking away from me to join him . . .
THAIS: That's what
    I felt like.
THRASO: Then give back Pamphila now. Or else I take her by
    force!
CHREMES: You won't get her back. You won't even touch her,
    you . . .
GNATHO:
    You shut up!
THRASO (*To* CHREMES): Just what do you mean? She's mine; I'll
    touch her.
CHREMES: Yours, you bastard?

GNATHO: Be careful, youngster. You obviously don't know whom
 you're addressing.

CHREMES (*To* GNATHO): Get out of here!
 (*To* THRASO)   —Do you know how you
 stand at present?   800
 You start the least little fuss here now, and I'll give you a reason
 To remember this day, and this place, and me, as long as you
 live.

GNATHO: Boy, it grieves me to see you making an enemy of such
 An important person.

CHREMES: Get Out of Here, or I shall personally
 Knock your block off.

GNATHO: You will, will you? Where's your manners,
 You sonofabitch?

THRASO: Who *are* you? What are you aiming at?
 What possible concern is this girl of yours?

CHREMES: I shall inform you.
 Point One: She is a freeborn . . .

THRASO: Pah!

CHREMES: . . . Athenian citizen . . .

THRASO: Tchah!

CHREMES: . . . Also, my sister.

THRASO: Insolent puppy!

CHREMES: Major,
 I therefore enjoin you from any show of violence against her.
 —Thais, I'll go get the nurse, Sophrona, and bring her back
 To see the evidence here.

THRASO: You'd really prevent me from touching
 A girl that belongs to me?

CHREMES: Exactly. I will prevent you.
 I have spoken.
 (*He disappears from the window, leaves* THAIS's *house, and
 stalks off right* [15])

GNATHO (*To* THRASO): Hear that? He as good as confesses to
 theft. That's all you need.

THRASO: You agree with that fellow, Thais?   810

[15] *and stalks off right:* Alternatively, Chremes might merely disappear from
the window, and be presumed, by those for whom such presumptions are necessary, to have left by a back door.

THAIS: Find somebody else to
  answer
Your questions. I'm through.
(*She closes the shutters.* THRASO *turns to* GNATHO)
THRASO: What now?
GNATHO: Well, let's go home. She'll come there soon
  enough
On her own. And on her knees.
THRASO: You really think so?
GNATHO: Certainly.
  I know the female mind: Say yes, and they say no.
  Say no . . . and they suddenly find that there's nothing they
    want so much.
THRASO: Excellent thought.
GNATHO: Should I dismiss the army now?
THRASO: Whenever you like.
GNATHO: —Sanga, as befits a soldier in the field,
  Turn your thoughts to the fires of home.
SANGA: My heart has never
  Left my broiler.
GNATHO: Good boy.
THRASO: —This way, men. Forward, march!
  (THRASO, GNATHO, *and the army struggle off left*)

ACT V

Scene 1

THAIS *and* PYTHIAS *enter from* THAIS's *house.*

THAIS: Oh, damn you, Pythias, please stop talking in riddles.
  "I know . . . but no, I don't know . . . he's gone . . . I heard . . .

I wasn't there . . ." Unravel this tangle of words
And tell me straight—what *is* all this?
                                        I've got
A virgin in there in tears; her dress is in tatters;   820
She won't say a thing. And what I haven't got
Is a eunuch. Why? What happened?
                                        Well, say something!
PYTHIAS: Oh, dear. How do I start?
                                        People are saying
That wasn't a eunuch.
THAIS: What was it, then?
PYTHIAS: Uh . . . Chaerea.
THAIS: What's a Chaerea?
PYTHIAS: Phaedria's teen-age brother.
THAIS: Don't gossip, you witch. That's a poisonous thing to say.
PYTHIAS: It's true. I checked it out.
THAIS: But what could he want
In our house? Why did they bring him?
PYTHIAS: I don't know . . .
(*A threatening gesture from* THAIS)
But I *think* that he might have been in love with Pamphila.
THAIS: Oh, hell. If what you're telling me is true,
You jinx, my reputation's dead and buried.
                                        This can't
Be the reason the girl's in tears?
PYTHIAS: I think it can.
THAIS: It can't have happened. You're lying.
                                   I warned you against
That very thing when I left!   830
PYTHIAS: And what was I
Supposed to do? I followed your orders to the letter:
Put him in charge, you said, alone. I did.
THAIS: You set the wolf to watch the lamb. Oh, damn you!
It nauseates me to be taken in like this.
What sort of a man can he be?
PYTHIAS (*Looking off left*):   Oh, mistress, shhhh!
Please shhhh. We're saved.
                                   We've got the man in question.

THAIS: Where is he?

PYTHIAS: Look over there to your left. You see him?

THAIS: I see him . . .

PYTHIAS: Quick, now, have him arrested!

THAIS: Idiot.
What would we do with him then?

PYTHIAS: Do you have to ask?
What do you see when you look at that face? Impudence,
No?

         You agree?

                    Oooh, what a cocky type!

Scene 2

CHAEREA, *still wearing* DORUS's *clothes, enters left* [16] *and stops.*
He does not immediately see the women.

CHAEREA: Antipho's father and Antipho's mother were both   840
    At home. You'd think they'd planned it, placing themselves
    Just where I couldn't get in without being seen.
    So, while I was standing outside their door, an acquaintance
    Began to move in my direction. At this,
    I tore out of there as fast as I could and ducked
    Down an alley. Nobody around. And then from there
    To another alley, and then another, running
    Away. And more than half out of my mind with fear
    That someone who knew me might see me wearing these
        clothes.
    —But isn't that Thais?

    [16] *enters left:* The one wing entrance in this play whose direction is definitely
specified in the text (by Pythias' line slightly earlier). The fact that it is not the
direction by which Chaerea departed is, I think, sufficiently motivated by his
remarks immediately after this on his confusion. An analogous confusion (I've
been looking all over and can't find the girl) underlies his first entrance in the
play, where (in this version) he has lost Gnatho's procession and debouches into
his home street by a different route.

It is.
                                                I'm stuck: What shall
I do? No matter—what will she do to me?
THAIS (*To* PYTHIAS): Let's go meet him.   850
   (*To* CHAEREA)   —Greetings, Dorus. De-
      lighted
To see you. Tell me, now: Did you run away?
CHAEREA: Yes, ma'am. It comes to that.
THAIS: You're pleased with your-
      self?
CHAEREA: No, ma'am.
THAIS: You think you'll get off easy, perhaps?
CHAEREA: Please pardon this first offense. If I ever commit
   Another, put me to death.
THAIS: But why did you do it?
   Did I look like such a vicious mistress?
CHAEREA: No, ma'am.
THAIS: Then what was the reason?
CHAEREA (*Indicating* PYTHIAS): Her. I was afraid
   She'd go to you and accuse me.
THAIS: What had you done?
CHAEREA: It's nothing, really.
PYTHIAS: *Nothing Really?* That's
   Too much! You raped a freeborn Athenian virgin—
   You call that Nothing Really?
CHAEREA: I thought that she
   Was one of us slaves.
PYTHIAS: Was one of us slaves! Of all
   The unnatural . . . I'm using all my control, or I'd tear   860
   Your hair out.
                       —All this, and he comes to laugh at us!
THAIS: You're raving; get out of here.
PYTHIAS: Why should I? What sort
   Of damages would I have to pay for assaulting
   A thug like him—a self-admitted slave?
THAIS: Let's drop this nonsense.
                             —Chaerea, what you've done
   Is horribly wrong. I may deserve an affront

Like this in the highest degree; regardless, you had
No right to commit it. And now I swear to god
I don't have the least idea what course to follow
About this girl. You've overturned all my planning.
How can I give her back to her people the way
She should have gone, the way I wanted her   870
To go? And tell me, Chaerea, what becomes
Of the tangible thanks I hoped to get out of this?
CHAEREA: At least I hope it's the start of a permanent bond
Between us, Thais. In affairs like this one, appalling
Beginnings often lead to lasting friendships.
There may be a god behind it all—who knows?
THAIS: Yes. There's an interpretation I'm happy to accept.
CHAEREA: Please do. There's one thing you can be sure of. I didn't
Do this to cause you any affront; I did it
For love.
THAIS: I know you did, and that's what makes me
All the more disposed to forgive you. I'm not
Exactly a stranger to human nature, Chaerea,   880
Or inexperienced. What love can do, I know.
CHAEREA: I swear to heaven, Thais, I love you, too.
PYTHIAS (*To* THAIS): Better watch out for him; it's your turn now.
CHAEREA: I wouldn't dream . . .
PYTHIAS: I don't believe a word.
THAIS (*To* PYTHIAS): Stop it!
CHAEREA: And now I humbly beg your assist-
ance
Out of this mess. I commend and commit myself
Into your keeping, I name you my advocate. Thais,
Help me: I'll die if I don't marry that girl.
THAIS: Yes, but your father . . .
CHAEREA: I guarantee he'll say yes.   890
As long as she's a citizen.
THAIS: If you can wait
A little, her brother should be back in a minute.
He went to get the nurse she had as a baby.
You can be there when she's identified, Chaerea!

CHAEREA: Fine; I'll stay.

THAIS: Then wouldn't you rather wait
Inside for him, instead of out here in the street?

CHAEREA: I'll jump at the chance.

PYTHIAS (*To* THAIS): And what, may I ask, do you think
You're doing?

THAIS: What's wrong now?

PYTHIAS: Do you have to ask?
Letting him in your house after what he did!

THAIS: Why not?

PYTHIAS: You take it from me, he'll start a nice, fresh
Fracas.

THAIS: Please do shut up.

PYTHIAS: You refuse to realize 900
Just how much of a menace this man is!

CHAEREA: I'll be quite harmless, Pythias.

PYTHIAS: I know you will,
Unless they let you get your hands on something.

CHAEREA: Well, then, Pythias, take me in charge yourself.

PYTHIAS: Not me. Take you in charge or put you in charge . . .
I wouldn't dare.
Now, *git!*

THAIS (*Looking off right*): Here comes her brother.
Just in time.

CHAEREA: Oh, hell. Oh, *No!* Please, Thais,
Let's get inside. I couldn't stand to have him
See me wearing these clothes on the street.

THAIS: Why not?
Modesty *now?*

CHAEREA: I'm afraid so.

PYTHIAS: Afraid so? A veritable
Virgin!

THAIS: You go ahead. I'll follow.
—Pythias,
You wait here for Chremes and bring him inside.
(*Exeunt* CHAEREA *and* THAIS *into* THAIS's *house*)

Scene 3

PYTHIAS: Idea, inspiration, hot flash—I need one now: 910
   Some way to pay back the slick pathological liar
   Who fobbed that bogus eunuch off on us. How?
   (CHREMES *and* SOPHRONA *enter right, very slowly*)
CHREMES: A little more speed, nurse. Come on, move.
SOPHRONA: I'm moving.
CHREMES: Which direction?
PYTHIAS (*Running up*):   Have you shown the nurse
   The evidence yet?
CHREMES: Every last item.
PYTHIAS: Well,
   What did she say? Could she identify them?
CHREMES: By heart.
PYTHIAS: That's marvelous news. I do so like
   The girl.
        Go right on in; my mistress has been
   Waiting for you for hours.
   (CHREMES *and* SOPHRONA *exit into* THAIS's *house.* PARMENO *enters from* DEMEA's *house and stops, not seeing* PYTHIAS)
               —Lo and behold,
   A noble soul advances . . . Parmeno. Such
   A leisurely pace. Please god, I think I've found
   A personal method for bringing this crook to book.   920
   First, I'll go inside and make quite sure
   The identification's secure; then back out here,
   To scare that scoundrel out of his scheming skin.
   (*Exit* PYTHIAS *into* THAIS's *house*)

Scene 4

PARMENO: Back for a check on Chaerea's progress. I hope
  He's managed the matter with some acumen; if so
  Imagine the praises accruing to Parmeno's account—
  So *rightly.*
                Just what have I done?
                                        I omit from mention
  The sheer achievement involved in effecting an affair
  As potentially clumsy and costly as this—the procural,
  From a hardened, tight-fisted pro, of the girl he loves—
  Without trouble, toll, or expense of any sort.
  Let all that pass. I pride myself on my second
  Success, my masterpiece, my moral breakthrough: 930
  I have developed a device whereby an innocent
  Youth can learn the true nature and mores of whores
  At an early age, and acquire a disgust to last him
  The rest of his life.
                        To see these broads abroad
  From their houses, daintily nibbling away at lunch
  With a lover, at intimate suppers, this is to conclude
  That no more tasteful, better-dressed, or sweeter
  Creatures exist.
                    But a stay inside those houses
  Shows *Truth:* The filth, the overall bathless squalor
  Of these soiled doves, their underlying ugliness,
  The greasy greed with which they slosh their hunks
  Of black bread in leftover soup and slobber it down.
  Such an education can be a boy's salvation.   940
  (*During this set piece,* PYTHIAS *has entered from* THAIS's *house
  and overheard*)
PYTHIAS (*Aside*): Heel. I'll make you eat those words . . . and
    your deeds
  As well. You've had your fun with us. You'll pay.

(*Loudly, pretending not to see* PARMENO)

—God save us, what a revolting development! Ohhh, the poor
    boy,
And so young, too! It's criminal, criminal—and Parmeno's
    guilty!
He brought him here.

PARMENO (*Aside*):   What's up?

PYTHIAS: He's such a pitiful sight,
I couldn't bear to watch. I ran out here before
They started that sickening punishment. How can they inflict
    such pain?

PARMENO (*Aside*): Oh god, what's all this uproar? Have I sunk
    myself somehow?
I'd better go see.

             —What's happened, Pythias? What's this mean?
Who's having such sickening pain?

PYTHIAS: What, *you?* And you need to
    ask?
In your single-minded zeal to put one over on us,   949
You have destroyed the boy you tried to pass off as a eunuch.

PARMENO: But how? Tell me what happened!

PYTHIAS: I'll tell you, but first
    you tell me:
The girl that Thais received as a gift today—who is she?

PARMENO: H-how should I know?

PYTHIAS: You didn't know that she's a
    citizen,
The sister of one of the best-connected men in town?

PARMENO: Er—no.

PYTHIAS: She is. They just found out. And that is the girl
Your unfortunate young man happened to rape. I say unfortu-
    nate:
Her brother heard about it—a violent man, and given
To shocking outbursts of . . .

PARMENO: What did he do?

PYTHIAS: Well, first he
    trussed
Your fellow up in a fashion that must be appallingly painful . . .

PARMENO: He trussed him up?

PYTHIAS: He did. In spite of Thais's prayers
    for mercy.

PARMENO: He didn't!

PYTHIAS: And now he's threatening him with the
    usual treatment
  Reserved for convicted rapists.[17] Ugly, disgusting business;
  I've never seen it, and I never want to.

PARMENO: He can't do that—it's
  Preposterous!

PYTHIAS: Preposterous? Pray tell me why.

PARMENO: What else can
    you call it?
  Whoever arrested a man for rape inside a whorehouse?   960

PYTHIAS: H-how should I know?

PARMENO: Well, here's an item you'd better
    know,
  Pythias, all of you: I hereby proclaim that that boy
  Is my master's son . . .

PYTHIAS: My goodness. Is he really?

PARMENO: So Thais
  Had better take care that no harm comes to him.
                             Matter
  Of fact, why don't I go in myself?

  (*He starts for* THAIS's *door, but* PYTHIAS *stops him*)

PYTHIAS: Parmeno, think:
  What can you accomplish? You won't help him and you'll ruin
    yourself;
  They've already got you down as the cause of the whole affair.

PARMENO: Then what the hell do I do? Is anything worth a try?
  (*Looking off right*)
  Now look at this—the old man, on his way home from the farm.
  Do I tell him or not?

---

[17] *reserved for convicted rapists:* Probably radical castration, which would
under the circumstances be peculiarly (if horribly) appropriate; Pythias has
obviously given the matter some thought. "Adulterers" may be closer to *moechis*
than "rapists," but its use here and later would evoke in a modern audience
different attitudes, not to say definitions, from the ones desired.

Oh god, I tell him. I know it ensures
Destruction for me, but I've simply got to do what I can
To help that boy.
PYTHIAS: Quite sound. I'll retire and leave him to you.
Do relate the events in sequence.   970
                         And don't leave anything out.
(*She exits into* THAIS's *house*)

Scene 5

DEMEA *enters right, and stops in front of his house.*

DEMEA: There's one advantage in having a farm close in:
City or country, I'm never bored with either.
Whenever one locale begins to cloy,
I switch.
(*He sees* PARMENO *in front of* THAIS's *house, and moves to him*)
     Hel-lo, isn't that Parmeno? Sure.
—Hey, Parmeno, why are you standing around over here?
Who are you waiting for?
PARMENO (*Stalling*):   Why, how can this be?
Oh, boss. I'm glad to see you got back safe and . . .
DEMEA: Who are you waiting for?
PARMENO (*Aside*):   Oh, hell. My mouth's
Gone dry.
DEMEA: What say? You're shaking—why? Are you
All right? Come on, speak up.
PARMENO: The first thing, boss,
I want you to know is the truth, and this is the truth:
Whatever happened, it wasn't my fault that it happened,   980
And that's the truth.
DEMEA: Eh?
PARMENO: A very intelligent question.
First, I should have told you what happened. Phaedria

Bought a eunuch to give as a gift.
(*Pointing to* THAIS's *house*)   To her.
DEMEA: To who?
PARMENO: To Thais.
DEMEA: He *bought* it? Tarnation. How much?
PARMENO: Twenty *minae*.
DEMEA: I'm bankrupt.
PARMENO: Then Chaerea fell
  In love with a girl in there who plays guitar.
DEMEA: He what? In *love*? At his age, he knows about whores?
  I thought he was still on the farm. Trouble breeds trouble.
PARMENO: Don't look at me, boss. I didn't force him to do it.
DEMEA: Let's not talk about you, you bastard. *You*
  I'll attend to, provided I live through this. But first   990
  An explanation: What is going on?
PARMENO: Well, Chaerea
  Got delivered to Thais. She took him for a eunuch.
DEMEA: For a *eunuch*?
PARMENO: That's right. And then they caught him in
    there
  And trussed him up. They took him for a rapist.
DEMEA: *Murder!*
PARMENO: Whores are very unprincipled people.
DEMEA: Is that the lot? Perhaps you missed a disaster?
  Or maybe a small foreclosure?
PARMENO: That's it.
DEMEA: Then there's
  No need to wait. I'll break my way in now.
  (*He hurriedly exits into* THAIS's *house*)
PARMENO: No doubt about it, this business can only end
  In punitive measures against me. Not puny ones, either.
  But it had to happen, and I do have this consolation:
  I'll be the cause of measures just as unpleasant
  Against that nest of whores. The old man's been sniffing   1000
  Around for a long time to find an excuse
  For lowering the boom on them. And now he's found it.

Scene 6

PYTHIAS, *laughing, enters from* THAIS's *house. She does not immediately see* PARMENO.

PYTHIAS: Never, for longer than I can remember, has a happy ending
　　Made me as happy as the ending that just turned out inside,
　　What with the old man stumbling in, a bundle of blunder.
　　I was the only one who saw anything funny—I knew what he
　　Was afraid he'd see.

PARMENO (*Aside*):　　What's up this time?

PYTHIAS:　　　　　　　　　　　　And now to go
　　See Parmeno. Where can he be?

PARMENO (*Aside*):　　　　　She's hunting me down.

PYTHIAS:　　　　　　　　　　　　　　Oh, there
　　He is. I'll go right over.
　　(*She moves to him, and breaks into whoops of laughter*)

PARMENO:　　　　　　　What is it, stupid? Why the chuckles?
　　What's so damned funny?
　　　　　　　　　　　Stop it!

PYTHIAS:　　　　　　　　　　Do spare a poor girl some
　　pity—
　　I've laughed at you till I'm pooped.

PARMENO:　　　　　　　And why, may I ask?

PYTHIAS:　　　　　　　　　　　　　　Do you
　　need to?
　　On my honor, I have never seen, nor do I expect
　　To see, a more consummate knucklehead. The innocent amusement　　　　　　　　　　　　　　　　　　　　　　1009
　　That you've supplied us inside is simply too great to relate.
　　I actually used to believe that you were cool and shrewd . . .
　　You! A man who'd swallow whatever I said without checking.
　　A man who was so ashamed of turning a lad to crime

That he'd double the young man's troubles by telling his father
  about it.
How do you think that Chaerea felt when his father saw him
Wearing those clothes? Well?

Admit it, you are through.

PARMENO: You slut, you mean that you were lying? And now you
  can laugh?
It gives you some twisted pleasure to make a joke of my life?
PYTHIAS: Pure bliss.
PARMENO: Provided you get home free.
PYTHIAS: Really?
PARMENO: I swear
I'll pay you back for this.
PYTHIAS: Doubtless. But Parmeno, threats
  Like yours are likely to be deferred for a bit; meanwhile,   1020
  You'll hang, on each or both of two counts: First, you led
  Your nitwit boy to a life of crime, and then you turned
  The same boy in. They'll get you either way.
PARMENO: I'm dead.
PYTHIAS: Which constitutes your reward for services rendered.

'Bye.

(*She exits into* THAIS's *house*)

PARMENO: Finished. Tangled and trussed in my very own vocal
  cords.

Scene 7

GNATHO *and* THRASO *enter left. They do not see* PARMENO, *and
he doesn't see them.*

GNATHO: And now? We're on the march, Thraso—but what's the
  objective?
What's the strategy? What do you hope to win?
THRASO: Er—me?
  Surrender, mine. To Thais. Her terms.

GNATHO: You mean . . . ?
THRASO: No less
Than Hercules. Slave to a queen in his time. Omphale.
GNATHO: A most
Impressive prototype.
(*Aside*)   I'd love to see her soften your skull
With her shoe.
(*Up*)   —There goes her door.
(CHAEREA, *still dressed as a eunuch,*[18] *bursts from* THAIS's *house*)
THRASO: Damnation. Another re-
     versal.
Never saw him before—a new one? Why such a rush?   1030

Scene 8

CHAEREA (*To no one in particular. He does not see* THRASO *and*
     GNATHO): Friends, neighbors, I ask you: Breathes there a
     luckier man
Than I?
                    The answer is No—nobody at all.
                                        Today
The gods have made me Exhibit A of their might, a showplace
For their powers, a dumping ground for the greatest number
     of boons
In the shortest possible time.
PARMENO (*Aside*):   Now, why should he be so
     cheerful?
CHAEREA: —Parmeno, friend and buddy—detector, director, and
     perfecter

_____

[18] *still dressed as a eunuch:* I adopt this stage direction in deference to
Donatus' interpretation: "Chaerea is in the eunuch's costume, but bursts forth in
manly self-assurance, frightening the soldier by seeming to appear as a new rival."
Alternatively, of course, if Dorus's clothes are distinctive enough, Thraso might
be startled at the appearance of a new eunuch. Or Chaerea just might, at long
last, have thrown something on over the costume.

Of all my joys! Do you realize how happy I am?
Do you realize they've found that Pamphila's really a citizen?
PARMENO: So I heard.
CHAEREA: Do you realize that we are engaged?
PARMENO: Thank god and congratulations!
GNATHO (*Aside to* THRASO):   Did you hear what I
    heard?
CHAEREA: And that's not all; I'm happy for Phaedria, too. His
    affair
Has finally found snug harbor. Just one big happy family:
Dad's taken Thais under his wing; now we're her official
Patrons, protectors, and sponsors.[19]   1040
PARMENO: And your brother's her only
    lover?
CHAEREA: Of course.
PARMENO: That means more cheer: The Major will get
    his discharge.
CHAEREA: Go find Phaedria fast as you can and tell him the news.
PARMENO: I'll see if he's home.
    (*He exits into* DEMEA's *house*)
THRASO (*Aside to* GNATHO):   No doubt about my predicament,
    Gnatho?
Annihilation, utter?
GNATHO (*Aside to* THRASO): I quite agree. No doubt at all.
CHAEREA: Whom should I put at the top of the list? Whom should
    I load
With the greatest praise?
                          Parmeno the planner, who formed the
    design?
Or myself the actor, who had the guts to try it out?
Or Lady Luck the conductor, who bought so many blessings
To bear on one short day? Or dear old Dad, for his gladness,
Good humor, and general zest?
                          O Jupiter, hear my prayer:
Stand by your bounty. Don't let our windfalls blow away.

[19] *patrons, protectors, and sponsors:* To the Roman audience this would
probably suggest the legally recognized client-patron relationship, though the
Athenian institution which it reflects is somewhat different: The sponsorship
(*prostasia*) of a resident alien by a responsible citizen.

Scene 9

PHAEDRIA *enters from* DEMEA's *house.*

PHAEDRIA: God save us all, what a staggering story Parmeno told
me.
But where's my brother?   1050
CHAEREA: Present.
PHAEDRIA: I couldn't be more delighted.
CHAEREA: I'm not surprised. No one deserves love more in this
world
Than Thais does yours. Given the favors she's done for the
family,
That girl's a positive philanthropist . . .
PHAEDRIA: Whoa! You really don't
need
To praise her to *me.*
(THRASO *and* GNATHO *converse apart*)
THRASO: Damnation. Lost. Yet passions swell
As prospects shrink. Gnatho, appeal to you. Last hope.
GNATHO: Just what would you like me to do?
THRASO: Secure me a beach-
head—size
No matter—in Thais's household. Use cash, cajolery, whatnot.
GNATHO: A rather large order.
THRASO: Motive all you need; know you.
Upon successful completion of mission, will undertake to supply
Reward. Your choosing. Ask and receive.
GNATHO: You mean it?
THRASO: Just so.
GNATHO: My conditions are these: If I succeed, I will receive
Carte blanche at your house whether you're home or not—a
permanent
Place at table.

THRASO: My absolute guarantee.
GNATHO: I shall gird my loins.
(*He and* THRASO *approach the brothers*)
PHAEDRIA: I hear somebody—who?   1061
                     Oh. Thraso.
THRASO: Good day to you
    both.
PHAEDRIA: You are, perhaps, in ignorance of what has happened
    here?
THRASO: Er . . . no.
PHAEDRIA: Then why do I descry you in this vicinity?
THRASO: Relying on you . . .
PHAEDRIA: I'll give you something to rely on,
    Major.
Now hear this: If, after today, I should ever chance
To meet you on this street, even if you should say,
"Just passing through; I have an appointment and this is a
    shortcut"—
You are a dead man.
GNATHO: Now, wait a minute. That's not a very nice
    Thing to say.
PHAEDRIA: It's said.
GNATHO: This arrogant air—it's just
    Not *you*, somehow.
PHAEDRIA: It's me, all right; the way I do things.
GNATHO: Before you do them, I have a few words I'd like you to
    hear.
Just let me have my say, then do whatever seems best.
CHAEREA: Let's listen to him.
GNATHO (*Pointing left*):   Thraso, clear off that way a little.
    (THRASO *obeys, and the three converse out of his hearing*)
I definitely want to establish one point with both of you
Before I begin: Whatever action I propose in this matter,
I do it entirely out of enlightened self-interest. *But,*   1070
If my proposal should prove to be to your interest, too,
It would, I believe, be folly for you to refuse it.
PHAEDRIA: What is it?

GNATHO: I advance the view that you should admit the Major as a
rival.

PHAEDRIA: What? *That I should admit* . . .

GNATHO: Now, don't be hasty.
Reflect:
This life which you enjoy with Thais, Phaedria—or rather,
This good, high living in which you rejoice with Thais—how
Is it maintained? By give and take. As it happens, of money.
But you have little to give, while Thais is so constructed
That she must take a great deal.

Problem: How to afford your
affair
Without undue expense to you. Solution: The Major,
Than whom there exists no source of funds more useful, or less
Inconvenient. *Item:* The Major is loaded, and throws the stuff
Around with unmatched abandon. *Item:* The Major is brainless,
Witless, and senseless, a dull hebetudinous clod who passes
His days and nights in snoring, and thus will afford you no
worry
As a possible object of Thais's affections. Besides, you can
always   1080
Kick him out; it's easy.

PHAEDRIA (*To* CHAEREA): Well?

GNATHO: One final *Item,*
To my way of thinking the most important: The Major stands
Alone as a host, and sets a table that knows no equal
For quality or for quantity.

CHAEREA: It may mean stretching a point,
But I think we ought to work him in.

PHAEDRIA: I tend to agree.

GNATHO: You're making no mistake.

Oh, one thing more—a
personal
Favor: Please let me join your crowd. I'm sick of rolling
That boulder uphill.

PHAEDRIA: You've joined, as of now.

CHAEREA: And welcome aboard.

GNATHO: By way of requital to you, Phaedria, and you, Chaerea,

I present the main course, a bountiful source of nourishment
    and laughs.
Eat hearty.
(*He indicates* THRASO)

CHAEREA: A dainty dish.

PHAEDRIA: Receiving its just deserts.

GNATHO: —Thraso, come back. Any time.

THRASO (*Running up*):   Well? Victory or defeat?

GNATHO: We won, of course. Our friends didn't know the real you.
    I had only to show them your inner nature and way of life,
    To tally up your achievements and appraise your peculiar
        virtues,   1090
    And I carried the day.

THRASO: Beautifully done. Extend my heartfelt
    Thanks.
                 The whole world over, have always attracted unalloyed
    Love.

GNATHO (*To* PHAEDRIA *and* CHAEREA):
    I told you. Finesse to the core.

PHAEDRIA: He's just as advertised.
    (*Conducting the rest to* THAIS's *door*)
    All right, men, this way.
    (*To the audience* [20])   —To you, farewell. Applause, please.
    (*Exeunt into* THAIS's *house*)

[20] *To the audience:* As in the *Phormio*, I have omitted the Cantor as a quasi-
character, and given the dismissal speech to that actor who is, at the moment,
directing the final exits.

PHORMIO

Translated by Douglass Parker

INTRODUCTION

Fifth of Terence's six plays in order of composition, *Phormio* was first presented at the Roman Games in September, 161 B.C., when the author was in his thirty-fifth year. It remains a monument to, among other things, dramatic lucidity. A complicated plot, which takes some pages even in the baldest summary, is fed to the audience at precisely the right rate for action and assimilation to coincide.

This lucidity is not attained at the expense of verve. *Prope tota motoria est:* One can only concur in the judgment of the fourth-century scholar-critic Aelius Donatus and admit that *Phormio*, once the slaves Geta and Davus have finished their ritualized face-off, is in almost ceaseless motion—but it is motion, not turmoil. This most economical play husbands its actual events carefully. It is built around one central fact, the parentage of the girl Phanium; the characters' responses to that fact, in various degrees of disclosure, accuracy, and truth, constitute almost all of the action. Technically, *Phormio* is not a "recognition play" and thus lacks a formal *anagnorisis* (although the Sophrona-Chremes confrontation in Act V, Scene 1, has its resemblances); but looked at one way, the whole play is a recognition that records the migration of a fact from fiction, to half-truth, to truth.

Phanium is in actuality the daughter of the Athenian Chremes, and hence niece to Demipho and cousin to his son Antipho, who, at the play's beginning, has become her husband. An out-and-out lie, which approaches this truth, has been formulated by Phormio to motivate the cooked-up suit that made the marriage possible, and it is to this rather illegal fiction (that Antipho and Demipho are Phanium's next of kin) that the characters, pro and con, respond through most of the play. So long as Demipho rejects it, it is a point to be pushed by Geta, Antipho's cousin Phaedria, and Phormio; when he accepts it, his desire to avoid the consequence of that acceptance may be employed as a source of funds to save Phaedria's affair with the courtesan Pamphila. During this time, however, the arrival of Chremes has shown us the fact from another angle—as the impulse behind Chremes' desire for the wedding that has in fact taken place. It only remains to put these two halves together and watch the result as the truth is disseminated to the members of the cast, including Chremes' wife Nausistrata. Phaedria's affair is the sole event that does not owe its origins to the problem of Phanium, but the two are linked early in the action by contrast and bound up inextricably in solution. The play, then, derives its unity from this central focus, to whose shifting truth-status the characters must continually realign themselves.

But there are other factors that weld the play together. *Phormio*, for example, is structured by processes-at-law, and teeters for its entire length on the edge of litigation. The initial dilemma is the product of Phormio's suit against Antipho on behalf of Phanium, a suit that Demipho feels compelled to restage, somewhat informally, twice. A second, even less formal action is the trial of Chremes before Nausistrata (for the prosecution, Phormio; for the defense, Demipho), which is still awaiting final adjudication by Phaedria at the play's end. The difference in defendants is one measure of the play's progress: Age is now in the dock instead of Youth. Indeed, the Greek original by Apollodorus of Carystus that Terence adapted even bore a legal title: *Epidikazomenos*, here translated the "petitioner," the one who initiates an action for assignment (i.e., Phormio), though it might just possibly mean the "assignee" (i.e., Antipho). But the first interpretation, with its overtones of action on another's behalf, does underline one important peculiarity of the play: It is a triumph of altruism.

In fact, *Phormio* stands as the most interesting early formulation of a great comedic truth: A character's control of an action varies in inverse proportion to his emotional involvement in it. No one, in this play, can advance his own fortunes very far (if at all), although he may do perfectly well for someone else. Phaedria can argue Antipho's case effectively; Chremes, at one point, can presumably solve Demipho's difficulties by the application of money—a solution from which Demipho is prevented by his avarice; Demipho can dismiss Chremes' fears and argue *his* defense before Nausistrata. But none of the three has any success as his own advocate. If this cluster of characters may be taken to define the center point on a bell curve, it is easy to see the extremes: negative, Antipho, a weak individual whom love and *pietas* reduce to the most startling degree of uselessness in Roman Comedy; positive, Geta, whose personal motive is the slave's minimum—to stay alive and fairly well—tempered by his loyalty to Antipho. And then, at the far end of the positive scale, we have Phormio, first in a long line of free-lance factotums (Mosca, Face, Scapin), whose managerial ability (hitherto a slave's prerogative) is enhanced by his fluid social position, but is raised to an instrument of power by his utter disinterest in the proceedings. He has no axe to grind; he will not suffer in any case; he is not involved.

Or not quite involved. One of Terence's certain additions to Apollodorus' play has been the gift to his hero of a stock parasite's stock motivation—the desire to live well at someone else's expense —and it is noteworthy that Phormio's nearest brush with disaster, his prolongation of the final debate (if that is the word) with the old men, develops directly from his wish to benefit from the situation at long last. Earlier, his principal motive has seemed to be delight in the game as game; at this later point, he desires to profit —and nearly loses his balance before winning his invitation to dinner.

Happily, this is a relatively minor lapse. For the most part, Phormio reigns serene in Olympian detachment and makes the play go. He does this in more senses than one: not only do his plans and maneuverings keep things in a whirl, but it is his huge enjoyment of role-playing that palliates the near-tragedies of the piece and places in focus the shortcomings of the other characters, who are relentlessly condemned to be themselves or (like Chremes) to make a hash of any attempted change.

Note: Phormio possesses no offstage questions on the order of the number of Lady Macbeth's children, but there is one point which has caused some trouble: How does Phormio happen to know

Chremes' alias Stilpo (or Stilpho) as early as line 356? The answer, I suppose, if answer is really needed, is that Phanium or Sophrona told him when he was devising the original suit; a good lie sticks as close to the truth as it can. Less happy is the problem of line 877, where, after Geta has disclosed Phanium's parentage to Antipho and Phormio, someone remarks that he's heard the story somewhere before. In the manuscripts, this someone is Phormio; modern editors assign the line to Antipho. I have followed the latter course because it seems to work better; Antipho's inability to think under any pressure whatsoever has been amply demonstrated. But the manuscripts may well be right: to take the opposite tack, Phormio is not omniscient, and there is no reason that he should have connected an Athenian tourist named Stilpo, who fathered a daughter fifteen years before, with Antipho's uncle. Even had he known of Chremes' business interests on Lemnus, such a conclusion would have smacked very much of coincidence, of a hopeless long shot. And Phormio does not play long shots.

Text and translation: As a basis for this version, I have used the Budé text of J. Marouzeau (1927), supplemented by the Oxford text of Kauer and Lindsay (1926). Departures are infrequent. I have preserved the traditional act divisions, though they do not go back to Terence first for ease of reference; secondly because I believe that Donatus' principle in creating such analytical breaks was sound. It is no small advantage for the reader, given Terence's plots, to be able to distinguish the workings of protasis, epitasis, and catastrophe under convenient spatial rubrics. Likewise, I have kept the traditional scene divisions, breaking when there is a change of personnel on stage. The advantage here may appear tinier, but the underscoring of slighter shifts in the action is certainly worth the unease that moderns feel at this sort of fragmentation. Roman Comedy, with its counterpoint of coincidence and cause-and-effect, is no place to demand sweep.

The language of the translation is American English, which I hope is as contemporary as I am. Its vehicle is a verse based, not on syllable-counting or an agreed-upon modulus, but on the regular occurrence of phrase-stress within the line. I have not attempted even the rather limited metrical polymorphism that

Terence allows himself with its shifts from iambic to trochaic, from senarius to septenarius to octonarius. Rather, I have employed a five-stress line to reflect the most common dialogue meter—the iambic senarius—and a six-stress line elsewhere. This will appear too loose to some, a regrettable attempt at pointless rigor to others. For myself, it was the only solution I could devise (prose was unthinkable) for any essay at reproducing the regularized richness of Terentian language.

DOUGLASS PARKER

PHORMIO

First Performance: The Roman Games, presented under the supervision of Lucius Postumius Albinus and Lucius Cornelius Merula, Curule Aediles.

Production: Lucius Ambivius Turpio and Lucius Hatilius of Praeneste.

Music: The entire piece scored for treble and bass flute by Flaccus, freedman of Claudius.

Greek Original: Epidikazomenos (The Petitioner) by Apollodorus.

The author's fourth play, written in 161 B.C. during the consulate of Gaius Fannius and Marcus Valerius.

CHARACTERS

DAVUS, a slave
GETA, slave of Demipho
ANTIPHO, a young man, son of Demipho
PHAEDRIA, a young man, son of Chremes
DEMIPHO, an elderly gentleman
PHORMIO, a man-about-town
HEGIO, a lawyer
CRATINUS, a lawyer
CRITO, a lawyer
DORIO, a pimp
CHREMES, an elderly gentleman, brother of Demipho

SOPHRONA, a nurse
NAUSISTRATA, wife of Chremes

*The scene is a street in Athens on which front three houses—
reading from stage right to stage left, the abodes of* DEMIPHO,
CHREMES, *and* DORIO. *There are two wing exits: stage right, to the
harbor; stage left, to downtown Athens and beyond.*

PROLOGUE

Yᵉ Olde Established Author (who shall be nameless [1])
Couldn't displace our playwright, consign him to silence,
Or freeze him out of the field. The present plan
Is slander, to scare him away from writing. It never
Varies: He claims our author's plays clothe shallow
Matter in shabby form. Translated, this means
They avoid the shopworn pseudoromantic conceits:
The lovelorn teen-age madman, ahunt in the hills,
Who seems to see a timorous doe (but no!   10
It is his darling), whoops his hounds upon her—
And horror-struck hears his sweetheart's last, despairing
Requests for assistance.
                    Well, If Yᵉ Olde Established
Author would only think back over the years
To his latest hit, and recall that its success
Was a one-man triumph, not for him, but for
The producer, he might be a lot less reckless with all
These slurs.
                    Oh—to you critics, vocal or not,
Who believe that, without the prior assault by Yᵉ Olde

---

[1] *who shall be nameless:* The reference is to Terence's constant opponent,
Luscius Lanuvinus, whose most glaring bit of literary obstructionism had occurred
earlier that year when he cried "Plagiarism!" in an effort to make the authorities
scrap the production of *The Eunuch.*

Established, our Up-and-Coming Author, lacking
A target for verbal attack, would have no prologue . . .
Poppycock. The prize for drama is, and should be,
Open to every practicing playwright; but Established
Has tried to make this young man quit his career
And starve. Thus, these remarks are not attack,
But rebuttal. No need for nastiness; a kindly rival's
Kind words would have been repaid in kind.
Things being as they are, I trust Yᵉ Olde can see   20
That he got as good as he gave. With that, I stop
My comments on the subject, in spite of the subject, whose spite
Goes on and on.
                    To my purpose. Attention, please.
I now present you a never-before-adapted
Comedy called, in the Greek, *The Petitioner.* Terence
Titles his version *Phormio,* taking its name
From the lead: Phormio the fat cat, paragon of parasites,
Prime mover of the plot—as the slightest modicum of courtesy
Will permit you to learn. Please do pay attention. Listen   30
Politely, in silence: The hullaballoo once drove
Our troupe offstage ²—and, frankly, that's an experience
We'd rather not have to repeat. Indeed, our return
To the boards was only effected by our producer's skill ³—
Supported by your unfailing fairness and good will.

---

² *The hullaballoo once drove our troupe offstage:* This was the disastrous conclusion to the abortive first performance of *The Mother-in-Law* four years earlier.

³ *by our producer's skill:* The skill of Lucius Ambivius Turpio, who with his
troupe gave all six of Terence's comedies their first performances, extended to more
areas than that of production: In his time, he was accounted Rome's best actor.

ACT I

Scene 1

DAVUS *entering left, carrying a small bag, as he makes his way
to a point in front of* DEMIPHO's *house.*

DAVUS: Geta's my best friend. We're from the same home town.
So, when he came over yesterday about the balance
On that little loan. . . . Well, it wasn't much.
He asked me to get the money; I got the money.
Here it is.
(He holds up the bag)
        They say his masters' son got married.
He's probably scrounging enough to buy the new wife
A present.   40
        What a system! No justice. Always
The same: subtract it from the poor, and add it to the rich.
Poor Geta. He'll go without, and cheat himself
Of fun, and scrimp back bits of his food allowance,
Grain by grain—and down she'll swoop, and snatch it
All in a lump. She won't give a damn for the labor
That nest egg cost him.
              But once she's on the nest,
Once she labors and has a son—poor Geta
Is hit for another present.
                 And then the boy
Has a birthday every year, and then his confirmation.[4] . . .

---

   4 *confirmation:* This perhaps unhappy analogue is an attempt to follow Terence's own practice. He has blurred the Greek original's clear reference to the Samothracian mysteries, making instead a vague statement about "initiation" that his audience could assimilate to comparable Roman phenomena without giving the matter much thought.

And mama will annex everything. The boy'll be a blind,
A dropbox for donations.   50
(GETA *enters from* DEMIPHO's *house*)
                         But isn't that Geta now?

Scene 2

GETA: If a redheaded man [5] comes looking for me . . .
DAVUS: He's here.
    Save your breath.
GETA: Oh, Davus. I was on my way
    To meet you.
DAVUS (*Handing him the bag*): Here you are. Nice, fresh money.
        Every
    Bit I owe you. Check; it's all there.
GETA: Thanks
    For not forgetting. You've done me a real favor.
DAVUS: So much for public morals. Things are bad.
    Pay your debts, it's a real favor.
                             Still gloomy?
    Trouble?
GETA: *Trouble?* The fear and trembling at our house
    You wouldn't believe.
DAVUS: What do you mean?
GETA: I'll tell you.
    Provided, of course, you can keep a secret.
DAVUS: Now, *there's*
    A stupid remark. You trust a man with money,   60
    But worry about words?
                     And what could I make by telling?
GETA: Then listen to me.
DAVUS: I pledge my earnest attention.
GETA: You know my master . . .
DAVUS: Old Demipho? Yes.

[5] *a redheaded man:* The stock slave's costume in Roman Comedy was topped
off with a fright wig.

GETA: And his son . . .

DAVUS: Antipho.

GETA: Do you know the old man's elder brother,
Chremes?

DAVUS: Of course.

GETA: And *his* son, Phaedria?

DAVUS: I don't know
You any better.

GETA: Well, some time back, both fathers
Had to go abroad. Chremes to Lemnus, on business.
My master to Cilicia, for friendship's sake. An old friend
Wrote from out there with a deal that guaranteed a solid gold
Mountain, or something.

DAVUS: Greedy? As rich as he is?

GETA: He's also consistent. True to himself.

DAVUS: Not fair.
If *I* were a plutocrat, now . . .   70

GETA: When the old men left
Their final act was to put me in charge of the boys.
Sort of a moral tutor.

DAVUS: Oooh. You took on
A tough assignment, Geta.

GETA: So I found out.
The hard way. The old men left me in charge; my luck
Just left me.

First, I started with discipline, strictly
Enforced—but why go further? A slave is a slave.
Keeping my word meant losing my skin.

DAVUS: I thought
That'd happen. Never kick against the pricks—
It's just not horse sense.

GETA: I changed my tactics. Started
To help them out. Went along with their slightest whim.

DAVUS: Good business: only as much as the traffic will bear.

GETA: And so disaster. Antipho kept clean for a while,   80
At least; but Phaedria ran across some slip
Of a girl and fell with a crash. Instant passion.
A slave. She played the guitar, no less.

                                                        Property
Of the most unprincipled pimp in town. The boys
Had nothing to pay with—their fathers showed that much sense.
So Phaedria's affair was chaste and gratis: hungry
Looks, discreet pursuit . . . walk the girl
To guitar school, walk her home. And Antipho and I
Had nothing else to do; we helped him.
                                                        Usually,
While she was taking her lesson, all of us waited
Across the street in the barbershop. One day   90
We're sitting around when a fellow comes in—he's just
About Antipho's age—and we're surprised to see
He's crying. We ask him why.
                                                "Poverty," he says.
"I just saw a girl in mourning, here in this neighborhood.
Her mother's dead. I'd never realized before
What an awful, desolate thing it is to be poor.
The corpse laid out before her . . . that was all;
Not a friend, not a relative, no one she knew. Only
Some little old woman to help her keep the wake.
I couldn't stand it. And such a beautiful girl."   100
I don't have to tell you we all were shaken up.
Antipho reacted first: "Do you want to go see her?"
"Good, let's go," says somebody else. "You lead
The way." And then we went, and then we saw . . .
She *was* a charmer. But more than that: certainly
Her charm didn't get a bit of outside help:
Hair all loose and straggly, bare feet, tearstains,
Filthy clothes—enough to smother any
Looks that lacked a natural, inborn beauty.
Phaedria, of course, was faithful to his guitarist.
His only remark was, "Very pretty." But Antipho . . .   110
DAVUS: I know, I know. He fell in love.
GETA: I suppose
You know how hard? Wait; see how it turns out.
Next day he marches over to the old girl, falls
On his knees and begs her to sign him up with the girl.
But granny refuses; calls him immoral; claims

The charmer's an Athenian citizen, excellent family.
If he wants to marry her legally, fine—otherwise,
No. Which put our boy in a quandary. Mad
For marriage, afraid of his father—even away.

DAVUS: Couldn't he wait till his father got back to get
Permission?

GETA: From *Demipho?* To marry a girl of no family?
Without a dowry? He'd never allow it.   120

DAVUS: So what's
The upshot?

GETA: The upshot? Well, there's a fellow called Phormio.
Profession, sponger. Character, cocky. Deserves
To be damned by every god who can spare the time.

DAVUS: And what did he do?

GETA: Phormio supplied a plan
(And I quote):

                    "There's a law on the books which orders female
Orphans to marry their next of kin. The same law
Orders their next of kin to marry *them.*
Ergo, Antipho, I shall depose that you
Are this girl's kin, and institute suit against you,
Representing myself as a valued friend of her dear departed
Father. Her father's name, her mother's, the precise   130
Degree of relationship she holds to you . . . all details
Such as these I shall, of course, devise.
Most advantageously for me, I might say. Inasmuch
As you will not contest this data, I shall,
Obviously, win the case.

                    On your father's return,
I imagine, charges will be lodged against *me*, but no matter:
The girl will be ours."

DAVUS: That's very pert impertinence.

GETA: And convincing, to Antipho. That's the way it went:
Trial, verdict, wedding.

DAVUS: You really mean it?

GETA: You heard me.

DAVUS: But, Geta, what's going to happen to you?

GETA: No idea. The only thing I know is this:
  (*Striking a pose*)
  Forever forbearant will I bear whatever
  Fortune bears.
DAVUS: Excellent. A hero's function.
GETA: *My only hope is centered in myself.*
DAVUS: Bravo!
GETA: I only hope I find a good lawyer to argue
  My case to the master: "Please forgive him this time,   140
  Sir, and I will never take his part again."
  That's his plea. It's not very far from saying,
  "Wait till I leave; and then, if you want to, kill him."
DAVUS: And the monitor? The one who walks the girl guitarist
  To school? How's his suit going?
GETA: So-so. He isn't
  Pressing it very hard.
DAVUS: He doesn't have much
  To give her, I suppose.
GETA: Phaedria has nothing but hope,
  Pure, undiluted hope.
DAVUS: Is his father back?
GETA: Chremes? Not yet.
DAVUS: And that old man of yours—Demipho:
  When do you expect him?
GETA: I'm really not quite sure.
  I just heard that a letter had come from him and was waiting
  For me down at Customs. I'd better go get it.   150
DAVUS: Well, Geta, anything else I can do for you?
GETA: Be healthy; be happy; fare well.
  (*Exit* DAVUS, GETA *addresses the house*)
                               Hey, boy, come out here!
  (*A pause*)
  Where is everybody?
  (*Enter a boy slave, from* DEMIPHO's *house.* GETA *gives him the
  bag*)
                          Give this money to my wife.
  (*Exeunt,* GETA *to the right, the boy into* DEMIPHO's *house*)

Scene 3

ANTIPHO *and* PHAEDRIA *enter from* DEMIPHO's *house.*

ANTIPHO: What a dreadful development, Phaedria! He loves me,
    looks out for me—
But when I even think that he might come home, I'm frightened
To death of my very own father. How could I be so thoughtless?
Oh, just to be anxious to see him again, like a proper son!
PHAEDRIA: What's the matter now?
ANTIPHO: The matter? Well, you should
    know;
You were my accomplice in all this madness.

                                        —Oh, why did
    Phormio
Have to suggest it. Why did I have to be so eager
To let him twist my arm? Success in love—that's what started
This mess. If I'd lost her . . . maybe a week or two of pain,
But not this ceaseless anguish, gnawing at my heart, day in . . .
PHAEDRIA: I know, *I know.*   160
ANTIPHO: . . . Day out, while I wait for some-
    one to blast
My happiness.
PHAEDRIA: Most lovers starve for affection; you're choking
    on it.
You're glutted with love, Antipho. Yours is the life, the logical
Object of all desire.
                      I swear to god, if I could buy
That much free time with the girl I love, I'd kill myself
To make the down payment. Just contrast our situations.
    Balance
The profits accrued to me from my poverty, to you from your
    surplus.
Not to mention your acquisition, at absolutely no expense,

Of a well-bred lady on your own terms—I mean, as a *wife*
Whom you can be proud to show your friends.

By any reckoning,
You are happy—all you need is the brains to stay
That way. If you had to haggle with the pimp I take from,
   you'd understand.   170
So much for human nature: we can't abide what we've got.
ANTIPHO: No, Phaedria, I can't see it. *You're* the happy man.
   Nothing hampers your power of choice; your love is yours
   To keep or lose. Then look at me—completely powerless:
   I can't do either.
(*Looking off right*)

—What's this? Someone in a hurry. It isn't
Geta?

—It's Geta. No doubt he's bringing me news.

—I'm afraid.

Scene 4

GETA *enters at a run from the right. He does not see* ANTIPHO
and PHAEDRIA.

GETA: Dig up some new maneuver *now*, Geta, or else
   You're null and void. Disaster's due to break soon, and you
   Aren't ready.   180

I can't avoid it; I can't even see any way
Of coming out alive.
ANTIPHO (*Aside to* PHAEDRIA): He's upset. I wonder why?
GETA: And only a minute to fix things. The boss is back.
ANTIPHO (*Aside to* PHAEDRIA):   What's
   wrong?
GETA: When he hears about this, he'll have a fit. How do I cure it?
   Confess? That's fuel on the fire.

Keep still? That's a spur in the
   side.
Clear myself? That's washing dirt.

                              What an absolute mess!
I'm not just shaking for *me;* Antipho's got me on the rack.
I pity *him;* I'm afraid for *him;* I stay here for *him.*
I should have looked out for myself and made the old man pay
For his anger; I ought to be packed and on my way out of here.

ANTIPHO (*Aside to* PHAEDRIA): *What's he up to? Theft, or*
   desertion?   191

GETA: But where do I find
Antipho? Where should I start to look?

PHAEDRIA (*Aside to* ANTIPHO):   I heard your name.

ANTIPHO (*Aside to* PHAEDRIA): He's brought some news. It's
   bound to be terribly bad.

PHAEDRIA (*Aside to* ANTIPHO): Now, look. . . .

GETA: I'll go on home. He's generally there.
   (*He starts for* DEMIPHO's *house, again at a run*)

PHAEDRIA (*Aside to* ANTIPHO):   Let's call him back.

ANTIPHO (*Shouting after* GETA): Stop this instant!

GETA (*Not stopping or turning*): I don't know your name, but
   you're bossy as hell.

ANTIPHO: *Geta!*

GETA (*As he stops and turns*): Just the man I wanted to meet.

ANTIPHO: Hurry
up
And tell me the news. And please be brief. One word, if you
   can.

GETA: Agreed.

ANTIPHO: Proceed.

GETA: The dock, just now.

ANTIPHO: My . . . ?

GETA: Yup.

ANTIPHO: I'm dead.

PHAEDRIA: Uh—pardon . . .

ANTIPHO: What can I do?

PHAEDRIA (*To* GETA):   Please, what did you
  tell him?

GETA: I told him
I saw his father. Your uncle.

ANTIPHO: All of a sudden, a victim.

How can I cure catastrophe? 200

—Phanium, if this is my fate,

To be wrenched away from you, I have no wish to live.

(*He slumps in dejection*)

GETA: Given the situation, Antipho, you certainly ought to try

Staying awake. Remember, Fortune Favors the Brave.

ANTIPHO: I'm beside myself.

GETA: That's not the place to be *now*,

Antipho.

If your father finds out you're afraid, he'll think it's a clear

admission

Of guilt.

PHAEDRIA: That's true.

ANTIPHO: And that's the way I am. I can't change.

GETA: What if you had to handle something even worse?

ANTIPHO: I'm badly off in this; I'd be worse off in that.

GETA: That's it, Phaedria—nothing. The game's all over.

Well,

No point in wasting time around here. I'm going.

PHAEDRIA: Me, too.

ANTIPHO (*In terror as they start to leave*): No, wait! Please wait!

Suppose I pretend?

(*Striking an attitude as they turn back*)

This good enough?

GETA: You're joking.

ANTIPHO: Watch my expression. 210

(*Managing a scowl*)

Is *this* good enough?

GETA: Er

. . . no.

ANTIPHO: How about this?

GETA: That's closer.

ANTIPHO: Well, then, this?

GETA: That's *it*.

Keep that one. Give him back word for word, and tit for tat;

Otherwise he'll curse you right off the field.

ANTIPHO (*Slumping again*): I know.

GETA: Remember:
You didn't want to marry her.
PHAEDRIA: You acted under compulsion.
GETA: Forced by the law.
PHAEDRIA: Coerced by the court.
GETA: Got it? Good.
(*Looking off left*)
—But look . . . who's that old man at the end of the street?
It's him!
ANTIPHO (*Starting off right*): I simply can't stay here.
GETA: Oh, now . . .
Antipho, what are you doing?
Where are you going? STOP!
ANTIPHO: I know myself. I did wrong.
I trust you both. I leave my Phanium and my future in your
hands.
(*He exits right. A pause*)
PHAEDRIA: Well, Geta, what next?   220
GETA: Unless I'm wrong, tongue-lash-
ing for you
And lashing for me. And yet, we ought to take the advice
We just gave Antipho.
PHAEDRIA: Don't be so tentative. Give me orders.
GETA: Do you recall the defense the two of you had worked out
Back when we began this—you know, that no guilt would
attach
Because the cause was just? It was simple, surefire, perfect.
PHAEDRIA: I do indeed.
GETA: Well, that's the defense we need, unless
There's one that's better and shrewder.
PHAEDRIA: I'll do the best I can.
GETA: Now you make the first attack, and I'll lie here in ambush—
An auxiliary force, in case you need reserves.
PHAEDRIA: All right.   230

ACT II

Scene 1

DEMIPHO *entering from the left.*

DEMIPHO: Marry without my permission—how could Antipho
    do it?
I don't expect respect for authority—but isn't he even
Afraid—not to say ashamed—at such infamous independence?
    And Geta—
What a prince among guardians.
GETA (*Aside*):   I thought you'd never get there.
DEMIPHO: How can they possibly plead? Where can they find a
    defense?
GETA (*Aside*): Don't worry; I'll think of something.
DEMIPHO: Maybe Coer-
    cion: "I *had*
To marry her, father—the Law is the Law." Granted. Agreed.
GETA (*Aside*): Mighty gracious.
DEMIPHO: But your mind was your own. To
    shut your mouth
And make your opponents a present of the case—is *that* the
    Law?
PHAEDRIA (*Aside*): That's a rough one.
GETA (*Aside*):   I'll smooth it over. Simple.
DEMIPHO: Uncertainty,
Lack of decision—that's my trouble. I didn't have the slightest
Idea that this could happen. And the shock's upset me so   240
That I'm simply not up to rational thought.
                          It shows the importance

Of planning: *When in Prosperity, always rehearse for Adversity.*
The joyous return from a trip abroad should always be tempered
With a tally of possible trials and losses: the slip of a son,
The death of a wife, the disease of a daughter. Once you see
That these things happen to everyone, once you ready your
    mind
To await disaster in all its forms—why, then, it follows
That you can enter any and all surprises as profit.

GETA (*Aside*): There's wisdom for you, Phaedria; but I'm way
    ahead of my master.
The troubles I'll have when he gets home are all thought
    through:
Weeks of sweat in the workhouse, flogging, flaying, and fetter-
    ing,
Tiresome toil in the country.   250
                        And now that I've readied my mind
To await disaster in all its forms—why, then, it follows
That I can enter any and all surprises as profit.
—Well, hurry. Say hello to the man. Speak gently and soften
    him up.

(*He pushes* PHAEDRIA *toward* DEMIPHO)

DEMIPHO: Who's the reception committee? Oh, my brother's boy.

PHAEDRIA: Well, uncle, you *are* welcome!

DEMIPHO: Hello. Where's Antipho?

PHAEDRIA: I must say you're looking . . .

DEMIPHO: I'm sure I am. Where's
    Antipho?

PHAEDRIA: No worry about him; he's around. But how about you?
    Everything in order?

DEMIPHO: Now that you mention it, no.

PHAEDRIA: Whatever's the matter?

DEMIPHO: The matter, as you damn well
    know, is
That magnificent marriage the two of you masterminded
While I was away!

PHAEDRIA: The marriage? But why should Antipho's
    Wedding upset you?

GETA (*Aside*):   Now, *there* is perfect technique.

DEMIPHO: I should be happy? I have only one desire—   260
　　To give my son a personal demonstration of what
　　He's done to me—turned an indulgent daddy into
　　An utter bastard.
PHAEDRIA:　　　　　Don't be so bitter, uncle.
　　Antipho hasn't done anything *wrong*.
DEMIPHO:　　　　　　　　　　　Here it comes—
　　The same old story: birds of a feather, thick
　　As thieves, alike as peas.
PHAEDRIA:　　　　　　　That's hardly fair.
DEMIPHO: If A slips up, B's there to cover up;
　　When B's in trouble, up trots A. A brotherhood
　　Of backscratchers.
GETA (*Aside*):　　For a man who doesn't know the facts,
　　He paints a pretty clear portrait.
DEMIPHO:　　　　　　　　That's the way of the world.
　　You wouldn't back him up otherwise.
PHAEDRIA:　　　　　　　　　Now, look here, uncle.
　　If Antipho's really guilty of neglecting the family   271
　　Honor or assets, I don't defend him; let him
　　Get his just deserts. However, if some
　　Unprincipled person has set a successful trap
　　For our **youth** and inexperience, who's guilty? Are we?
　　Or is **the jury**—the jury, which generally soaks
　　The rich, in jealousy, and pays the poor, out of pity?
GETA (*Aside*): I'd take that for absolute truth—if I hadn't seen
　　The trial.
DEMIPHO: What jury can judge your case on its merits,
　　When you won't let it know what those merits *are*? Antipho
　　Wouldn't say a single word.   281
PHAEDRIA:　　　　　　　He behaved in a manner
　　Befitting a well-brought-up young gentleman. He simply
　　Could *not* address the jury; his retiring nature
　　Was struck completely dumb by his ingrained modesty.
GETA (*Aside*): Applause is in order. Still, I'd better hurry
　　And say my helloes.
　　(*Advancing to* DEMIPHO)

                    Well, master, welcome! I'm glad
    You're back home safe and sound.
DEMIPHO: Hail the sterling
    Overseer, prop and bulwark of the household, trusted
    Guide and tutor of an absent father's son.
GETA: I've spent the last few minutes hearing your complaints.
    They're unfair to all of us, mostly unfair to me.   290
    Just what did you expect me to do in court?
    Argue the case? Give evidence? Both illegal:
    I'm a slave, remember?
DEMIPHO: I yield to your arguments.
    (*To* PHAEDRIA)
    He's young, ignorant, retiring . . . I grant the point.
    (*To* GETA)
    And you, I must agree, are a slave.
                                    —But still,
    No matter how related she was, please, *Why*
    Did he marry her? It wasn't required; the law
    Has a loophole. Just give her a dowry and find her another
    Husband. But bring home a penniless bride—
    What was he using for brains?
GETA: Brains he had;
    What would he use for money?
DEMIPHO: Borrow it somewhere.
GETA: Somewhere. Easiest thing in the world—to *say*.   300
DEMIPHO: At the worst, if all else failed, he could borrow at
    interest.
GETA: Another pretty word. And who'd extend him
    Credit, while you were still alive?
DEMIPHO: No,
    Dammit, no! I refuse to let this happen—
    It's monstrous! For them to spend a single day
    As man and wife—unthinkable. Drastic action
    Is what they deserve . . . and what they'll get. This fellow—
    What does he look like? Where does he live? I want
    To see him.
GETA: What fellow? Phormio?

DEMIPHO: The friend and sponsor
Of that female.
GETA: I'll have him here in less than no time.
DEMIPHO: And where might Antipho be?
GETA: Antipho's out.
DEMIPHO: Phaedria, you go find him and bring him here.
PHAEDRIA: Certainly. By the quickest route . . .   310
(*He exits right.* GETA *looks after him*)
GETA: . . . Straight to
Pamphila.
(*He exits left*)
DEMIPHO: First, I'll stop by the house to give thanks for my safe
Return. And then I can go downtown and solicit
The assistance of a friend or two. I need help.
And when that Phormio comes, I want to be ready.
(*He enters his house*)

Scene 2

PHORMIO: Let's see: For fear of his father, the boy has, shall we
say, blown?
GETA: Absolutely.
PHORMIO: Phanium's forsaken?
GETA: Completely.
PHORMIO: Father's furious?
GETA: Oh boy.
PHORMIO: Well, Phormio, there's the sum; all yours to solve.
You mixed this mess, and now you eat it. All. Courage,
Man. Make ready for war.
GETA: I'm on my knees.
PHORMIO (*To himself*): His probable
First demand . . .
GETA: We're depending on you.
PHORMIO (*To himself*): Contrariwise,
If he replies . . .   320

GETA: You drove us to it.
PHORMIO (*To himself*):   On the whole, I think so.
    Yes.
GETA: For god's sake, *Help!*
PHORMIO (*To* GETA):   Trot out the father. Strategy
    Settled; ultimate objectives in view.
GETA: What objectives?
PHORMIO: Yours:
    Phanium still a bride; Antipho snatched from reproach;
    The full force of Daddy's anger diverted to the hapless head
    Of yours truly . . . Adequate?
GETA: Phormio, you're a hero; what's
    more,
    A friend. But all this bravery can only lead to jail.
PHORMIO: Hardly. I know the bit, and the pitfalls. Each step is
    plotted.
    consider the staggering casualty rate among my opponents—
    Thousands battered and bleeding. But do you ever see me
    Subpoenaed for assault and battery?
GETA: Why not?   330
PHORMIO: Absurdly simple:
    No one sets nets for birds of prey—for hawks, or kites.
    The work would be wasted; who traps trouble? No; the nets
    Are spread for innocent birds; *they* pay off. Any man
    With a smidgin is vulnerable—he can be fleeced somehow. Not
    me.
    I'm widely known to have nothing.
                            Don't bring up enslavement
    for debt:
    They *could* attach my person—but who would knowingly attach
    Such a notorious appetite? Not my enemies. And I
    Applaud their logic: They avoid returning good for evil.
GETA: My master can never repay you.
PHORMIO: Tut. I never lose.
    It's always the patron who pays. Just put yourself in my place—
    My place at dinner, of course:
                            You haven't expended a cent,

But there you are, fresh from a bath and massage, free from
worry,
The while your host is conspicuously consumed by bills and
bother.   340
Your every desire is seen to, to the tune of his grinding teeth.
So smile, and drink the first drink, and take the best place:
Your meal
Is ready and moot.
GETA: My meal is *moot?*
PHORMIO: So much on the menu,
The question is where to begin. Now tot up those viands and
goodies,
Reckon their sheer expense. Then look at your host, the founder
Of the feast—here is a god in the flesh.
GETA (*Looking off right*):   And here's the old man.
So tend to your business. Remember, the first onslaught is the
deadliest:
Get through that alive; then play with him any way you please.

Scene 3

DEMIPHO *enters from the left, followed by* HEGIO, CRATINUS, *and*
CRITO.

DEMIPHO: I trust you admit that you've never heard of more insult
Added to injury than in my case. Therefore, gentlemen,
I beg your assistance.
GETA (*Aside to* PHORMIO): He's annoyed.   350
PHORMIO (*Aside to* GETA):   Just watch;
I'll send him into fits.
(*Raising his voice*)
                          In the name of all that's holy!
Does Demipho dare deny that Phanium's his kin?
Can Demipho claim she's *not* his kin?
GETA (*Raising his voice*):   He can.

PHORMIO: But can he claim he's forgotten her father?

GETA: He can.

DEMIPHO (*To his companions*): I fancy that's the fellow I meant;
  this way.

PHORMIO: Deny he knows the name of Stilpo?

GETA: He can.

PHORMIO: Because the poor girl's a penniless orphan, her father's
  Forgotten, and she's to be cast aside. Behold
  The deeds of greed.

GETA: Don't charge my master with malice;
  He'll call you every name in the book.

DEMIPHO (*To his companions*):   Sheer insolence.   360
  I'm to be charged? I tell you, he goes too far.

PHORMIO: As for the lad, reproach is pointless; he couldn't
  Have known her father. Venerable chap, quite poor,
  Kept to the country, wresting what living he could
  From a farm. My father's tenant. How many times
  Has he told me the sorry tale of his kinsman's neglect!
  And such a man. The finest I ever laid eyes on.

GETA: Yourself excepted, of course.

PHORMIO: Please go to hell.
  Finest I said, and finest I meant. Otherwise,
  Why should I feud so fiercely against your household   370
  To help his daughter? Whom, I might add, your master
  Rejects in a manner which betokens an utter
  Lack of breeding.

GETA: Flinging more muck on a man
  Who can't defend himself?

PHORMIO: A purely objective
  Appraisal.

GETA: Appraisal, you refugee from jail?

DEMIPHO (*Coming up*):   Geta.

GETA: Bloodsucker! Blackmailer! Charlatan! Shyster!

DEMIPHO: GETA!

PHORMIO (*Aside*): Answer him.

GETA: Why, who can that be?
                                          —Oops.

DEMIPHO: SHUT UP!

GETA: This man's insulting you, sir. Says horrible things
  That fit him better than you. He just won't stop.
  Gone on all day.
DEMIPHO: Enough!
  (*To* PHORMIO)   —Excuse me, sir.
  I should like to ask you (at your discretion and pleasure,
  If possible) this one small question: Can you inform me
  Just who this so-called friend of yours was, who claimed   380
  To be my relation?
PHORMIO: Angling, eh? Sly rogue—
  As if you didn't know.
DEMIPHO: You mean I knew him?
PHORMIO: Of course.
DEMIPHO: I say I didn't; you say I did—
  So joggle my memory.
PHORMIO: Really, now . . . you've forgotten
  Your cousin?
DEMIPHO: Stop this torture and tell me his name.
PHORMIO: His name?
DEMIPHO: Precisely.
                              —Well? Speak up!
PHORMIO (*Aside*):   Damnation.
  Forgot the name.
DEMIPHO: What was that?
PHORMIO (*Aside*):   Geta,
  What was the name we used? Try to remember.
  (*To* DEMIPHO)
  I'll tell you nothing; I'm onto your game—pretending
  You didn't know him.
GETA (*Aside*):   Stilpo.   390
PHORMIO: And yet, why not?
  His name was Stilpo.
DEMIPHO: Pardon?
PHORMIO: Stilpo. Have you
  Forgotten Stilpo?
DEMIPHO: I never knew him. Neither
  Did I ever have any relation with a name like that.

PHORMIO: You stick to your story? All these witnesses, and still
  No shame? —Of course, if he'd left an estate, amounting
  To, say, ten talents . . .
DEMIPHO: Oh, damn and blast you!
PHORMIO: . . . you'd lead
  The pack in producing a pedigree, tracing your line
  Back to your grandfather, and thence to your grandfather's
    grandfather.
DEMIPHO: True; I agree. If I'd gone to court, I'd have made
  A statement of the girl's relationship to me. So now
  You do the same—tell me, how *are* we related?
GETA (*To* DEMIPHO): A point for our side.
  (*Aside to* PHORMIO)   Better look out.
PHORMIO: I gave
  A plain deposition before the proper authorities.
  If what I said at the trial was false, why didn't   400
  Your son refute it?
DEMIPHO: Don't mention my son to me;
  His brainless behavior refuses to go into words.
PHORMIO: But you have brains. Why not apply to the court
  To have your case retried? Your word, I imagine,
  Is law in Athens; doubtless they'll make an exception,
  Reopen the case for *you.*
DEMIPHO: I've suffered a grievous
  Miscarriage of justice—but still, to avoid perpetual
  Litigation (*and* the sound of your voice), I'll grant
  The point—she *is* a relative. Take her away,
  And I'll pay you the dowry the law prescribes—five *minae.*   410
PHORMIO (*Laughing*): You're generous to a fault.
DEMIPHO: My offer is per-
    fectly fair
  And legal. Shouldn't I start to receive *some* justice?
PHORMIO: Come, now: you make it sound like a law for whores:
  Take your pleasure, pay her, dismiss her, forget her.
  You know its intent—to keep an impoverished Athenian
  Lady from a life of shame. That's why it demands
  That she marry the next of kin. But you're repealing
  The laws.

DEMIPHO: All right, but how are *we* the next
Of kin? And, come to think of it, why?
PHORMIO: Tut.
Remember the proverb: "What's done is done."
DEMIPHO: It's done, eh?
By the time I'm done, it'll be *un*done!   420
PHORMIO: Words, words.
DEMIPHO: You wait!
PHORMIO: What business we have with you, Demipho,
Is, in the final analysis, nil. The court
Condemned your son to marriage; I'm afraid it felt
That you were a bit overage.
DEMIPHO: You will please remember
That my son says exactly what I say here—or else,
Believe me, my door is closed to him and that wife
Of his!
GETA (*Aside*): He is annoyed.
PHORMIO: You'd better close
That door to yourself.
DEMIPHO: Look, idiot, did you come prepared
To attack me on *everything?*
PHORMIO (*Aside to* GETA):   He's trying hard to conceal it,
But we've got him scared.
GETA (*Aside to* PHORMIO):   You've made a terrific start.
PHORMIO (*To* DEMIPHO): Bear what's to be borne, behave in a
    fashion befitting   430
The real you; and—who knows?—we might be friends.
DEMIPHO: Friendship with *you?* Sooner than seek the sight
Of that face, or the sound of that voice. . . .
PHORMIO: Remember the
    girl.
She's charming. Cultivate her, and you'll have a comfort
For your declining years.
                         Show some respect for old age.
DEMIPHO: Keep all her comfort for yourself!
PHORMIO: Temper, temper.
DEMIPHO: Now listen. We've talked enough. Look smart, and take

That woman away, or I'll throw her out. And that,
Phormio, is that.
PHORMIO: If you lay a finger on her,
Except as befits a freeborn lady, I'll sue
You so hard you won't be able to walk. And that,
Demipho, is *that*.
(*Aside to* GETA)
I'm home if you need me. 440
GETA (*Aside to* PHORMIO): Got you.
(PHORMIO *exits left*)

Scene 4

DEMIPHO: Just look at the woe and worry my boy's producing
For me. His marriage has both of us tied in knots.
Doesn't even show his face.
Then I could at least
Find out what he has to say, or what he thinks
About this business.
(*To* GETA) Go see if Antipho's home yet.
GETA: Yes, sir.
(*He enters* DEMIPHO's *house*)
DEMIPHO (*To* HEGIO, CRATINUS, *and* CRITO): You see the situation.
What do I do?
Tell me, Hegio.
HEGIO: Me? I believe Cratinus
Should speak, if it's all the same to you.
DEMIPHO: Very well.
Cratinus?
CRATINUS: You want my opinion?
DEMIPHO: Yours.
CRATINUS: Well, now.
I feel that you should act for your own advantage. 450
I reason thus: When a son concludes a contract
In his father's absence, it is only fair and proper

That it be rendered null and void. Therefore,
The court will reverse this decision. And that is that.
DEMIPHO: And now you, Hegio.
HEGIO: My colleague's opinion shows
    careful
Thought; I respect it. Opinions, however, are as many
And varied as the men who hold them; each has his own.
And mine is this: An action performed under law
Cannot be annulled. To attempt such annulment were heinous.
DEMIPHO: And now you, Crito.
CRITO: My judgment is, that a matter
So fraught and weighty demands extended deliberation.
HEGIO: May we aid you further?
DEMIPHO: You've done an excellent job. . . .
    (*As* HEGIO, CRATINUS, *and* CRITO *exit left*)
Now I'm really confused.
GETA (*Entering from* DEMIPHO's *house*): They say he's still out.
DEMIPHO: I guess I'll have to wait for my brother. He's sure   460
    To give me some good advice; I'll do what he says.
    I'll hurry down to the harbor, and find out when
    He's due to arrive.
    (*He exits right*)
GETA: I'll hunt for Antipho. He needs
    To know about all this.
    (*Looking off left*)
                              Here he comes. Just in time.

ACT III

Scene 1

ANTIPHO *enters left. He does not see* GETA.

ANTIPHO: Antipho, the dirty names that you and your chicken
    heart deserve
Are almost endless. Deserting! Leaving your life to be saved
By other people! Did you really think that they'd manage your
    interests
Better than you?
               At the very least, you should look after *her*.
You brought her home; do you want her destroyed simply
    because
She trusted you?
            Poor girl, what awful luck: her hopes,
Her fears, her prospects all depend on one man—you.   470
GETA: That's just what we've done all the time you've been away,
    boss:
Given you hell for deserting . . .
ANTIPHO: You're just the man I wanted.
GETA: . . . Not that we've slackened our efforts on that account.
    No, sir.
ANTIPHO: I'm begging you. Let me know where I stand. What are
    my chances?
Does Dad suspect?
GETA: Not a thing.
ANTIPHO: Is there any hope?
GETA: Who knows?
ANTIPHO: Oh, god!

GETA: There's one thing: Phaedria hasn't faltered.
   He's in there
   Pushing for you.
ANTIPHO: He always did.
GETA: And Phormio's in there,
   Acting the part of a man of action.
ANTIPHO: What did *he* do?
GETA: Your father blew up just now, but Phormio put the lid on.
ANTIPHO: Good boy, Phormio!
GETA: I'm in there, too. I did what I could.
ANTIPHO: Geta, you're great. I love you all.
GETA: Well, so much
   For the first encounters. The action's quieted down for the time
     being.
   Your father's decided to wait for your uncle.   480
ANTIPHO: Why my uncle?
GETA: Your father said that he'd take his advice about this business.
ANTIPHO: And now I'm afraid that my *uncle* will come home safe
   and sound!
   He'll decide my life or death with a single vote.
GETA: Look, here's Phaedria.
ANTIPHO: Where?
GETA: Just coming out of gym class.

Scene 2

PHAEDRIA *and* DORIO *enter from* DORIO's *brothel. They do not see
the others.*

PHAEDRIA: Dorio, listen.
DORIO: I won't.
PHAEDRIA: A little?
DORIO: Let go of me.
PHAEDRIA: Won't you hear what I have to say?

DORIO:　　　　　　　　　　　　　　　　　I've heard it a
　　thousand times.
　　It nauseates me.
PHAEDRIA:　　　　This time it's different. You'll like it.
DORIO:　　　　　　　　　　　　　　　　　　　Go on,
　　I'll listen.
PHAEDRIA:　　Can't I persuade you to wait for just three days?
　　—Where are you going?
DORIO:　　　　　　　　　　No change at all. I should have known.
ANTIPHO (*Aside to* GETA): I don't like this. I'm afraid that pimp
　　may . . .　　　　　　　　　　　　　　　　　　491
GETA (*Aside to* ANTIPHO): Sew himself
A shroud? It bothers me, too.
PHAEDRIA:　　　　　　　　　　But don't you trust me?
DORIO:　　　　　　　　　　　　　　　　　You're read-
　　ing
　　My mind.
PHAEDRIA:　　I'll give you my word . . .
DORIO:　　　　　　　　　　　　　Cheap fiction.
PHAEDRIA:　　　　　　　　　　　　　Do me this
　　favor;
　　You'll get it back with interest.
DORIO:　　　　　　　　　　　Drivel.
PHAEDRIA:　　　　　　　　　　Trust me. I swear
　　To god, you'll thank me for it. And that's the truth.
DORIO:　　　　　　　　　　　　　　　　Daydreams.
PHAEDRIA: Take a chance—it's only three days!
DORIO:　　　　　　　　　　　　　　You're singing the
　　same old song.
PHAEDRIA: You are my friend, my family, my father, my brother,
　　my . . .
DORIO: Bull.
PHAEDRIA: Your heart's too hard and relentless. Neither pity nor
　　prayers
Can make you relax and do a generous act for once.　　　500
DORIO: Your head's too soft and shameless. You think you can
　　butter me up
With fancy phrases and get my girl away for free.
ANTIPHO (*Aside to* GETA): Fine sort of pity *that* is.

PHAEDRIA: Dammit, I can't
   fight truth!
GETA (*Aside to* ANTIPHO): At least, they're both consistent.
PHAEDRIA: And why
   did the blow have to fall
On me when Antipho had his own troubles—if that's what they
   are?
ANTIPHO (*Going up to* PHAEDRIA): What's the matter, Phaedria?
PHAEDRIA: It's
   the luckiest man alive!
ANTIPHO: I'm lucky?
PHAEDRIA: You're lucky. You've got your loved one safe
   at home.
You've never had to struggle with this sort of godawful mess.
ANTIPHO: *Safe at home?* I'll tell you what I've got. I've got a wolf
   By the ears, like the proverb: I can't let go, I can't hang on.
DORIO (*Indicating* PHAEDRIA): That's just my relation to him.
ANTIPHO: No way for a pimp to talk.
   (*To* PHAEDRIA)
He hasn't done anything, has he?
PHAEDRIA: Oh, yes! He's just not human!
   It's Pamphila—that man sold her!   510
ANTIPHO: Sold her?
GETA: Sold her?
PHAEDRIA: Sold her!
DORIO: An utterly heinous crime, to sell a girl I paid for.
PHAEDRIA: I can't persuade him to break his bond with her buyer
   and wait.
Just for three days, until my friends can raise the money.
   (*To* DORIO)
If I don't pay you then, you don't have to wait a minute more.
DORIO: Hammer away.   520
ANTIPHO: He isn't asking for much time; let him
   Have it. Whatever favor you do him, he'll pay back double.
DORIO: Words, words.
ANTIPHO: Can you really allow that girl to be shipped
   out of town?
Are you willing to take the blame for ripping two lovers apart?
DORIO: I'm no more to blame than you are.

GETA: May heaven settle your
hash!

DORIO (*To* PHAEDRIA): Much as it's galled me to do it, I've stood
you, month in, month out—
Promises, tears, but never money. But that's all changed:
I've found a man who pays cash instead of crying. Give way
To a better man than you.

ANTIPHO: But, Phaedria, I'm sure I remember
That sometime back you both agreed on a day for payment.

PHAEDRIA: We certainly did.

DORIO: Who says we didn't?

ANTIPHO: Did the day go
past?

DORIO: Oh, no. Today came first.

ANTIPHO: That's downright fraud! Doesn't it
Make you ashamed?

DORIO: Not when it pays.

GETA: You open sewer!

PHAEDRIA: Honestly, is this the way to behave?

DORIO: I am what I am.
If you like it, do business with me.

ANTIPHO: I can't stand to see him
cheated.

DORIO: You've got it backwards, Antipho. *He* cheated *me.* He
knew
My methods; I thought I knew his . . . as it turned out,
wrongly. But he's
The deceiver; I'm the same man I always was.   530
                                        Forget that;
Here's what I'll do. The Captain promised to bring me the
money
Tomorrow. If you can bring it today, Phaedria, I'll follow
My established rule:
                  First paid, first served.
                                    And so farewell.

(*He enters his establishment*)

Scene 3

PHAEDRIA: What do I do now? Where can a man in my state raise
   That amount on such short notice? My assets are less than
   nothing.
   Oh, for just three more days! They'd promised to get me the
   money!
ANTIPHO: Geta, we can't let a comrade suffer like this. You've told
   me
   How much he's helped me. Such kindness has to be repaid.
   Let's try. He certainly needs it.
GETA: I suppose. It's only fair.
ANTIPHO: Get started. You're the only one who can save him.
GETA: How?
ANTIPHO: Dig up the money.   540
GETA: I'd love to. Where, for instance?
ANTIPHO: Dad's
   back.
GETA: I know he's back. So what?
ANTIPHO: You know. A word to the wise . . .
GETA: *That's* your idea?
ANTIPHO: That's it.
GETA: Oh god, what lovely advice—
   Go away!
           I've had my success: you're married and I'm still alive.
   And now you want me to go and borrow disaster for *him*?
ANTIPHO (*To* PHAEDRIA): He does have a point.
PHAEDRIA: But, Geta, am I a
   stranger?
GETA: Of course not.
   But the old man's wild with all of us now. Isn't that enough?
   Why should we roil him up any more? We won't have a prayer.
PHAEDRIA: Will another tear her from before my eyes and bear her
   away
   To an unknown land?

       Then while you can, and while I remain,
  Talk to me, Antipho, Geta, rest your gaze on my face.   550
ANTIPHO: Well, why? What are you planning to do? What is it?
PHAEDRIA: Wherever
  In all this world they abduct my darling, my firm resolve
  Is to follow.
       Or else to die.
GETA: Good luck, whatever you do . . .
  But take your time.
ANTIPHO: You've got to help him. Think of something.
 GETA: Something? *What?*
ANTIPHO: At least make an effort. He might . . .
  you know.
  We'd never forgive ourselves, Geta.
GETA: I'm trying, I'm trying.
  (*Pause for thought*)
                I think
  I've got him home safe.
       But it doesn't look too good for me.
ANTIPHO: Don't worry. We're with you. Good or bad, we'll suffer
  together.
GETA: Tell me, how much do you need?
PHAEDRIA: It's only thirty *minae.*
GETA: *Thirty minae!* Phaedria, that girl's mighty expensive.
PHAEDRIA: Not this girl. She's *cheap!*
GETA: All right, all right, I'll get
  you the money.
PHAEDRIA: What a wonderful fellow!
GETA: Enough of that.
PHAEDRIA: I need it now.
GETA: You'll have it now; but I need Phormio to help me out. 560
ANTIPHO: He's ready. Never hold back with him. No matter how
  heavy
  Your burden, he'll carry it through. Best friend a friend can
  have.
GETA: Then let's go see him *now.*
ANTIPHO: Do you need my help anymore?

GETA: We don't. Go home, reassure your wife. She's probably
    Scared to death.
                —Go on!
ANTIPHO: There's nothing I'd enjoy doing more.
    (*He exits happily into* DEMIPHO's *house*)
PHAEDRIA: How will you do this?
GETA: Tell you on the way. Come on,
    let's leave.
    (*They exit left*)

ACT IV

Scene 1

CHREMES *and* DEMIPHO *enter from the left.*

DEMIPHO: Have a successful trip to Lemnus, Chremes?
    Bring your daughter back with you?
CHREMES: No.
DEMIPHO: Why not?
CHREMES: Her mother. She saw I was staying at Athens longer
    Than usual, and didn't feel that the girl, given
    Her age, could wait on my lack of fatherly concern.   570
    When I got there, they told me she'd taken the entire staff
    And gone to Athens to meet me.
DEMIPHO: Well, why did you stay there
    So long, then, after you'd heard the news?
CHREMES: Oh, lord,
    I had to stay. I was sick.
DEMIPHO: What with? Where did
    You catch it?

CHREMES: Not that; old age in itself is an illness.
Anyway, the captain of the ship that brought them informed me
They all arrived safely in Athens.
DEMIPHO: You heard what happened to my son while *I* was away?
CHREMES: I certainly did, and that's upset my plans.
If I have to find her a husband outside the family,
I'll have to declare her relationship to me in detail.   580
You, you're loyal; I'd trust you as I trust myself.
But some outsider who decides to become my in-law—
He'll keep my secret as long as we stay close;
But if there's a break . . . well, then, he'll know too much.
And I'm worried about my wife. If *she* finds out
Somehow, well, all I can do is clean out my pockets
And clear out.
                    The only thing I own is me.
DEMIPHO: I know how it is with you. It's my worry, too.
I won't wear out, I'll never slacken my efforts
Until I fulfill in full the promise I made you.   590
(*They continue talking as* GETA *enters left. They do not see
him, nor, at first, does he see them*)

Scene 2

GETA: For sheer shrewdness, I've never seen the man to equal
Phormio. I went up to him to tell him we needed
Money, and how we could get it. I'd barely reached
The halfway mark in my story, when he saw everything.
He was tickled, congratulated me, and asked how to find
The old man. He gave the gods thanks for a chance to show
That he was just as much Phaedria's friend as Antipho's.
I told him to wait downtown; I'd deliver the old man
There.
(*He sees* DEMIPHO)
                    And here he is. Who's that behind him?
                                        Ouch!

Phaedria's father's back home!   600
                              —Of all the nitwits;
What was I worried about? Because I've got
A pair to swindle instead of a single? I always
Say, it's better to carry a spare. I'll make
My pitch to the man I started out to see;
If he comes across with the money, that's it. If nothing's
Forthcoming there, I'll attack the new arrival.

Scene 3

ANTIPHO *enters from* DEMIPHO's *house, and stops by the door,*
unperceived by DEMIPHO, CHREMES, *and* GETA.

ANTIPHO: I'll wait to see how quickly Geta gets back.
  —Look. There's my uncle. He's with my father. Oh, no!
  He's come back home and I'm afraid. Just what
  Will he push Dad into?
GETA (*Aside*): I'll approach.
  (*He moves up to* CHREMES)
                              —Well, Chremes! Greetings!
CHREMES: Greetings,
    Geta.
GETA: Most happy to see you home safe.   610
CHREMES: I'm sure you are.
GETA: And how's it going? The usual bunch of surprises
    To greet the returning traveler?
CHREMES: More than enough.
GETA: Of course. You've heard what happened to Antipho?
CHREMES: Every-
    thing.
GETA (*To* DEMIPHO): Were you the one who told him?
                              —Oh,
    Chremes, a shocking
    Business. Such flagrant fraud!

CHREMES: We were just discussing it.
GETA: What a coincidence! I've just been handling the matter
    Myself, working it over. And now I think
    I've found a solution.
CHREMES: What, Geta?
DEMIPHO: What solution?
GETA: Well, when I left you, I happened to run into Phormio.
CHREMES: Who's Phormio?
DEMIPHO: The fellow who brought her to . . .
CHREMES: Oh. Of
    course.
GETA: I decided to test his sentiments. I take him aside.
    "Phormio," I say, "why don't you figure out a settlement,   620
    And leave us all with good feelings rather than bad ones?
    My master's a well-bred gentleman, and shy of legal
    Action, but he's got you. Those friends of his just rendered
    A unanimous opinion: they said he should kick the girl out."
ANTIPHO (*Aside*): What is he starting? Where's it going to end?
GETA: "You'll probably say," I say, "that the law will punish
    My master if he ejects her; that's all thought out.
    I swear you'll sweat if you tangle with him; the man
    Is solid eloquence. But let's suppose he loses—   630
    It's not a capital offense. He'll pay a fine."
    I begin to see that my speech has softened him up.
    "We're all by ourselves," I say. "How much will you take?
    Cash on the barrel: my master avoids litigation,
    The girl clears out, and you stop bothering us."
ANTIPHO (*Aside*): I think he's lost his mind.
GETA: "He's an honorable
    man,"
    I say. "I'm sure that if you offer him terms that
    Are just the least bit reasonable and honest, you'll end
    This whole ungodly mess in three words or less."
DEMIPHO: Who authorized you to speak for me?
CHREMES: Now, look!
    There couldn't be a better way to reach our goal.   640
ANTIPHO: I'm ruined!
DEMIPHO: Continue your tale.

GETA: He raved like a madman
At first.
CHREMES: How much is he asking?
GETA: How much? Too much.
As much as he could think of.
CHREMES: How much is that?
GETA: He wanted one talent. Sixty *minae*.
DEMIPHO: He wanted
To lose the skin off his back. Absolutely shameless!
GETA: That's just what I said to him. "Now look," I say,
"Do you think my master's marrying off his only
Daughter? There goes his profit in never raising
A girl, if a girl's been found to demand a full-scale
Dowry!"
            To cut this short and leave out his insolent
Nonsense, his final proposal ran as follows:
"From the first," he says, "I've wanted to do the right thing,
And marry my friend's daughter. I've always thought   651
How awkward it is when a poor girl marries a rich man—
That's not matrimony, it's slavery. To be frank, however,
I needed a wife who could bring me a little something
To pay my debts. But even now, if Demipho's willing
To give me as much as I'll get from my present fiancée,
There's no girl I'd rather have for my bride than Phanium."
ANTIPHO (*Aside*): Why is he doing this? Stupidity, or just plain
    spite?
Is he clever or clumsy? I don't have the slightest idea.   660
DEMIPHO: What if he's up to his ears in debt?
GETA: "There's a field,"
He says. "The mortgage comes to ten *minae*."
DEMIPHO: Marvelous!
He can marry her now. I'll pay it.
GETA: "Next, a cottage—
Ten *minae* more."
DEMIPHO: Oh, hell! Too much.
CHREMES: Don't squeal;
I'll refund the ten.

GETA: "I must buy my wife a maid,"
He says, "and then we need a little more furniture,
And then the wedding itself. For all these items,
Let's say," he says, "you put down ten more *minae.*"
DEMIPHO: He can also put down five hundred suits against me.
I give him nothing. To think that scum like that
Can laugh at me!
CHREMES: Please quiet down. I'll pay it.
Just make your son marry the wife we want him to marry.   670
ANTIPHO (*Aside*): Oh, Geta, I'm lost! Your tricks have meant my
    death!
CHREMES: She's being thrown out for my sake. It's only fair
That I should lose the money.
GETA: "Let me know,"
He says, "as soon as you can, if they give me Phanium.
I'll have to break off with the other girl. I can't
Stay on the fence; her people have promised to pay me
The dowry today."
CHREMES: He can have the money now,
And break his engagement, and marry this girl.
DEMIPHO: Much good
May it do him!
CHREMES: What luck—I've brought some money along
From Lemnus—the rent from my wife's farms there. I'll take it
Out of that, and tell my wife you needed the cash.   681
(CHREMES *and* DEMIPHO *enter* CHREMES' *house*)

Scene 4

ANTIPHO *angrily moves from his place by* DEMIPHO's *door to*
GETA.

ANTIPHO: Geta!
GETA: Well!
ANTIPHO: Just what have you done?

GETA: I've conned
  The old men out of the cash.
ANTIPHO: Is that all?
GETA: I'm damned
  If I know. It's all I was told to do.
ANTIPHO: You rat!
  I asked one question, you answered another!
GETA: So what
  Did you mean?
ANTIPHO: So what did I mean?
                         The only recourse
  That's left for me is the rope, and it's all your fault.
  May all the gods and goddesses, in heaven and hell,
  Damn you to unspeakable torments!
                       Just look at this man;
  Entrust him with any task. He'll steer you out
  Of still water, straight onto a rock!
                   What was more futile
  Than touching that wound, or mentioning my wife? You've only
  Given my father hope of throwing her out,   691
  That's all!
          For future reference, tell me this: If Phormio
  Gets the dowry, he has to marry the wife—
  What then?
GETA: Oh, he won't marry her.
ANTIPHO: Of course he won't.
  And when they ask for their money back, for the love
  He bears us, he'll choose to go to jail.
GETA: There's nothing
  That can't be debased by telling it badly, Antipho.
  You cut out all the good and mention the bad.
  So listen to the other side:
               If he keeps the money,
  He'll have to go through with the marriage, just as you say.
  I grant the point. However, he'll have some time   701
  To prepare for the wedding, and send invitations, and arrange
  The ceremony proper. Meantime, those friends will supply
  The money they've promised. He'll pay it back out of that.

ANTIPHO: But why? What sort of excuse can he give?

GETA:　　　　　　　　　　　　　　　　　　　　That's easy:
　　"The number of evil omens I've received since I
　　Was engaged! A strange black dog ran into my house;
　　A snake fell off the roof right into the cistern;
　　A hen went cockadoodledoo; a soothsayer said I shouldn't;
　　A diviner forbade it; I can't undertake a new business
　　Before the shortest day of the year"—and *that's*
　　The best excuse there is. That's what'll happen　　　　710

ANTIPHO: I wish it would.

GETA:　　　　　　　　　　It will. Just trust in me.
　　Here comes your father.

　　　　　　　　　　　　Tell Phaedria the money's here.
　　(ANTIPHO *exits left as* DEMIPHO *and* CHREMES *emerge from*
　　CHREMES' *house*)

Scene 5

DEMIPHO: I tell you, don't worry. I can handle this; he won't cheat
　　us.
　　I'll never be so rash that I give him the money except
　　In front of witnesses. And then I'll recite the recipient's name
　　And the reason for payment.

GETA (*Aside*):　　　　　　　　That man's a perfect model of
　　caution,
　　When it isn't needed.

CHREMES:　　　　　　Yes, that's the way you have to do it.
　　But hurry, while he's still in the mood. If the other girl fusses
　　And prods, it's always possible that he'll reject our offer.

GETA (*Aside*): Just so. You've hit it.

DEMIPHO (*To* GETA):　　　　　So lead me to him.

GETA:　　　　　　　　　　　　　　　This very·
　　minute.

CHREMES: When you're done with this, come over to my wife, and
　　ask her to visit

The girl before she has to leave. And have her tell her
That we're giving her to Phormio in marriage (just so she won't
    get angry),   720
And that Phormio's a better husband for her because she's
    known him
Longer, *and* that we haven't strayed one step from our duty,
But we've given her as large a dowry as her husband demanded.
DEMIPHO: What in hell does this mean to *you?*
CHREMES: A great deal,
    Demipho.
It's not enough to do your duty; Public Opinion
Has to approve it. I want this to happen with the girl's consent;
That way, she won't be able to claim that we threw her out.
DEMIPHO: I could do the job myself.
CHREMES: A woman's better for a woman.
DEMIPHO: I'll ask your wife.
    (GETA *and* DEMIPHO *exit left*)
CHREMES: Now where can I find those women
    from Lemnus?

ACT V

Scene 1

SOPHRONA *enters from* DEMIPHO's *house. She does not see*
CHREMES.

SOPHRONA: What am I to do? In all this trouble, where can I find
    A friend to consider my plans,
                    A friend to grant me assistance?
I'm afraid my advice will cause my mistress to suffer horribly.
They say the young man's father is furious at what we've done.

CHREMES (*Aside*): Who's this old woman who came from my
  brother's? She's scared to death. 732
SOPHRONA: I knew the marriage wouldn't last, but poverty made
  me do it:
  I needed time to devise a way to keep us alive.
CHREMES (*Aside*): Oh, lord—unless my mind's playing tricks, or
  my eyes won't work,
  That's my daughter's nurse!
SOPHRONA: We haven't encountered a trace . . .
CHREMES: What shall I do?
SOPHRONA: . . . of her father.
CHREMES (*Aside*): Do I go up to her, or
  wait
  And listen until I'm absolutely sure?
SOPHRONA: Oh, to find him!
  I wouldn't have a fear in the world.
CHREMES (*Aside*): It *is* the nurse. I'll go up
  And speak.
SOPHRONA: Who's that talking?
CHREMES: Sophrona!
SOPHRONA: He knows my name!
CHREMES: Turn around. Look at me. 740
SOPHRONA: Merciful heavens! It's *Stilpo!*
CHREMES: It's not!
SOPHRONA: You deny it?
  (*They are now near the door of* CHREMES' *house. He beckons
  her away*)
CHREMES: Move away from that door a bit,
  Sophrona, *please*. Over here.
  (*She complies. He whispers*)
  Never call me that name again.
SOPHRONA: What? Aren't you the man you always said you
  were?
CHREMES: Shhhh!
SOPHRONA: Why *are* you afraid of that door?
CHREMES: Terror lurks behind it—
  My wife. About that name: It isn't mine. I told you

It was to keep you from blurting out my real name by accident.
I thought my wife might find out somehow.

SOPHRONA: Well, I declare!
That's why we never could locate you in all our troubles.

CHREMES: That house you came out of—what's your connection
with the family inside?
Where are the others?

SOPHRONA: Oh, dear!

CHREMES: What's this? Are they alive?

SOPHRONA: Your daughter's alive. After all this grief, her mother
died.   750

CHREMES: What a dreadful blow!

SOPHRONA: That left me, a poor old woman,
deserted,
Penniless, unknown. I did my best; I married the girl
To the young man who's master of this house.

CHREMES: To *Antipho?*

SOPHRONA: That's
the man.

CHREMES: You mean he has two wives?

SOPHRONA: No! *This* man only has one.

CHREMES: But the other one, the one they call his relative?

SOPHRONA: That's
this one.

CHREMES: You don't mean that.

SOPHRONA: It was all a plan to let her lover
Marry her without a dowry.

CHREMES: Oh heavens above, how often
Fortune brings events you wouldn't dare to pray for!
I return to discover my daughter married to the man I wanted
In the way I wanted. The goal we both were struggling to
reach,   760
She attained alone by her own exertions, without our aid.

SOPHRONA: Consider what we have to do now. The young man's
father
Is back, and people say he's very opposed to the match.

CHREMES: No danger there; but in heaven's name, and earth's
name, too,
Don't let anyone learn that she's my daughter.

SOPHRONA: Not
From me.

CHREMES: Follow me. You can tell the rest of the story inside.
(*They enter* DEMIPHO's *house*)

Scene 2

DEMIPHO *and* GETA *enter left.*

DEMIPHO: Roguery's profitable now, and it's all our fault. And
why?
Because we're too eager to have the name of *honest* and
generous.
Stay in your own back yard, they say. Wasn't it enough
To suffer at that man's hands? But no, we throw money at him,
To keep him alive until he achieves another crime.

GETA: Indubitably.   770

DEMIPHO: These days, there's a prize for turning right
into wrong.

GETA: Incontrovertibly.

DEMIPHO: How stupid we were to let ourselves be
duped!

GETA: I only hope we come out all right, and Phormio marries her.

DEMIPHO: Is there any doubt about that?

GETA: I'd hate to say. You know
What he's like; he just might change his mind.

DEMIPHO: What! Change
his mind?

GETA: I don't really know. I say *might.*

DEMIPHO: I'll take my brother's suggestion,

And bring his wife across to talk to the girl. Geta,
Go on ahead and tell them she's coming.
(*He enters* CHREMES' *house*)
GETA: We've got the money
For Phaedria; utter silence about the suit; for the moment,
The girl stays here.
                       But what of the future? What will happen?
You're stuck in the same old mud, Geta; you borrowed to pay
   off   780
Your debts—and the new loan's just about due. Immediate
   troubles
Can wait for a while, but future whippings mount up, unless
You watch out. Now I'll go home and explain to Phanium;
   otherwise,
She's bound to be frightened by Phormio and scared of the
   lady's speeches.
(*He enters* DEMIPHO's *house*)

Scene 3

DEMIPHO *and* NAUSISTRATA *enter from* CHREMES' *house.*

DEMIPHO: Now, Nausistrata, ply your usual tact to make her
   Happy, wanting to do what has to be done.
NAUSISTRATA: I'll do that.
DEMIPHO: Lend your efforts to help me now, as recently you lent
   me
Your purse.
NAUSISTRATA: Delighted to help. I really feel I can't
   Do everything I should. My husband's fault.
DEMIPHO: Why, what do you
   mean?
NAUSISTRATA: Gracious! That man's so careless in handling my
   father's honest
Savings! Every time the rent on his farms came due,

Daddy collected *two talents!* But some men, it seems, are different
From others.

DEMIPHO: Two talents? Really?   790

NAUSISTRATA: And money went further in those days.
Two whole talents!

DEMIPHO: Amazing!

NAUSISTRATA: What's your opinion?

DEMIPHO: It's obvious.

NAUSISTRATA: I wish I'd been born a man; I'd show that . . .

DEMIPHO: I'm sure you would.

NAUSISTRATA: . . . Just how . . .

DEMIPHO: Please conserve yourself to talk with the girl.
She's rather young. Might wear you out.

NAUSISTRATA: I'll take your advice.
—Oh, here's my husband. Coming out of your house.
(CHREMES *rushes excitedly out of* DEMIPHO's *house. He does not see* NAUSISTRATA)

CHREMES: Oh, Demipho!
Did you pay the money already?

DEMIPHO: I paid it at once.

CHREMES: Too bad.
(*Aside, as he sees* NAUSISTRATA)
—Oops, my wife! I almost said too much.

DEMIPHO: Why "too bad,"
Chremes?

CHREMES: It's all right now.

DEMIPHO: I trust you talked with the girl
And told her why we're bringing your wife?

CHREMES: I arranged it all.

DEMIPHO: What was her answer?

CHREMES: She's not to be removed.

DEMIPHO: Why not?

CHREMES: Because they're in love with each other.   800

DEMIPHO: What's that to
  us?
CHREMES: A great deal.
  What's more, I learned she's a relative of ours.
DEMIPHO: You're out of your
  head!
CHREMES: You'll see. I'm not speaking rashly; I got my memory
  back.
DEMIPHO: Are you mad?
NAUSISTRATA: Now, please, if she's a relative, let's not
  Harm her.
DEMIPHO: She's *not* a relative!
CHREMES: Don't be too sure. She got
  Her father's name wrong; there's where you made your mis-
  take.
DEMIPHO: She didn't
  Know her *father?*
CHREMES: Of course she did!
DEMIPHO: Then why the wrong name?
CHREMES (*Aside to* DEMIPHO): Won't you ever give in and under-
  stand?
DEMIPHO: Talk sense, and I'll try.
CHREMES (*Aside to* DEMIPHO): You're ruining me!
NAUSISTRATA: I wonder what
  all this means?
DEMIPHO: I swear
  To god that *I* don't know.
CHREMES: Would you like to?
                                            As Jove is my judge,
  She has no closer relatives in the world than you and me.
DEMIPHO: Good lord, let's go and see her. I want us all to learn
  The truth together.
  (*He moves toward his door.* CHREMES *catches his sleeve*)
CHREMES: Oh, no!
DEMIPHO: Now what?   810
CHREMES: How can you have
  Such little faith in me?

DEMIPHO:　　　　　　　　　You want me to take your word?
You want me to take the question as settled?
　　　　　　　　　　　　　　　　　All right, it's settled.
—Now, what about our friend, the one with the daughter? What
Will happen to her?

CHREMES:　　　　　　　It's all right.

DEMIPHO:　　　　　　　　　　And so we drop the daughter?

CHREMES: What else?

DEMIPHO:　　　　　　　And the other girl stays?

CHREMES:　　　　　　　　　　　Of course.

DEMIPHO:　　　　　　　　　　　　　Well,
　　then,
I guess you can go home, Nausistrata.

NAUSISTRATA:　　　　　　　　　I'd like to say
That it seems much nicer for everybody, having her stay here
Rather than go. The one time I saw her, I thought she was quite
Well-bred.

(*She enters the house of* CHREMES. DEMIPHO *turns to* CHREMES)

DEMIPHO:　　　What *is* this business?

CHREMES:　　　　　　　　　Is the door shut yet?

DEMIPHO:　　　　　　　　　　　It's shut.

CHREMES: Oh Jove, the gods are with us! I've learned that my
　　daughter has married
Your son!

DEMIPHO:　　　How could that have happened?

CHREMES:　　　　　　　　　　It isn't safe
To tell it outdoors.

DEMIPHO:　　　　　　All right, then. Come indoors and tell it.

CHREMES: But let's be careful. I don't even want our sons to find
　　out.

(*They enter* DEMIPHO's *house*)

Scene 4

ANTIPHO *enters left.*

ANTIPHO: I'm happy. Except for my anguish. My cousin's got what
    he wants.   820
   I envy that prudent approach to passion: Be smart, and choose
   Desires that you can repair with ease when trouble strikes.
   He found his money and sloughed his worry in a single motion.
   But me . . . I'm trapped, wrapped up in troubles—and no re-
    lease.
   While my secret's kept, I'm afraid; if the truth comes out, I'm
    ruined.
   I wouldn't be going home now, except for a hint of hope
   That I might stay married.
                               But where can I find Geta?
   He'll be able to tell me when I should interview Dad.

Scene 5

PHORMIO *enters right. He does not see* ANTIPHO.

PHORMIO: Cash collected, paid to pimp. Female removed,
   Duly delivered—free and clear—to Phaedria's keeping.   830
   Leaving me one last job: a vacation. I'll make the fathers
   Supply me some time to get drunk in. Take a few days off.
ANTIPHO: It's Phormio.
            —Well?
PHORMIO: Well, what?
ANTIPHO: Well, Phaedria: What's
   his next move?
   How does he propose to . . . slake his passion?

PHORMIO: He'll take
  A turn at playing your part.
ANTIPHO: What part?
PHORMIO: Avoiding father.
  In turn, he has a request for you: Play his. *You* plead
  His case for a while. He'll be at my house, drinking. Myself,
  I'd better tell the old men that I'm off for Sunium market,
  To buy that maid that Geta just mentioned. I'd hate to have
  My absence make them think I might be depleting their funds.
  —That sounded like your door.   840
ANTIPHO: See who's leaving.
PHORMIO: Geta.

Scene 6

GETA *enters from* DEMIPHO's *house. He sees neither* ANTIPHO *nor*
PHORMIO.

GETA: Thank you, Luck! You, too, Good Fortune! for loading
  today
With such a sudden bale of blessings for my master Antipho . . .
ANTIPHO (*Aside to* PHORMIO): What does he mean?
GETA: . . . And thanks for unloading that burden of worry
  From all his friends!
               —I'm wasting time. I ought to be loading
  My cloak on my shoulder and running to find him, tell him
  what happened.
ANTIPHO (*Aside to* PHORMIO): Do you understand what he's
  saying?
PHORMIO: Do you?
ANTIPHO: Not a word.
PHORMIO: We're even.
GETA (*Starting off*): I'll go to the pimp's; they should be there.
ANTIPHO: Hey,
  Geta!

GETA: I knew it.

Never fails. Start, and somebody calls you back.

ANTIPHO: Geta!

GETA: Oh god, persistent.

(*Without stopping or turning around*)

—I'm sick of that bit. You'd better give
up.

ANTIPHO: Wait up!

GETA: Dry up. 850

ANTIPHO: Pull up, or I'll hang you up. To dry.

GETA: A threat, a palpable threat. It must be one of the family.

(*He stops and turns*)

The man I'm looking for: yes or no?

Yes!

(*To himself*) Advance at once.

ANTIPHO: What's up?

GETA: You are, O best-supplied of men alive.

No room for argument, sir: The gods love you alone.

ANTIPHO: I'd like that.

I'd also like you to give me a reason to
think so.

GETA: I'll smear you with ecstasy, sir. That reason enough?

ANTIPHO: You'll
kill me.

PHORMIO: Come on, dispose of these guarantees. Deliver the
goods.

GETA: Oh, Phormio. You here too?

PHORMIO: Here too. Get on with it.

GETA (*To* PHORMIO): All right, listen: We gave you the money
and went straight home

From the market.

(*To* ANTIPHO)

Not long, and the master sent me to see your
wife. 860

ANTIPHO: What for?

GETA: I won't develop that point; it isn't pertinent.

—I'm just starting into the women's wing when up runs Mida,

Catches my cloak from behind and hauls me back. I turn

And ask him why the delay. "No admittance to the mistress'
rooms,"
He says. "Sophrona just brought in the old man's brother—
Chremes. He's in there with them now." Well, when I heard
this,
I tiptoed soundlessly up to the door, reached it, halted,
Held my breath, applied my ear . . . and applied myself
To catching the conversation.

PHORMIO: Good boy, Geta.

GETA: And oh,   869
What a stunning story I heard. I damn near bawled for bliss

ANTIPHO: What story?

GETA: Guess.

ANTIPHO: I haven't the slightest.

GETA: Simply
staggering:
Your uncle turns out to be Phanium's father.

ANTIPHO: What do you
mean?

GETA: He had an undercover affair with her mother once in
Lemnus.

PHORMIO: Piffle. The girl would certainly know her own father.

GETA: Believe
me,
Phormio, there's an explanation. But they were all inside:
How much do you think I could hear through the door?

ANTIPHO: Of
course!
Someone told me something about this.

GETA: And here's more proof:
After a while, your uncle leaves and goes outside;
A little later he charges back inside, dragging your father:
Both give you their permission to keep your wife.   880
                                        And lastly,
They sent me to find you and take you in.

ANTIPHO: So here I am.
Snatch me away—don't stall!

GETA (*Grabbing him up*):   It's as good as done.

ANTIPHO (*As* GETA *carries him into* DEMIPHO's *house*): Oh Phormio,
Good friend Phormio—goodbye!
PHORMIO: Goodbye to *you*, Antipho.
I swear to heaven, a lovely job. Their joy is mine.

Scene 7

PHORMIO: The lucky pair. Such unforeseen felicity. . . . For me,
The perfect opportunity to con the codgers and resolve
Phaedria's financial worries. Relieve him of dependence
On the charity of friends. The money, unwillingly given
Or not, is his already. And his it shall remain.
This affair has furnished me sufficient force 890
To assure it.
Now to adopt a different appearance,
A new expression. Slip into this handy alley,[6]
Make my entrance when they're out here in the street.
That trick about going to market?
I just won't go.
(*He slips into the alley between the houses of* CHREMES *and*
DORIO)

Scene 8

DEMIPHO *and* CHREMES *enter from* DEMIPHO's *house. They do not
see* PHORMIO.

DEMIPHO: Brother, I *do* thank the gods. I'm in their debt.
They've turned our troubles to quite a successful account.
Our immediate task, however, is turning up Phormio:

[6] *this handy alley:* I have followed tradition and located this *angiportum*
between houses. Some scholars reject the possibility of such hiding places on stage,
in which case "side street" might be a better translation, and Phormio would
retire into the wings, stage left.

We've got to get those thirty *minae* refunded
Before he slings them all over the landscape.

PHORMIO (*Cutting sharply out of the alley, as if coming from the
Forum, and making for* DEMIPHO's *house*):

                                                  I'll drop

By Demipho's, see if he's in, and say . . .   900

DEMIPHO: Ah, Phormio.

Just on our way to your place.

PHORMIO: The usual reason,

By any chance?

DEMIPHO: Of course.

PHORMIO: Suspected as much.

Why come to my place?

DEMIPHO: This is no time for joking.

PHORMIO: Were you afraid that I would fail to perform
A task once undertaken? Gentlemen, please!
Impoverished I may be; my straits are great.
But through it all I have preserved one thing—
My Honor.

DEMIPHO (*To* CHREMES): Perfect gentleman. Didn't I tell you?

CHREMES: Exactly.

PHORMIO: Wherefore, my visit's object. I come
To proclaim that *I am ready.*

                              Convey me my wife
At your convenience; my own affairs are shelved,
A move I made immediately I discerned
Your urgent concern. It seemed, after all, only fair.

DEMIPHO: Er—yes. The fact is, Chremes here has made me   910
Reverse my stand. "Don't give her away," he protested.
"What will people say? The time is past
For taking a step like this with any honor.
To chuck her out without a husband *now*
Would bring disgrace." Er—matter of fact, he brought up
Almost the very same objections you raised
Against me yourself a little while ago.

PHORMIO: This humor at my expense is pretty inhuman.

DEMIPHO: I don't understand.

PHORMIO: Of course you do. You've ruined me:
   I can't even marry the girl I used to have.
   I jilted her. What pretty complexion am I
   Supposed to put on that? How can I make her
   Take me back?
CHREMES (*Aside to* DEMIPHO): Try this: "What's more, I've dis-
   covered
   That Antipho isn't disposed to discard her."
DEMIPHO: What's more,
   I've discovered my son is not at all disposed   920
   To discard the girl. So trot on down to the bank
   And have them retransfer the cash to my account.
PHORMIO: The cash already disbursed to settle my debts?
DEMIPHO: Well, what are we going to do?
PHORMIO: The decision is yours:
   You betrothed me a wife: Convey her to me as agreed,
   I'll marry her; choose for her to remain with you . . .
   And the dowry remains right here.
                     I forsook an equally
   Affluent fiancée solely to save your good name;
   Is it fair for you to defraud me of the money too?
DEMIPHO: Take your highbrow bluster and go to hell,   930
   You displaced peon! You know we know what you are
   And what you're up to!
PHORMIO: You're beginning to crack my com-
   posure.
DEMIPHO: I suppose you'd marry the girl if we handed her over?
PHORMIO: Try me and see.
DEMIPHO: So my son can set up housekeeping
   With her at your place—that's your grand design?
PHORMIO: Now, *there's* a novel theory.
DEMIPHO: You give me my money!
PHORMIO: You give me my wife.
DEMIPHO: I'm taking you to court.
PHORMIO: Not a bad idea. You know, if you two persist
   In this irksome behavior . . .
DEMIPHO: Just what are you going to do?

PHORMIO: I'm glad you asked. Perhaps you imagine I act
  As unpaid legal adviser solely for dowerless
  Women. If so, you're mistaken. I perform the service   940
  For those *with* dowries as well.
CHREMES: What's that to us?
PHORMIO: Not a thing.
                        I knew a dowried woman in town
  Whose husband married another . . .
CHREMES: Oops.
DEMIPHO: What's up?
PHORMIO: . . . wife on the island of Lemnus . . .
CHREMES: I'm dead.
PHORMIO: . . . begot
  A daughter, and brought her up on the sly . . .
CHREMES: And buried.
PHORMIO: The woman knows nothing. I think I'll supply her the
    details
  Right this moment.
CHREMES: I implore you, *don't!*
PHORMIO: Dear me,
  Were you the man?
DEMIPHO: He's making us look like idiots.
CHREMES: We're letting you off, free and clear.
PHORMIO: A likely story.
CHREMES: What more do you want? You'll keep the cash; it's a
    gift.
PHORMIO: Of course it is.
                        I resent this revolving derision
  At my expense. You blither along and exhibit
  The mental stability of babies:
                        Yes, no, maybe so,
  Yes, and no again. Receive her; return her.   950
  You unmean meanings, you disagree on agreements. . . .
CHREMES (*To* DEMIPHO): How did he find out? Who told him?
DEMIPHO: I don't
    know.
  I'm only sure I didn't.

CHREMES: God help us all.
It looks like an omen.
PHORMIO (*Aside*):   A wee bit of stone for their insteps.
DEMIPHO: Ooooh god. Imagine him making off with that money,
   With all that money, and laughing us straight in the face.
   I'll drop dead first.
   (*To* CHREMES)
                         All right, man, up to the mark!
A little courage, a little presence of mind.
—Look, Chremes, your secret is out, your sin is discovered.
You can't keep your wife from learning any longer.
She's bound to hear it from somebody sooner or later;   960
Why not from us? That way, we'll increase our chances
Of calming her down.
                         And then we can turn our attention
To this pariah, and take our personal, private
Revenge.
PHORMIO: Damnation. If I don't pick my steps, I'm stuck.
   They're shifting over to offense—no holds barred.
CHREMES: I'm frightened. We can't appease her.
DEMIPHO: Nerve, man,
      nerve.
   I'll work you back in her graces. Our best point's this:
   The hand that rocked the cradle has—er—passed beyond.
PHORMIO (*To both*): Which neatly disposes of me? A clever
      assault.
   (*To* DEMIPHO)
—By god, your goading has gone too far, and your brother
Will bear the brunt.
                         —Now, Chremes, tell me the truth:
Did you really expect to take a foreign holiday   970
From all morality, devise a modern method
For cheating on a high-grade wife, execute same
With never a quiver—and then return to wash
Your iniquity whiter than snow with a prayer or two?
Well, think again. I tell you, when I've had my say,
That woman will be so stoked with hate you'll never

Put out the fire, not even by trickling away
Every last atom of your being in tears.

DEMIPHO: May every
God in heaven cover that clod with catastrophe!
No man ever lived with such a stock of cheek;
They ought to ship him off (at state expense)
To a desert island.

CHREMES: But where does that put me?
I'm so confused I absolutely don't know what   980
To do with him.

DEMIPHO: I do.

(*To* PHORMIO)

                                    We're going to court.

PHORMIO: To court? Of course,

(*Starting for* CHREMES' *house*)

                                    But court's being held over here,
If you don't mind.

CHREMES (*To* DEMIPHO): After him! Hold him off!
I'll get your slaves.

(*He starts for* DEMIPHO's *house as* DEMIPHO *grabs* PHORMIO *by
the arm*)

DEMIPHO: I can't do it all alone.
Quick, help!

PHORMIO: A charge for you: Assault, one count.

DEMIPHO: Then take it to court.

PHORMIO (*As* CHREMES *grabs his other arm*): A second count for
   you.

CHREMES: Drag him away!

(*A wild struggle ensues, the brothers attempting to keep* PHOR-
MIO *away from* CHREMES' *house*)

PHORMIO: No time for half-measures; I'll use
My voice:
                NAUSISTRATA! OUT HERE!

CHREMES: Stop up his mouth!

DEMIPHO: The bastard's strong enough.

PHORMIO: I repeat: NAUSISTRATA!

CHREMES: Shut up!

PHORMIO: Who, me?

DEMIPHO: Beat him in the belly until he
Comes along.

PHORMIO: Or why not scoop out an eye?
Revenge will be sweet, gentlemen.

                                        And here she comes.

Scene 9

NAUSISTRATA *enters from* CHREMES' *house. Action freezes.*

NAUSISTRATA: I heard my name. Who called?   990
                                        My goodness.
(*To* CHREMES)
                                                        Darling,
What's all this commotion?

PHORMIO (*To* CHREMES):
                              Tongue-tied? I wonder why.

NAUSISTRATA (*To* CHREMES, *indicating* PHORMIO):
Who's that?
                    Why don't you answer?

PHORMIO: He doesn't know how
To answer. Doesn't even know where he is.

CHREMES (*To* NAUSISTRATA): Don't you believe a word he says!

PHORMIO (*To* NAUSISTRATA, *with a wave at* CHREMES):   Try
touching
The body. I'll stake my life he's solid ice.

CHREMES: There's nothing to it.

NAUSISTRATA: Nothing to what? What's that man
Saying?

PHORMIO: You'll know in a moment. Attention, please. . . .

CHREMES (*To* NAUSISTRATA): Why do you persist in believing
his lies?

NAUSISTRATA: So what's
To believe? He hasn't said anything yet.

PHORMIO: Sad case.
Stark mad with fear.
NAUSISTRATA: I know there must be some reason
For you to be so afraid.
CHREMES: *Afraid?* Who, me?
PHORMIO: Oh, certainly not. And since you're a stranger to fear
And there's nothing to what I say,   1000
                              You tell her the story.
DEMIPHO: Tell it to save *your* skin, you scum?
PHORMIO: Ah, Demipho—
Ceaselessly zealous at minding your brother's business.
NAUSISTRATA: Dear, tell me the story.
CHREMES: But . . .
    (*He stops*)
NAUSISTRATA: What sort of a
    story
Is "But"?
CHREMES: It isn't worth telling.
PHORMIO: For you, I agree.
For *her*, however, it *is* worth knowing.
    (*A pause*)
                                        Once,
On the island of Lemnus . . .
DEMIPHO: What are you saying?
CHREMES: Shut *up!*
PHORMIO: . . . All unbeknownst to you . . .
CHREMES: Oh, no—not that!
PHORMIO: . . . He married. A wife.
NAUSISTRATA: Oh, no, sir. I hope I deserve
Better of heaven.
PHORMIO: It's true.
NAUSISTRATA: I'm crushed. My life
Is over.
PHORMIO: There's more: He begot a daughter on her,
While you were sleeping alone.
CHREMES (*To* DEMIPHO):   Now what do we do?
NAUSISTRATA (*Erupting*): Ye gods! Of all the contemptible
    crimes!

PHORMIO (*To* CHREMES): It's done.

NAUSISTRATA: I never conceived of such hideous, odious baseness!
   —These men! When they get around to their wives, they're
   all of a sudden   1010
   Too old.
             —Demipho, I'll talk to you. I don't have the stomach
   For words with *that*.
                      Was this the cause of the constant treks
   To Lemnus, the extended stopovers? Was this the local de-
   pression
   That reduced our rents?

DEMIPHO: I will not claim that Chremes was
   blameless
   In this affair, Nausistrata. I do maintain that he
   Deserves your pardon. . . .

PHORMIO: A most affecting funeral sermon.

DEMIPHO: His slip did not reflect any change in his feelings for
   you,
   No loss of concern, no lessening of love.
                       Fact is, he was drunk.
   A lightning affair: He—er—ravished the woman, she bore him
   a tiny
   Daughter, and that is all. In the fifteen years that have passed
   Since that encounter, he's never touched her again.
                            And now
   She's dead, and the trouble she might have caused is out of
   the way.
   This makes my plea quite logical: Be your usual self,
   Forgive and forget, be broad-minded.   1020

NAUSISTRATA: How can I be broad-
   minded?
   I only want this wretched mess to be over and done with,
   But what guarantees do I have for the future? He'll settle down
   Because age makes men behave? He was ancient when all this
   happened.
   I'm younger and prettier now than I was then, more able
   To hold a man? Can you supply me with a solitary reason
   To hope or expect that this won't happen all over again?

PHORMIO: For those disposed to attend the final rites of dear,
Departed Chremes: On your marks!
                              —And that's my method.
Let any potential foe of Phormio attack at will;
I'll see that he meets demolition that's quite as effective as this.
(*Aside*)
—All right, all right. I'll let him back in his wife's good graces.
I've got sufficient revenge: His wife has enough material
To nag him about for the rest of his life.   1030
NAUSISTRATA: And this, I suppose,
Is what I deserve? I was an ideal wife to him.
Should I give an itemized list of my virtues?
DEMIPHO: I know them all
As well as you do.
NAUSISTRATA: Then *is* this what I deserve?
DEMIPHO: Oh, no.
Certainly not. But no recriminations can change the past
Or revise what's happened. So grant him a pardon and take
him back.
He offers you prayers, confessions, excuses . . . what more do
you want?
PHORMIO (*Aside*): Before she takes him back, I'd better provide
for my future.
Phaedria's, too.
                       —Ahoy, Nausistrata. Before you commit
Yourself to an ill-considered reply, I have a word.
NAUSISTRATA: What word?
PHORMIO: I abstracted thirty *minae* from your
good husband
By a confidence ploy, and gave the money to your son. He
used it
To pry his mistress loose from a pimp.
CHREMES: Eh? What did you say?
NAUSISTRATA (*Rounding on* CHREMES): Oh, aren't we moral all of
a sudden? All right for you   1040
To have two wives, but your poor son, a growing boy,
Can't have one measly mistress?
                              Where is your sense of shame?

How can you look him in the eye and reproach him for bad
behavior?
Answer me that, if you can?
(*Pause*)

DEMIPHO: I'm sure he'll do just as you please.

NAUSISTRATA (*To* CHREMES): Now listen while I render you my
considered opinion:
There won't be a single reply, or pardon, or promise from me
To you until I consult with my son. I'm turning the whole case
Over to him for judgment, and his decision, whatever
It is, is final with me.

PHORMIO: Madam, your wisdom is peerless.

NAUSISTRATA (*To* CHREMES): Satisfied?

DEMIPHO: He is, he is.

CHREMES (*Aside*): I certainly am. Success
Beyond my wildest dreams.

NAUSISTRATA (*To* PHORMIO): You haven't told me your name.

PHORMIO: My name? It's Phormio, madam. Ever a faithful friend
To you and yours. Particular chum to your son Phaedria.

NAUSISTRATA: From this day forward, Phormio, I'll do my utmost
for you. 1050
Your will is my command to word or action.

PHORMIO: You are too kind.

NAUSISTRATA: It's only what you deserve.

PHORMIO: All right, I'll start today.
Here's an idea that will give me pleasure and do your husband
One in the eye.

NAUSISTRATA: I'd love it! What is it?

PHORMIO: Invite me to dinner.

NAUSISTRATA: Of course! I invite you to dinner.

PHORMIO: I accept. Let's go
inside.

NAUSISTRATA: But where can Phaedria be? We need him to judge
the case.

PHORMIO: I'll have him here in a minute.
(*To the audience* ⁷)

---

⁷ *To the audience:* The manuscripts assign the succeeding half-line to a per-
sonage designated by the Greek letter Omega. This is usually taken to mean the

To you, farewell.

Applause, please.

(*Exeunt omnes,* NAUSISTRATA, CHREMES, *and* DEMIPHO *into* CHREMES' *house,* PHORMIO *to the left, in search of* PHAEDRIA)

---

cantor, whose main function throughout the play, presumably, was to sing the lyric monologues while the appropriate actors mimed. But the extent of this worthy's employment by Terence is far from certain, as is the line assignment; and the monologues of this version are designed to be spoken, not sung. I have therefore dispensed with the *cantor* altogether and given the speech to Phormio.

THE BROTHERS

(*ADELPHOE*)

Translated by Constance Carrier

INTRODUCTION

All Terence's plays except *Her Husband's Mother* have double plots. That of *The Brothers* is less involved than the plots of *The Eunuch* and *Phormio* because there is more misunderstanding than intrigue at work. Both pairs of brothers in this play act out their misunderstandings, and the unexpected reversals at the end assume nearly Euclidean proportions as the final reconciliations and balance of positions are aligned against the initial oppositions and cross-purposes. The Roman audience seeing this play presented for the first time in 160 B.C. under the sanction of a younger Scipio, the adoptive grandson of the great Africanus, may well have applauded the young poet Terence (from Africa) for his skillful managing of the lines of action. At the play's end they may have felt, if not like shouting Bravo, at least like murmuring Q.E.D. Back home afterwards they may have said to themselves, "Like father, like son."

One of Terence's main preoccupations, a theme in all his writing, is: the generation gap, and why bridge it? He dramatizes the plight of his *adulescentes*. Once they achieve their immediate ends, of marriage, or attachment to the object of their affections, they are more or less doomed to maturity. The old men, *senes*, long since married or committed in some way, know all too well what the young men are letting themselves in for. But they can't always get the message across at the right time. It has to be spelled out in action.

So Terence plunges into the predicaments, combining pleasure and dismay, mix-up and fix-up, passion and reason, youth and age, comic confusion and tragic sobriety. Here there are two sets of brothers, both forming a supposedly contrasting pair. Old

Demea is married, auctoritarian, not very rich, strict (*durus*), but proud of what he believes to be his son Ctesipho's restrained behavior. His other son Aeschinus has been adopted by Demea's brother Micio, who is unmarried, permissive, rich, and ready to indulge Aeschinus' penchant for Pamphila (or any other girl). As the play opens Micio is a bit worried about Aeschinus' riotous behavior but still prepared to lecture Demea on the proper way to treat young people, tolerantly and with understanding. "You are his father by nature, I by my anxiety": *natura tu illi pater es, consiliis ego* (l. 126). Demea can hardly tolerate such talk from his rich brother, but Micio has taken Aeschinus off his hands and it is expensive to bring up two boys.

Unfortunately, Ctesipho, the model son of a *durus pater*, has fallen in love with a lute-girl. Aeschinus offers to help him by bodily abducting the girl from her owner, the slave-dealer Sannio, and thereby "by action of freedom," claim possession of her. He will buy her for Ctesipho. Syrus, Micio's slave, maneuvers Sannio into accepting ten instead of twenty *minae*.[1] What can Ctesipho do but sing a song of praise to his brother for so generous and chivalric a deed? Inevitably, though, when the abduction becomes public knowledge, misunderstandings crowd in, first on Sostrata, Pamphila's mother, who infers that she and Pamphila have been deceived as to Aeschinus' good intentions toward Pamphila. The nature of Aeschinus' relationship with Pamphila is made lamentably plain by the two offstage lines assigned her, cries in childbirth. Also, Aeschinus has kept the true nature of this attachment from Micio, his "father." Micio learns the facts from Hegio, the friend called in for counsel by Sostrata. Demea, meanwhile, has learned that Ctesipho, his model son, has also been involved in the lute-girl's seduction. He is sent off by Syrus on a spurious hunt through town in search of Micio and when he returns from his fruitless chase discovers Ctesipho carousing in Micio's house with his newly acquired possession. While Demea is on this walk, Aeschinus confronts Micio and confesses his plight. Micio handles this situation, equipped with prior knowledge, with such tact and understanding that Aeschinus can hardly believe his ears, marvels,

[1] I calculate the *mina* at the rate of $25. The girl's price is reduced from $500 to $250.

and says, "Is this being a father, or this being a son? If he had been a brother or close friend, how could he have been more agreeable?" *Hoc est patrem esse aut hoc filium esse? Si frater aut sodalis esset, qui magis morem gereret?* (ll. 707–708).

There ensues a second scene of confrontation between the older brothers, rather like a reprise of the opening of the play. In the second argument Demea seems to become somewhat reconciled to Micio's point of view and says he will let Ctesipho keep the lute-girl. But after Micio goes indoors, Demea soliloquizes on their contrasting attitudes and decides to show how over-indulgence works. He becomes the most generous and accommodating person in the cast, awarding everyone everything he wants; he even maneuvres Micio into marrying Sostrata, who is, after all, his son's wife's mother. Demea has the last word, virtually, with a short lecture to Micio on how fathers should treat their sons. Pamper them, you'll win their affection, but they'll get around you and misbehave. Reprove, restrain, and control them, they'll respect you. And while you may not be so popular with them as you might wish, they will conduct themselves well.

PALMER BOVIE

THE BROTHERS

First Performance: The funeral games in honor of Aemilius Paulus, under the auspices of Q. Fabius Maximus and P. Cornelius Africanus.[2]
Production: L. Ambivius Turpio and L. Hatilius of Praeneste.
Music: Scored for equal Tyrian flutes by Flaccus, freedman of Claudius.
Greek Original: Menander.
In the consulship of Gallus and Cethegus (160 B.C.).

CHARACTERS

DEMEA } old Athenians, brothers
MICIO

HEGIO, old Athenian, a relative of SOSTRATA
SOSTRATA, a widow, mother of PAMPHILA
AESCHINUS, son of DEMEA, adopted by MICIO
CTESIPHO, son of DEMEA, brother of AESCHINUS
SANNIO, a procurer, a slave-dealer in women
GETA, a slave, servant of SOSTRATA

SYRUS } slaves, servants of MICIO
DROMO

CANTHARA, old nurse in the household of SOSTRATA

[2] Adopted by the son of Scipio the Great, this man became known in history as Publius Cornelius Scipio Africanus Minor.

Mute Characters

*PAMPHILA,[3] a young woman loved by AESCHINUS
*BACCHIS,[4] a courtesan loved by CTESIPHO, a lute-girl
*PARMENO, a slave, servant of MICIO

SCENE: *Athens, in front of the house of Micio and Sostrata.*

PROLOGUE

Because his work's unjustly criticized
And this same play which we're about to act
Has been attacked by his competitors,
The author has decided he'll be witness
And you the judges in this case against him—
Whether his work deserves acclaim or scorn.
Diphilus'[5] comedy, *Those Linked in Death,*
(*Synapothnescontes*) is used by Plautus
For his *Commorientes,* done in Latin.
In the original Greek, there's a young man
Who in the first act carries off a girl
From a slave-monger. Plautus didn't use this,　　　　10
But our playwright translates it word for word
Into *The Brothers,* which you'll see today.
Whether this is a theft, you must decide,
Or whether the rescue of a long-lost scene.
As to what his ill-wishers say as well—
That he has had as his collaborators
Men of high standing, that they work with him—
Envy considers such a charge disgraceful,

---

[3] PAMPHILA is assigned two lines, offstage cries in childbirth (ll. 486–487).

[4] BACCHIS is the name of the lute-girl, referred to in the play only as *puella citharistria,* or a *psaltria.*

[5] A poet of the Greek New Comedy, contemporary with Menander.

* Denotes mute part.

But he himself looks on it as an honor
That he can please men whom the country praises,
Whom you admire, whose skill in carrying out
The management of war and peace you all   20
Have used unchallenged in your own affairs.

Do not expect a summary of the plot:
The old men who appear first will begin
To clarify the action, and the rest
Moves with the play. Keeping an open mind,
You'll give the poet further heart for writing.

ACT I

Scene 1

MICIO

MICIO: Storax! [6] . . . So Aeschinus has not come back
    From last night's dinner—he nor his escort-slaves.
    People are right who say if you're away
    Or late returning, better have happen to you
    Whatever your wife calls down, or what she is thinking,   30
    Angry as she may be, than what parents fear.
    If you're late, your wife is sure you've begun an affair,
    Or been caught up in one, or else are drinking and gaming—
    That tho' she can't do without you, you can do without her.
    When my son stays out, what horrors I can imagine,
    What trifles worry me!—that he has caught cold,
    Or fallen down somewhere and broken a bone.

    [6] MICIO calls back inside to a house servant.

Only a fool would take something into his heart
And set it up like an idol dearer than self—
This isn't even my own son; it's my brother's,   40
And the brother and I as different as night and day.
My life's been a good one: all the joys of the city,
No profession, no wife—how many envy me that!
He's at the opposite pole: he lives in the country,
He worships thrift and simplicity, has a wife
And a couple of sons. The elder boy I adopted
As a child, and look on him now as my own—indeed,
He's my pride and joy, the thing that I hold most dear.
I hope with all my heart I'm as dear to him.   50
I support him, don't often punish, try not to nag,
And as a result, while others are pulling the wool
Over their fathers' eyes, he's honest with me.
That's simply the way that I've managed to bring him up,
For a boy who's used to lying to his father,
Who dares to deceive him, will trick other men the more.
Keep a lad in check by teaching him what's honor,
What's character—that works much better than fear.
My brother doesn't agree; he keeps on coming
To me and crying, "What are you up to, Micio?   60
You're losing the boy for us—why? And why let him do
And drink as he likes? Why underwrite his expenses,
Why give him carte blanche at the tailor's? You're out of your
    mind!"
He can be harsh beyond belief and justice,
And to my mind he's wholly wrong in his thinking
That an authority based on force is stronger
Or longer-lasting than one that springs from friendship.
My reasoning is this: I'm quite persuaded
One who behaves from fear of punishment
Behaves while he's in danger of detection—   70
Or thinks he is; if not, he'll lapse from virtue.
You'll find him willing, if kindness binds him to you,
Eager to match you, ready to be trusted.
A father aims to train his son to choose
The right himself, and not be threats to others.

If he can't, he's not fit to be a father.
But isn't that the man I've been speaking of?
He seems a little gloomy; I can expect
The usual arguments. Welcome back, Demea!   80

Scene 2

MICIO, DEMEA

DEMEA: A lucky meeting; I've been looking for you.
MICIO: Why such a long face?
DEMEA: Why, with Aeschinus?
  You ask me why?
MICIO: I could have told you so.
  What has he done?
DEMEA: Done? Why, he has no shame
  And no respect—he's even beyond the law.
  I won't even mention his earlier escapades.
  And what has he done this time?
MICIO: What is it? Tell me.
DEMEA: Breaking and entering; beating up the owner,
  Family, slaves, almost to death; kidnapping   90
  A girl he's in love with. The whole town's in an uproar
  Over the story. Every man I meet
  Tells it—O! it's a crying scandal, Micio.
  Why, if he needs examples, can't he use
  His brother, living quietly in the country?
  Nothing like that for him. And when I shout
  At him, I shout at you—it's you who've ruined him.
MICIO: The most unjust are the unsophisticated;
  Nothing seems right to them but their own actions.
DEMEA: And the point of that remark?
MICIO: —Is that you're quite wrong
  No young man is breaking the law, believe me,   101
  When he's whoring or drunk—no, I swear he isn't, not even

When he's breaking down doors. If we never did these things
It was only that we were too poor; can you credit yourself
With a virtue you owed to poverty alone?
That's not honest: given the wherewithal
We'd have done it ourselves. And if you had any sense,
You'd turn a blind eye, forgive him because he's young,
And not make him wait till he's bundled your corpse to the
 grave,
To sow his wild oats at a far less suitable age.   110
DEMEA: Good god, you can drive a man to insanity!
Because the boy's young, you think this isn't a crime?
MICIO: Just listen, don't think that repeating delivers the punch.
You gave me your son for adoption; now he is mine,
Whatever offense he commits, Demea, I tell you
Is done against me; I bear the brunt of the business.
The cost of his elegant banquets, his liquor—I pay it;
My money, so long as I have any, goes for his girl;
Perhaps, when it's gone, he'll find her doors shut in his face.
The locks that he forced will be fixed; the clothes that he tore
A tailor can mend; there's money enough, thank God, 121
For such things still—I haven't been bankrupt yet.
Either give up or call in someone to judge—
I can show him, I think, that most of the fault is yours.
DEMEA: Learn fatherhood from those who are truly fathers!
MICIO: Your fatherhood came via nature, mine by design.
DEMEA: You talk of design?
MICIO: Go on like that and I'm leaving.
DEMEA: That's no way to treat me.
MICIO: I'm sick of hearing you talk.
DEMEA: But he's all I think of--
MICIO: And I. But Demea, look:
What we ought to do is share our worries, you taking 130
One boy, I the other. If you insist on both,
It's as if you wanted back the son that you gave me.
DEMEA: O no, no—
MICIO: I think so.
DEMEA: Well, if that's what you want—
Let him go to hell if he wants; it's not my doing.
If I hear one word of this later—

MICIO: More temper, Demea?

DEMEA: Do you doubt my word? Have I asked that you return
    him?

  I'm worried. I'm not uninvolved. If I argue—O well,

  You've left me one son to watch out for, and he is, thank
    heaven,

  All I could ask for. The other—well, he'll find out

  Some day—no, I don't want to be too harsh—(*Exit*)   140

MICIO: There's truth in what he says, but not the whole truth.

  I don't say I'm not upset; I'd certainly rather

  He didn't know how much. The way to calm him

  Is to resist him, face him down, alarm him,

  However furious he gets. If I fed the flames

  Or even seemed to him to share his anger,

  I'd be crazy as he is. Still, Aeschinus

  Can't be let off; no question that he's disgraced me.

  He's fallen in love with a dozen prostitutes   150

  And paid them well, then, tired of them all,

  Claimed he was all for settling down to marriage.

  That made me hopeful that his blood was cooling;

  Fine, I thought, fine!—Till it all began again.

  I need the facts. Let me look for him in the forum.

ACT II

Scene 1

SANNIO, AESCHINUS

SANNIO: Help, help! I'm innocent, I'm being cheated—
  Help me!

AESCHINUS (*To the girl*):

        Be calm; stand right there for a minute.

What are you looking back for? There's no danger:
With me here he won't touch you.
SANNIO: I don't care who—
AESCHINUS: He's not going to run the risk of another beating.
SANNIO: Aeschinus, you know you knew what I am: 160
A dealer in slaves—
AESCHINUS: I know.
SANNIO: —but an honest man.
And your "I didn't mean any harm," your apologies—
I'm not having any of those. I'll take you to court
Where you'll pay for your insults, and pay with more than
words.
I can hear you: "Sorry about that; on my oath
You didn't deserve any wrong"—when I've just been man-
handled.
AESCHINUS (*To* PARMENO): Go on, hurry up, open the doors.
SANNIO: Are
you deaf?
AESCHINUS (*To the girl*): Get in with you now.
SANNIO: I won't let
her—
AESCHINUS: Parmeno, stand near him—
You're too far away; get closer. Ah, that's what I want.
Now don't take your eyes from my face for so much as a second.
The minute I nod to you, give him your fist in his face   171
SANNIO: Let him try it—
AESCHINUS: Watch out—take your hands off the girl—
SANNIO: Dirty pool!
AESCHINUS: He can double it if you're not careful.
SANNIO: Ow! Ow!
AESCHINUS: That came without signal—Parmeno, a very wise error.
Go in, girl.
SANNIO: What are you, Aeschinus? the dictator here?
AESCHINUS: If I were, you'd be wearing the emblems your virtues
deserve.
SANNIO: What's our tie-up?
AESCHINUS: There is none.

SANNIO: You know what I
am?

AESCHINUS: I don't care to.

SANNIO: Have I laid hands on something of yours?

AESCHINUS: If you have
you'll regret it.

SANNIO: Then what gives you the right to make off with a girl that
I bought?
Tell me that.

AESCHINUS: You'll do well to stop shouting in front of this
house. 180
If you don't, you are likely to find yourself dragged off inside
And whipped till you're bloody.

SANNIO: A free man whipped?

AESCHINUS: That's
what I said.

SANNIO: You devil!—and this is the city where free men are equal?

AESCHINUS: Slaver, listen to me, if you've come to the end of your
ranting.

SANNIO: Who's doing the ranting?

AESCHINUS: Forget it and come to the point.

SANNIO: What point?

AESCHINUS: Do you want me to tell you your business
myself?

SANNIO: Why not? A fair deal, though.

AESCHINUS: Fair deals with a dealer in
slaves?

SANNIO: Okay, I'm a pander, then, dangerous to the young,
Lying, perverting, all that—but I've done you no harm.

AESCHINUS: That's still in the future, no doubt.

SANNIO: Let's start this
again. 190

AESCHINUS: The devil take the money you bought her with—
I'll pay you for her.

SANNIO: Supposing she's not for sale?
You'd force me?

AESCHINUS: No.

SANNIO: I was afraid you might.

AESCHINUS: She shouldn't be sold, she's free—I so declare her.
    You have your choice: the cash, or a case to plead.
    Till I come back, then, pimp, think it over.
SANNIO: Good God!
    No wonder people go crazy from things like this.
    He breaks in, beats me up, makes off with the girl,
    And leaves me bloody and sore in fifty places.
    In return, he'll buy the girl at the price I paid.   200
    Well, if he's that generous, let him; he's got his rights.
    I want whatever he'll give—but I talk like a fool:
    If I agree to his offer, some witness will prove
    That I sold her, the cash goes in smoke, and it's "come back
      tomorrow."
    I could even stand that if he'd pay, though it makes me see red.
    But I can face up to the truth; when you start in my line,
    You've got to expect such insults and learn to take them.
    In this case nobody pays, so the talk's all useless.

Scene 2

SYRUS, SANNIO

SYRUS: Say no more, sir; I'll find him and make him see light
    And admit it's all fair. Why, Sannio, what's this about?   210
    You've been on the mat with my master?
SANNIO: The phoniest match
    That I ever saw, or you either—that's what we had.
    He's as worn out with giving the knockout as I am with taking.
SYRUS: *Your* fault.
SANNIO: What should I have done?
SYRUS: Let him have his
    way.
SANNIO: Who better? I let him smash my teeth.
SYRUS: What I think is
    Sometimes it's wise not to seem too hot for the cash.

Now you were afraid if you gave up some of your rights,
If you played along—O you fool!—you wouldn't be getting every-
thing back with interest.
SANNIO: I buy sure things.   219
SYRUS: You'll never get rich, you won't; you don't know the tricks.
SANNIO: Like you do, of course—I've never been smart enough
To wait for the bird in the bush when there's one in the hand.
SYRUS: Come on, I know you. What's a couple of thousand
To do him a favor? Besides, aren't you off to Cyprus?
SANNIO (*Aside*): O damn—
SYRUS: —and so much to take that you've hired
a boat.
Hard to decide? Well, settle when you come back.
SANNIO: I won't budge an inch. (*Aside*) It's this that started it all.
SYRUS (*Aside*): He's scared, with that bee in his bonnet.
SANNIO (*Aside*):   The devil!
Now look,
He hits where it hurts. The women and all that I bought
Have got to be sent off to Cyprus, and no time to lose—   230
If I get to the market too late, they won't leave me my shirt.
If I let this thing go and begin it again when I'm back—
No good; it'll be stone-cold. They'll say, "*Now* you come?
Why did you wait? Where were you?" I might as well
Give up my case as stay here or go to court late.
SYRUS: Well, have you figured out what's coming your way?
SANNIO: Does a gentleman act like this? Did Aeschinus plot
A surprise attack from the first, to get the girl?
SYRUS (*Aside*): He's on the skids. (*Aloud*) Just this: see if it's
okay.
Rather than take the chance of losing it all,   240
Save yourself such a blow; be happy with half.
Somewhere or other he can scrape that much up.
SANNIO: Am I running the risk, God help me, of losing, then?
Hasn't he any shame? He's shaken my teeth loose,
My head is sore all over from his punching,
And he's going to cheat me as well? I stay here.
SYRUS: As you choose.
Anything else before I leave?

SANNIO: Wait, Syrus—
  No matter how I've been treated, rather than sue,
  Let me get back what she cost me first, anyway.
  Up till now I know we've never been friends,   250
  But you're going to find that I don't forget a favor.
SYRUS: I'll make it my business—but here's the brother, excited
  About his girl.
SANNIO: And what we were speaking of—?
SYRUS: Shortly.

Scene 3

CTESIPHO, SANNIO, SYRUS

CTESIPHO: A good turn done by anyone is welcome
  In a tight spot, but best when the right man does it.
  How can I praise a brother like you? I'm certain
  There are no words to do you adequate justice.
  In this one thing I'm the luckiest man in the world—
  Who else has a brother with every possible virtue?   259
SYRUS: Hello, sir.
CTESIPHO: O, where's Aeschinus?
SYRUS: At home, and waiting.
CTESIPHO: Wonderful!
SYRUS: Sir?
CTESIPHO: Through him I'm still alive.
  He puts my interests above his own,
  Takes the blame for my foul-mouthed trouble-making—
  Who could do more? Who's coming out?
SYRUS: Your brother.

Scene 4

AESCHINUS, CTESIPHO, SYRUS, SANNIO

AESCHINUS: Where is that God-forsaken—
SYRUS: It's me he's after.
  Is he holding anything? I can't make out.
AESCHINUS: Ctesipho! I've been looking for you. How goes it?
  Everything's settled; let's have no more of that gloom.
CTESIPHO: No more of it, not with you for my true blood-brother.
  Aeschinus, if I praised you as you deserve   271
  And to your face, you'd think it was flattery.
AESCHINUS: Come, don't be foolish; by now we know each other—
  I'm only sorry we found out almost too late
  For anybody, no matter how willing, to help.
CTESIPHO: I was ashamed.
AESCHINUS: Not ashamed, only simple-minded—
  To banish yourself for a trifle like that? Absurd!
  God forbid—
CTESIPHO: I was wrong.
AESCHINUS: What does Sannio say?
SYRUS: He's calmed
  down.
AESCHINUS: I'm off to the market to pay him. Go find your girl,
  brother.
SANNIO (*Aside*): Urge him!
SYRUS: Come on; any minute he's leaving for
  Cyprus.
SANNIO: There's not all that rush; I can stay and I will—
SYRUS: O, he'll pay
  you.
SANNIO: In full?   280
SYRUS: Yes, in full; keep quiet now, follow him.
SANNIO: Right.
CTESIPHO: Hi, Syrus!

SYRUS: What?
CTESIPHO: Pay off that creature, for heaven's sake
  —let him
  Lose his temper again and my father hear of it, I'm ruined.
SYRUS: O no sir; cheer up and enjoy yourself with the lady.
  Have them set the table and get things ready for dinner.
  When I've finished my errand I'll come home with the food.
CTESIPHO: That's fine. Things have gone so well we must celebrate.

ACT III

Scene 1

SOSTRATA, CANTHARA

SOSTRATA: Nurse, tell me, how are things going?
CANTHARA: Now, now, don't
    worry;
  Everything's fine. Your pains, poor child, are beginning.
  (*To* SOSTRATA): I swear you're as nervous as though you'd never
    seen
  A birth before this, or borne a child yourself.   290
SOSTRATA: O dear, we're alone, I've no one, not even Geta,
  To send for the midwife, or to go for Aeschinus—
CANTHARA: Don't worry; he'll be here. Never a day goes by
  But he comes.
SOSTRATA: He's my only comfort in all my troubles.
CANTHARA: All things considered, ma'am, things could be much
    worse.
  She's been seduced, but think what the young man's like:
  Good heart, fine character, well-known family—
SOSTRATA: You're perfectly right; I pray the gods let us keep him.

Scene 2

GETA, SOSTRATA, CANTHARA

GETA: The way things are, no matter what anyone does,
　　However they try to help, there isn't a thing   300
　　Will save my mistress or her daughter or me.
　　It's as though a wall was around us we can't break through—
　　Violence, poverty, loneliness, disgrace.
　　What a world full of wrongs and wrongdoers, and he most of
　　　all!
SOSTRATA (*Aside*): Great heavens, why is he rushing so fearfully?
GETA: Nothing of honor, of promise, of pity, has held him back
　　Or changed his course, though her time is near, poor lady
　　That he's treated so badly.
SOSTRATA (*Aside*):　　　　　I can't make out a word
　　He's saying.
CANTHARA:　　Let's go a bit closer, ma'am.
GETA: I'm burning with anger, almost out of my mind—   310
　　There's nothing I'd like better than to have
　　That crew where I could pour out my fury on them
　　While it's still fresh. I'd kill the old man first,
　　That devil's father. Syrus, who led him on—
　　God be my witness, how I'd mangle him!—
　　Catch him around the waist, lift him up, then drop him
　　Head down to split his skull and let his brains
　　And blood spatter the pavement. And the young man—
　　I'd tear his eyes out, throw him over a cliff.
　　Why put off telling this horror to my mistress?   320
SOSTRATA: Call him back! Geta!
GETA:　　　　　　　　　Whoever you are, don't stop me.
SOSTRATA: I'm Sostrata.
GETA:　　　　　　Where are you? It's you I've been seeking,
　　Waiting for. Lucky we met each other. But ma'am—

SOSTRATA: What is it? Why are you shaking?

GETA: O—

SOSTRATA: Why such a
    hurry?
  Catch your breath.

GETA: We are wholly

SOSTRATA: Wholly—

GETA: Done for.
  It's over.

SOSTRATA: Speak out, explain.

GETA: Now—

SOSTRATA: Now what, Geta?

GETA: Aeschinus—

SOSTRATA: What about him?

GETA: He's broken all ties.

SOSTRATA: God help us! You're sure?

GETA: He's fallen in love with some
  woman.

SOSTRATA: O no!

GETA: Doesn't hide it; has kidnapped her now from the slaver,
  Bold as brass.

SOSTRATA: You know this?

GETA: Sostrata, I saw it myself.

SOSTRATA: O misery—who's to be trusted? what can I believe?   330
  Our Aeschinus, dearer than life, our hope and our future,
  Who swore that he couldn't face life, not a day more, without
    her!
  That he'd put the child in his father's arms, and in that way
  Beg him, persuade him, to let him marry our girl!

GETA: Don't cry, ma'am. Better plan what to do: should we
  Just take it, or tell someone?

SOSTRATA: Why, man, are you mad?
  You think this ought to be told anywhere?

GETA: No, I don't.
  First off, what he's done shows how little he cares for us.
  If we make it public, he'll only deny it all;
  There'll be a blot on your name and your daughter's future.   340
  And even if he confessed, you would hardly let her

Marry a man who's announced that he loves another.
We had better say nothing.
SOSTRATA: Not for all the world.
   I shan't!
GETA: What then?
SOSTRATA: I'll tell.
GETA: Ma'am, think what you're doing.
SOSTRATA: What can be worse than things the way they are?
   She has no dowry; even the next best thing
   Is lost—she can't be given as a virgin.
   Then what? If he denies it, I'll show this ring.
   He lost it; I shall make it my witness now.
   Since in all conscience I haven't been involved
   In this affair, have given no bribes, done nothing wrong,
   Nothing to shame her or myself—I'll go to court.   350
GETA: What's left to say? Your argument's convinced me.
SOSTRATA: Run then, and tell the facts to Hegio,
   My husband's kin and friend. He loved us all.
GETA: Did he, indeed? Well, no one loves us now.
SOSTRATA: See that the midwife is on call, Canthara;
   Then when she's needed, there'll be no delay.

Scene 3

DEMEA, SYRUS

DEMEA: Confound it—now I hear that Ctesipho
   Is as involved in this as Aeschinus.
   My luck's gone if so promising a lad
   Can be led into evil by his brother.
   Where shall I find him? In some filthy bar,
   No doubt—Aeschinus will have shown the way, I'm sure.   360
   O, here comes Syrus: he will give me news—
   Yet he's one of that crew. If he finds out

I'm looking for him, he won't talk, the bastard.
I shan't say what I want.
SYRUS: I've just described
The whole thing to the old man, just as it happened.
Nobody ever was more pleased.
DEMEA (*Aside*):   God, what a fool!
SYRUS: He praised his son, said I'd advised him wisely—
DEMEA (*Aside*): I could explode!
SYRUS: —And counted out the money.
He even gave me extra for expenses.   370
(I've made good use of that already.)
DEMEA (*Aside*):   Ah, see?
Give him an order and the thing's done right.
SYRUS: O sir, I hadn't seen you. What's the trouble?
DEMEA: Trouble? I marvel at your goings-on.
SYRUS: They're pretty silly, yes; to put it frankly,
Downright ridiculous. Dromo, clean these fish—
Not the big eel, though; he can enjoy the water
A bit till I come back; then he'll be boned.
Not now.
DEMEA: Disgraceful!
SYRUS: I don't like it either,
And I make it known. Stephanio, be careful
To soak these salt fish well.
DEMEA: Great God in heaven,   380
Is he doing this with a purpose? Does he want praise
For driving the boy to ruin? Trouble, trouble!
I see that a day will come when he hasn't a penny
And runs away to enlist.
SYRUS: Demea, that's wisdom,
If I may say so, sir—not only to see
What's under your nose but what's in the future, too.
DEMEA: Look here, is that lute-playing girl at your place still?
SYRUS: That she is.
DEMEA: Will he keep her there?
SYRUS: I suppose so:
He's crazy enough.
DEMEA: Incredible!   390

SYRUS: It's his father—
Wrongheaded, easy-going, indulgent—
DEMEA: I tell you,
I'm sick of my brother.
SYRUS: O sir, the difference
Between you (and I don't say this just to your face)!
Every inch of you is solid wisdom;
He's a fool. You wouldn't have let your son
Act so.
DEMEA: Let him? I'd have been on his trail
Six months before he'd even so much as got involved!
SYRUS: No need to tell *me* of your clear-sightedness.
DEMEA: If he'll stay as he is—
SYRUS: You each find your son as you want
him.
DEMEA: Have you seen mine today? 400
SYRUS: Your son, sir? (I'll drive the
old man.
To the country.) I think he's been working out at the farm.
DEMEA: You're sure about this?
SYRUS: I went with him, sir.
DEMEA: Very well.
I was worried that he might stay here.
SYRUS: And O what a temper!
DEMEA: Over what?
SYRUS: He swore at his brother right there in the
market
About the lute-girl.
DEMEA: You mean it?
SYRUS: He gave him the works.
The money was being counted when who should arrive
But our hero. "Aeschinus!" he shouted. "To think
That you would commit such a crime, that you would degrade
Our family so!"
DEMEA: O Syrus, I weep for joy!
SYRUS: "It isn't money you're wasting; it's your life." 410
DEMEA: Bless him, he's worthy of all his forebears.
SYRUS: Yes.

DEMEA: He's learned their precepts well.

SYRUS: I'm not surprised:
He had his teacher right at home.

DEMEA: I work
At it, I never miss a chance, I train him
To look into men's lives as if into
A mirror, and to take example from them.
"Do this," I say—

SYRUS: How wise!

DEMEA: "Not that."

SYRUS: How clever!

DEMEA: "Well done," for this—

SYRUS: Great!

DEMEA: "Shame on you!" for that.

SYRUS: A perfect system.

DEMEA: Furthermore—

SYRUS: I'm sorry,
Sir, but I've no more time. I found some fish,   420
Fresh-caught, and I must have them see that they're cooked
    just right.
It's quite as wrong for servants as for you, sir,
Not to do what you've just said, and I try
To train the other slaves by the same rule:
"This is too salty—overdone—not clean.
That's just right. Mind you do it so next time."
I give the best advice I'm able to:
Tell them to look into each dish as if
Into a mirror, and show them what to do.
People may think these acts of ours are silly,   430
But never mind. Give each man what he wants.
What's your wish, sir?

DEMEA: A better brain for you.

SYRUS: You're leaving for the country?

DEMEA: Yes.

SYRUS: No good
To stay in town where no one hears your teaching.

DEMEA: The country—yes, I'm leaving; that's where he is,
The boy who's both my own and my concern.

Let Micio, if he will, see to the other.
But who's that in the distance? Is it Hegio,
My old compatriot? Can I trust my eyes?
It is! My friend from boyhood—why, God bless him, 440
The state has few to equal him these days
In good old-fashioned faithfulness and courage.
This land will never suffer harm from him.
I'm glad to see him, as I'm always glad
To find there's some trace left of that old breed.
I'll stop to greet him and to talk a bit.

Scene 4

HEGIO, DEMEA, GETA, (PAMPHILA)

HEGIO: By Jove, a nasty business this is, Geta;
  You're sure it's true?
GETA: Quite true, sir.
HEGIO: Such an act
  To come from such a family! Aeschinus,
  I swear you're not your father's son! 450
DEMEA: He's heard, then,
  About the girl, and though we're not his kin,
  He's far more shocked than Micio ever was.
  If only he'd been here and overheard!
HEGIO: Unless they mend their ways, they'll suffer for it.
GETA: Hegio, you're our one and only hope:
  You must be her defender now, her father.
  The old man, when he died, made you our guardian.
  If you leave us, we're lost.
HEGIO: Don't even suggest it:
  Of course I will not break my faith with him.
DEMEA: I'll speak to him. Hegio, I hope you're well. 460
HEGIO: O, I've been looking for you. How do you do?
DEMEA: Looking for me?

HEGIO: Yes, Aeschinus, your son,
  Whom you allowed your brother to adopt,
  Has proved himself a ruffian and a cad.
DEMEA: In what way?
HEGIO: Simulus, our long-time friend—
  You knew him?
DEMEA: Yes, of course.
HEGIO: Your son has raped
  His daughter.
DEMEA: Heaven forbid!
HEGIO: There's worse to come.
DEMEA: What can you say that could be worse than that?
HEGIO: Plenty. We might have found excuses for him—
  Darkness, and passion, a young man's hot blood: 470
  That's human nature. When he knew, he came
  To the girl's mother, freely, wept with shame,
  Begged for their pardon, swore he'd marry her.
  He was forgiven, everything hushed up,
  His word believed. The girl's long overdue,
  And he, this worthy gentleman, has taken
  A lute-player to share his house—the other,
  May the gods punish him, he has deserted.
DEMEA: All this is true past doubt?
HEGIO: The girl's own mother
  Is here, the girl (she's proof enough), and Geta,
  A good slave as slaves go; hardworking, too.   480
  He, no one else, has been their sole support.
  Seize him and chain him up, to get the truth.
GETA: Torture me if it isn't true, Demea.
  He won't deny it; question him while I'm here.
DEMEA: I'm overwhelmed; what can I do or say?
PAMPHILA (*From within*): O, I can't bear the pain! Juno Lucina,
  Who helps in childbirth, help me now, I pray!
HEGIO: She is in labor?
GETA: Yes, indeed, sir.
HEGIO: Listen:
  She begs that you redeem your family's honor
  And do of your free will what law requires.   490

I pray to heaven you'll do things properly.
If you do not, I swear I'll stop at nothing
To guard her name and that of her dead father.
We were kin, he and I, and friends from childhood;
We shared our lives in war and peace; we weathered
The bitterness of lean years, side by side.
I'll work for this cause, struggle, go to court—
I'd give up life sooner than give them up.
What do you say, then?
DEMEA: I will see my brother.
HEGIO: Be sure that you consider this, Demea: 500
The better you live, and he—the greater you are
In power and rank and influence and wealth—
So much the more, then, should you recognize
Justice, if you would be considered just.
DEMEA: You need not wait. What must be done will be.
HEGIO: That's like you. Geta, take me to Sostrata.
DEMEA: This happens as I said it would. If only
It were all over! Too much freedom leads
Sooner or later to catastrophe.
I'll go find Micia and pour out the story.   510

Scene 5

HEGIO

HEGIO: Courage, Sostrata; do whatever you can
To comfort her. I'll look for Micio
In town and tell him what's been going on—
If he is ready to do his duty, let him;
If he has different views, why, let him tell me
So that I'll know at once how to proceed.

ACT IV

Scene 1

CTESIPHO, SYRUS

CTESIPHO: My father's gone from town?
SYRUS: Long since.
CTESIPHO: Please tell
   me—
SYRUS: He's at the farm and hard at work, no doubt—
CTESIPHO: I hope he is. I wish he were, not ill
   But so worn out he'd spend three days in bed.   520
SYRUS: I'd like that too, or anything that's better.
CTESIPHO: I want this day to end the way it started.
   The trouble with the farm is, it's nearby;
   He couldn't get back, otherwise, by nightfall.
   Seeing I'm not there, he'll return, I know it,
   Asking me where I've been—"You're gone all day!"—
   What shall I say?
SYRUS: No notion?
CTESIPHO: None.
SYRUS: You're hopeless.
   Look, you've got friends, dependents, sometime-guests?
CTESIPHO: Yes, but—
SYRUS: Say you were with them.
CTESIPHO: When I wasn't?
   I can't.   530
SYRUS: You can.
CTESIPHO: For daytime. Suppose I spend the night?
SYRUS: Too bad: no nightly business—deals with friends.

O well, relax; I know his way of thinking;
  I'll turn that raging bull into a lamb.
CTESIPHO: How?
SYRUS: He loves to hear you praised; I'll call you god
  And list your virtues.
CTESIPHO: Mine?
SYRUS: He'll weep for joy.
  Look there!
CTESIPHO: What is it?
SYRUS: The wolf in the fairy-tale.
CTESIPHO: My father?
SYRUS: Yes.
CTESIPHO: What—
SYRUS: Go inside. I'll manage.
CTESIPHO: You haven't seen me, hear?
SYRUS: Go in—keep still!

Scene 2

DEMEA, CTESIPHO, SYRUS

DEMEA: No luck at all, and no sign of my brother.   540
  Looking for him, I found one of my farm boys
  Who says my son's not at the farm. What next?
CTESIPHO (*To* SYRUS): Psst!
SYRUS: What?
CTESIPHO: He's after me?
SYRUS: Yes.
CTESIPHO: Lord!
SYRUS: Chin up;
DEMEA: What's this bad luck? I can't make out,
  Unless my birthright is to face misfortune.
  I'm first to sense our woes, first to define them,
  First to warn others—and what's done I'm blamed for.
SYRUS (*Aside*): Him first? A joke. He'll be the last to find out.

DEMEA: I'm back to see if Micio's returned.

CTESIPHO: Syrus, for heaven's sake don't let him in!   550

SYRUS: I'll work it. Quiet.

CTESIPHO: I've lost faith in you.
    I'll lock the girl up with me in some room—
    That's safe.

SYRUS: I'll get him out.

DEMEA: There's that wretch Syrus.

SYRUS: Who can stand living here unless things change?
    How many masters have I got? and troubles?

DEMEA: What's that he's mumbling? Is my brother at home,
    My good man?

SYRUS: "Good"? As good as dead.

DEMEA: What's up now?

SYRUS: Only that Ctesipho's given me a beating,
    And the lute-girl too.

DEMEA: What?

SYRUS: See? He cut my lip.

DEMEA: But why?

SYRUS: He says I made him buy her.   560

DEMEA: *You* said
    You'd gone to the country with him.

SYRUS: He came back crazy,
    Stark mad, no shame at beating an old man
    Who'd carried him around when he was a baby.

DEMEA: Ctesipho, good for you; you're your father's son.

SYRUS: Good for him? He should keep his fists to himself—

DEMEA: A fine job—

SYRUS: Beating a girl and a slave like me
    Who can't hit back: that's a fine job, you think?

DEMEA: None better. Like me, he sees you've caused it all.
    Is my brother there?

SYRUS: No.

DEMEA: I wish I knew where he is.

SYRUS: I know, but I'm not telling.   570

DEMEA: What's that?

SYRUS: That's it.

DEMEA: I'll break your head—

SYRUS: I know the place where he is
    But not the name of the man.
DEMEA: Well, tell me the place.
SYRUS: You know the colonnade by the butcher's?
DEMEA: Yes.
SYRUS: Go past that up the street until you find
    The hill in front of you; go down that; then
    There's a chapel on this side, and next to it an alley.
DEMEA: Which side of the street?
SYRUS: The one with the big wild fig
    tree.
DEMEA: I know.
SYRUS: Go down there.
DEMEA: That's dead-end.
SYRUS: You're right;
    I sound like a fool. Let's start this over again.
    There's a quicker way, and one where you won't get lost.   580
    You know where the millionaire Cratinus lives?
DEMEA: Yes.
SYRUS: Go past, turn left, then straight; at Diana's chapel
    Go right, near the pool, to a workshop next to the gate,
    Across from a mill. He's there.
DEMEA: But what is he doing?
SYRUS: He's ordered some seats with oak legs, for the garden.
DEMEA: For your drinking-parties? I must hurry to him. (*Exit*)
SYRUS: It's a workout for you, you gravestone [7]—be on your way.
    That Aeschinus is late, and dinner is spoiling,
    And Ctesipho's in love. I'll look out for myself—
    Go in and pick the tidbits for my plate,   590
    And spend the rest of the day in quiet drinking.

    [7] Literally *silicernium*, "dry bones" or "funeral feast," that is, fit only to die.
The term derives from *silex*, stone, applied to an old man's stooping posture: "he
looks at the stones," *silices cernit*.

Scene 3

MICIO: But Hegio, I don't deserve this praise;
 I must make amends for what was our offense,
 Unless you count me a man who feels insulted
 When people protest a wrong that he has done,
 And so insults them. Don't thank me that I do not.
HEGIO: No, no! I wouldn't want you changed at all.
 But when I see the girl's mother, come along,
 And tell her the things that you've already told me:
 That what she suspects is really Ctesipho's doing. 600
MICIO: If that's the course we should follow, let's go.
HEGIO: Very well.
 We can ease her mind—poor thing, she's wasted away
 With worry—and settle your conscience. If you choose,
 I'll tell her what you've said.
MICIO: No, no.
HEGIO: All right, then.
 A run of bad luck makes us all more likely
 To look for insult where there's none intended,
 To feel we're being mocked because we're poor.
 Apologize in person; that's most calming.
MICIO: Those are true words.
HEGIO: Come inside.
MICIO: That I shall.

Scene 4

AESCHINUS

AESCHINUS: It's agony to have such problems thrust   610
    Upon me without warning—What shall I do,
    How shall I deal with them? I'm shaking, shaking,
    With fear; my mind won't function; I'm too chilled
    To work up even the outline of a plan.
    What can I say? It seems they all suspect me,
    And rightly, from the evidence. Sostrata
    Thinks, the old woman says, I bought the lute-girl
    (When she went for the midwife, I rushed up
    To ask if Pamphila was near her time,
    If the midwife was on call. "Go away," she cried.   620
    "You're free with words, but we've no faith in you now."
    "Explain!" I begged, but she only said, "Goodbye—
    And now that you've got the girl you want, why, keep her!")
    What they felt was clear, and yet I held myself back:
    She'd spread the story if I named my brother.
    What then? Say the girl is his? It all must be
    Kept secret. I'll do my part—it may not get out.
    If it did, no one would believe it; too strong a case.
    I kidnapped her and I paid; she's at my house.
    O, I admit it all! If I'd only told my father   630
    What I had done, he might have let me marry.
    Well, I'm only wasting my time. Come on, wake up;
    Straighten things out with the women. There's the door—
    O Lord, I break out in cold sweat when I knock!
    Hello—it's Aeschinus. Please open the door—
    Wait: Who's coming? I'll hide.

Scene 5

MICIO, AESCHINUS

MICIO: Sostrata, you both
  Must do as I say; I'll tell Aeschinus what's settled.
  Who knocked at the door?
AESCHINUS (*Aside*):   My father. O Lord!
MICIO: Aeschinus!
AESCHINUS (*Aside*): What is all this?
MICIO: You were knocking? (*Aside*)
    No answer.
  I'll rib him a little, I think, as he deserves—
  A sort of reward for not confiding in me.   640
  (*To* AESCHINUS) Come, tell me, son.
AESCHINUS: Not at that door, as far as
    I know.
MICIO: So, I wondered what brought you here. (*Aside*) He's
    blushing.
  This will work out.
AESCHINUS: But father, I want to know
  What business you have in these parts.
MICIO: None, really.
  A friend has brought me up from town just now
  To act as witness.
AESCHINUS: Witness?
MICIO: Well, I'll tell you:
  Two ladies live here, neither one well off—
  Nobody you would know, I'm sure of that:
  They've come here recently.
AESCHINUS: Yes sir; go on.
MICIO: A girl and her mother—
AESCHINUS: Oh?
MICIO: The father's dead;   650

My friend is next of kin, and so, by law,
Must marry the girl.
AESCHINUS: My God, no!
MICIO: What's the matter?
AESCHINUS: It's all right; never mind.
MICIO: He's come to take her
Back to Miletus.
AESCHINUS: He's going to carry her off?
MICIO: Yes.
AESCHINUS: To Miletus?
MICIO: Why not?
AESCHINUS (*Aside*):   This is awful.
    What does she say, or her mother?
MICIO: Not a word,
    Though the mother tells some story that her daughter
    Had a child by someone else; she won't say who.   659
    But she thinks, because of him, my friend shouldn't wed her.
AESCHINUS: And you—good heavens, you surely think she's right?
MICIO: I don't.
AESCHINUS: But why? And will he take her away?
MICIO: Is there any reason why not?
AESCHINUS: I can only feel
    You have acted with neither pity nor kindness, father—
    Not—though I may sound harsh—like a gentleman.
MICIO: In what way, tell me?
AESCHINUS: You ask? How will he feel,
    The man who fell in love with her first and may
    Be still in love with her, for all we know,
    To stand there, helpless, while she's snatched away
    And carried off? Why father, it's criminal!   669
MICIO: Explain to me who promised, who gave her in marriage,
    Who married her? When? And who was her guardian?
    And why did her fiancé wed somebody else?
AESCHINUS: Should a girl—a woman—sit at home and wait
    Till some distant relative shall end her waiting?
    Why didn't you bring that up, and argue it too?
MICIO: You're silly to think I'd argue against the cause
    Of a man I was witness for. But all these things—

They've nothing to do with us. Come, what's the matter?
You're weeping?

AESCHINUS: Father, listen—

MICIO: My son, I've listened;   680
I know; for I love you; your woes are mine.

AESCHINUS: Just as I want to deserve that love forever,
So I'm ashamed to have committed this act—
Deadly ashamed.

MICIO: I know your sense of honor,
But in this business you've been woefully careless.
What land, indeed, do you think you're living in?
Seducing her, you've broken one of its laws:
Your first sin, great, but still a natural one
That good men have committed. But afterwards
Did you consider your sin, or choose a course
And a way to carry it out? How could I learn   690
What shame kept silent till ten months had passed?
You've wronged yourself as well as her and the child;
Or were the gods to right things while you slept?
To waft her to a bridal-chamber here
By magic? Must you be so feckless always?
Cheer up. You'll wed her.

AESCHINUS: I?

MICIO: I said "Cheer up."

AESCHINUS: It's not a joke?

MICIO: Why should I joke?

AESCHINUS: Who knows?
I want this so much—I don't dare believe it.

MICIO: Go back and pray that you may bring her home.   700

AESCHINUS: Bring home my wife?

MICIO: Now.

AESCHINUS: Now?

MICIO: Quick as you can.

AESCHINUS: Damn it, if I don't love you more than life—

MICIO: More than her?

AESCHINUS: Equally.

MICIO: Thanks.

AESCHINUS: O—your friend:
    Where's he?
MICIO: Gone, vanished, sailed. Get on your way!
AESCHINUS: *You* go: the gods hear you; you are far better
    Than I; your prayers are likelier to succeed.
MICIO: I'll go inside and start the preparation;
    If you are wise, you'll do as I have said.
AESCHINUS: So this is being a father, being a son?
    Who could do more? No friend, not even a brother.
    Who wouldn't love him, hold him in his heart?
    That generosity leaves me afraid   710
    I may, without intending to, displease him.
    I must watch out. But now I'll go inside
    For fear I find that I've delayed my wedding.

Scene 6

DEMEA

DEMEA: I ache from walking. Damn that slave's directions!
    I've trudged the town—all over, to the gate,
    The lake—and no shop, and nobody able
    To say he'd seen my brother. What I'll do
    Is sit down here and wait for his return.

Scene 7

MICIO, DEMEA

MICIO: I'll go and tell them that we won't delay.
DEMEA: Why, there he is! I've looked for you for hours.   720
MICIO: You have?

DEMEA: To bring you word of other crimes
   Of your young paragon.
MICIO: Indeed?
DEMEA: Yes, crimes.
MICIO: Absurd.
DEMEA: O, you've misjudged him.
MICIO: I have not.
DEMEA: You think I'm speaking of the lute-girl. Well,
   It's an Athenian, free-born—
MICIO: I know.
DEMEA: You know it and forgive him?
MICIO: Why not?
DEMEA: Tell me:
   Doesn't it drive you crazy?
MICIO: No; I'd rather—
DEMEA: The child's been born.
MICIO: Fine!
DEMEA: She is penniless—
MICIO: I've heard.
DEMEA: —But must be married, even so
MICIO: Of course.
DEMEA: What, then?   730
MICIO: Whatever suggests itself.
   She'll have to be brought over here.
DEMEA: Good Lord,
   You think so?
MICIO: There's no more that I can do.
DEMEA: No more? Look: if you're really not upset,
   At least be man enough to seem that way.
MICIO: I've given him the girl; the wedding's set;
   I've calmed their fears. This was my major aim.
DEMEA: Do you approve of him, really?
MICIO: No. If I could,
   I'd change things; since I can't, I'll bear them.
   Life is a dice-game: if you make a throw
   That's bad, why, you make up for it with skill.   740
DEMEA: Make up for it? Your skill has lost the cash
   You paid for the lute-girl—she must be sold
   For what she'll bring, or at worst given away.

MICIO: She isn't to be sold. I'm set against it.
DEMEA: Then what—
MICIO: She stays in my house.
DEMEA: Lord preserve us,
  Wife and kept woman under the same roof?
MICIO: Why not?
DEMEA: The bride learns music too?   750
MICIO: Of course!
DEMEA: You'll do a rope-dance with them both?
MICIO: I shall.
DEMEA: You will?
MICIO: And you shall be the fourth we'll need.
DEMEA: Have you no shame?
MICIO: O, that's enough, Demea;
  Calm down, calm down; be cheerful, show some joy
  As men should at the wedding of a son.
  I'm going to see them; then I'll come back here.
DEMEA: To lead a life like that—immoral! mad!
  Bride with no dowry, lute-girl settled in;
  Household he can't afford; son spoiled past saving;   760
  Father a fool. Salus, great Rome's protector,
  Could never rescue them, though she's a goddess.

ACT V

Scene 1

SYRUS, DEMEA

SYRUS: Syrus, my boy, hooray: you've lined your nest
  And managed this whole business very neatly.
  Let's go. I'm stuffed with all those goodies.
  A walk should do the trick.

DEMEA: Well, look at that!
  The way this house is run!
SYRUS: Ho, see who's here!
  Our old man. What goes on? Why sad?
DEMEA: You devil—
SYRUS: Shut up! Don't shoot your mouth off here, wise guy.
DEMEA: If *I* had hired you—   770
SYRUS: Think how rich you'd be:
  Your fortune would be made.
DEMEA: —You'd serve as warning
  To my whole house.
SYRUS: Why? What have I done now?
DEMEA: Done? In this evil-doing, this commotion—
  Which isn't settled yet—wretch, you get drunk
  As if it were.
SYRUS (*Aside*): I should have stayed inside.

Scene 2

DROMO, SYRUS, DEMEA

DROMO: Syrus! Hey! Ctesipho wants you back!
SYRUS: Go 'way!
DEMEA: Did he speak of my son?
SYRUS: No, No.
DEMEA: You devil,
  Is Ctesipho in there?
SYRUS: No.
DEMEA: But that fellow
  Mentioned his name.
SYRUS: Not him; some hanger-on.
  You know this guy?
DEMEA: I shall.
SYRUS: Don't move!
DEMEA: Let go—   780

SYRUS: I tell you, don't move.

DEMEA: Take your hands off me—
   Or shall I knock your brains out here and now?

SYRUS: He's gone. A great addition to a party,
   Especially Ctesipho's. Now what do I do?
   Maybe, till things calm down, I'd better find
   Somewhere to sleep until I sober up.

Scene 3

MICIO, DEMEA

DEMEA: Lord, what now? Shall I shout out my complaints?
   Great heaven and earth! Great god of all the seas!

MICIO: Oho, he's found out; that is why he's yelling—
   The case is ready; I must offer help.

DEMEA: Look at him, the corrupter of our sons!   790

MICIO: Master your anger, sir; control yourself.

DEMEA: All right. I've got control. No further outbursts.
   Let's think this over. Didn't we agree
   (And you proposed it) we'd not interfere
   In bringing up our sons?

MICIO: I don't deny it.

DEMEA: Why is he drunk, at your house? Why do you
   Keep him—my boy!—And buy a mistress for him?   800
   Can't you be fair with me as I with you?
   I don't bring up your son; don't bring up mine.

MICIO: That's not fair.

DEMEA: Why?

MICIO: Do you forget the proverb,
   "The truest friends share everything between them"?

DEMEA: You're quite a wit, but it's too late for speeches.

MICIO: Now listen, if that isn't too demanding.
   First, if what's bothering you is the money
   The boys spend, think of it this way, Demea:

You thought you could afford to raise the two
(Your income seemed enough then for them both)   810
And in those days, you were quite certain, too
That I would marry. Well, try that again:
Save, scrimp, invest, make every cent you can
To leave to them. That way you'll earn your glory.
Let them enjoy the windfall of my wealth.
You won't lose anything; don't be alarmed.
My contribution will be profit for you.
Just take your time and think the business over—
You'll find you've spared us all a lot of grief.

DEMEA: Who cares about the money? It's their morals.   820

MICIO: Wait. I will come to that. We all have traits
By which our character can be assessed.
Let two do the same thing, and you may say,
"One will be harmed, the other go scot-free."
The deed's the same; only the doers differ.
The more I see, the more I trust our boys
To turn out well, for they have common sense,
Good minds, respect, and fondness for each other.
Give them free rein—they can be checked at will.
Are you afraid they may be lax in business?   830
In other matters age can make us wiser—
The single vice it brings out in all men
Is to grow keener than they should for gain.
The passing years will sharpen our lads.

DEMEA: If
Your generalities don't ruin them,
And that permissiveness.

MICIO: Be still; it won't.
Let's have no more such talk; stay here today;
Stop frowning.

DEMEA: If I must, no doubt I must.
All right, but he and I will leave at dawn
Tomorrow for the country.   840

MICIO: Or tonight—
Just for today, be pleasant.

DEMEA: And I'm taking
  The lute-girl with me.
MICIO: You'll have won your fight
  And won your son besides, no question there—
  Only be sure you keep her.
DEMEA: I'll see to it;
  Out there, she'll cook and grind the meal until
  She's full of dust and smoke and ashes. Likewise
  I'll send her out to gather grain at noon,
  I'll get her sunburned till she's coal-black.
MICIO: Fine!
  I'd call that wise. And more: I'd force the boy   850
  Whether he wants or not, to sleep with her.
DEMEA: You mock me. Well, I'm glad that you can take it
  So easily. I feel—
MICIO: You've said.
DEMEA: I'm through, then.
MICIO: Come in; let's spend the day the way we should.

Scene 4

DEMEA

DEMEA: Whoever ordered life so well that time,
  Experience, circumstance, did not change it
  And teach him something? You come out not knowing
  The things you thought you knew; what seemed essential
  Loses importance when you test it out.
  It's been that way with me, too; I'd reject
  The life that I've been living all these years,   860
  Now that it's nearly over. Why? I've learned
  The hard way that there's nothing really better
  For any man than easy-going kindness.
  Compare my brother and me, if you need proof.
  He's lived in leisure; loved society;

Been calm and kind; hurt no one; smiled at all;
Lived for himself, and spared no luxury—
Everyone loves him and speaks well of him.
But I—a farmer, rough and mean, hot-headed—
I married—that was misery. We had sons:
More worries. So it goes! and in my struggles
To save for them, I've ground away life.
Now that I'm old, the payment for such toil?   870
Hate—while he lifts no finger and is loved.
They worship him, shun me, confide in him,
Value him, spend time with him, leave me lonely.
They wait my death, but pray he'll live forever.
Those whom I worked to raise he's made his own,
And at no cost; he reaps what I have sown.
Well then, it's about-face, and see if I
Can deal in softer words and acts, so challenged.
I want my kin to prize and cherish me.
Does that mean gifts and compliments? I'll show them!   880
What's bankruptcy to me, the elder brother?

Scene 5

SYRUS, DEMEA

SYRUS: O sir, your brother begs you not to leave.
DEMEA: What's that? My good man, how are things? How goes it?
SYRUS: Fine, sir.

        Great! (*Aside*) There! three unaccustomed phrases
  Worked in: *my good man, how are things, how goes it?*
DEMEA: Though you're a slave, there's nothing mean about you;
  I'd like to do you a good turn.
SYRUS: Why, thanks.
DEMEA: And Syrus—
  I really mean this, as you'll soon find out.

Scene 6

GETA, DEMEA

GETA: I thought I'd go see whom they're sending for
    The bride, ma'am—O hello, sir. Here's Demea.   890
DEMEA: Uh—you are—?
GETA: Geta.
DEMEA: Geta, I've decided
    This very day that you're a man to prize;
    The worthiest of slaves, I'd say, is one
    Whose master's interests are his own, like you.
    And so, if there's an opportunity,
    I'll do you a good turn. (*Aside*) I'm learning tact
    And very quickly.
GETA: Sir, you're kind indeed
    To speak so.
DEMEA (*Aside*): One by one I win them over.

Scene 7

AESCHINUS, DEMEA, SYRUS, GETA

AESCHINUS: I'm bored to death with all the fuss they're making
    Over a wedding: They've spent all day preparing.   900
DEMEA: Something's wrong, Aeschinus?
AESCHINUS: Is that you, father?
DEMEA: Your father, yes, in blood as well as spirit,
    Who loves you more than life. But why not bring
    Your bride home?
AESCHINUS: O, I want to—the musicians
    Are late, and those who sing the wedding-hymn.

DEMEA: Take an old man's advice—

AESCHINUS: Yes, sir?

DEMEA: —Forget them,
   Guests, torches, music, hymn singing—forget them,
   And have the garden wall pulled down at once.
   Then bring her in; make one house out of two,
   And all her household part of ours.   910

AESCHINUS: That's genius,
   And you're the best of fathers.

DEMEA: Great! I'm "best"—
   Micia's house will be an open road jammed
   With people—and the cost! But I don't care:
   I am the favorite. I'm "best." Tell Croesus
   To open up his wallet now for you.
   Syrus, get going.

SYRUS: Where, sir?

DEMEA: Break the wall.
   Aeschinus, lead them here.

GETA: God bless you, sir;
   I see you have the family's best interests
   At heart.

DEMEA: They're worthy of all favors.
   Don't you agree?

AESCHINUS: O yes!   920

DEMEA: Don't have her carried
   Up streets and down, a woman fresh from childbirth.

AESCHINUS: There couldn't be a better way than yours, sir.

DEMEA: Leave it to me. But here comes Micio.

Scene 8

MICIO, DEMEA, AESCHINUS

MICIO: My brother's orders? Where is he? Come, tell me:
   You ordered this?

DEMEA: I did, for in every way
  I'd make our households one—in mutual love,
  Support and unity.
AESCHINUS: I beg you, father—
MICIO: I'm not averse.
DEMEA: By heaven, it's our duty.
  First off, there's the bride's mother.
MICIO: Yes, What then?
DEMEA: A woman of good repute.   930
MICIO: I've heard.
DEMEA: Not young.
MICIO: I know.
DEMEA: She's past the age of bearing children:
  She's all alone—no one for her to turn to—
MICIO: What's this about?
DEMEA: You've got to marry her,
  And (To AESCHINUS) it's your business to be sure he does.
MICIO: Marry? I?
DEMEA: You.
MICIO: I? Absurd.
DEMEA (To AESCHINUS):   He'd do it.
  If you were a man.
AESCHINUS: Father!
MICIO: You heed him? Idiot!
AESCHINUS: No use: you must.
MICIO: You're mad.
AESCHINUS: Let me beg you—
MICIO: Get out of here, maniac!
AESCHINUS: As a favor, father?
MICIO: Are you out of your mind? I marry, at sixty-five,
  A doddering old woman? This you want?
AESCHINUS: O please—I've promised—   940
MICIO: Promised? You'd better limit
  Your generosity to what belongs to you.
DEMEA: He might ask something greater.
MICIO: There isn't any.
DEMEA: Give in.
AESCHINUS: You can't refuse.

DEMEA: Your word?

MICIO: Stop pestering!

AESCHINUS: Not till you yield.

MICIO: You threaten—?

DEMEA: Be generous.

MICIO: It all seems ill-advised, unnatural, mad—
    Still, if you're so determined—well, I'll do it.

AESCHINUS: Splendid!

DEMEA: You're worth my love, but—

MICIO: What?

DEMEA: I'll tell you,
    Now that I've won.

MICIO: Go on.

DEMEA: Their nearest kin,
    Our relative as well, is Hegio.
    He isn't rich; we should do something for him.

MICIO: What now?

DEMEA: That bit of land you rent outside of town—
    Let's give it to him!

MICIO: *Bit* of land?

DEMEA: Big, small—   950
    We must. He's been a father to her; also
    He is our relative, a good man. O, it's right
    To give it. It's your preaching that I practise;
    I heard you say it not long since: "Our failing
    Is, in old age, to think too much of money."
    Let us try not to; it is sound advice.

AESCHINUS: Please—

MICIO: Very well; you ask it, he shall have it.

AESCHINUS: Three cheers!

DEMEA: We're brothers in spirit as in blood.
    (*Aside*) I've turned his sword against him!

Scene 9

SYRUS, DEMEA, MICIO, AESCHINUS

SYRUS: Orders done, sir.
DEMEA: Good man! Today I've come to the conclusion
   That Syrus must be freed.   960
MICIO: You'll free him?
   Why?
DEMEA: Many reasons.
SYRUS: You're a kind man, sir.
   I've done my best to bring the two boys up—
   Taught them, and scolded them, and given the best advice
   I could.
DEMEA: That's clear: we trust you to buy food,
   Bring home a whore, make dinner on short notice—
   Not everyone can do the like.
SYRUS: O bless you!
DEMEA: Today, take note, he helped to buy the lute-girl—
   His work. Reward him: watch your slaves improve.
   Aeschinus wants you to.
MICIO: You do?
AESCHINUS: O yes, sir.
MICIO: Well then, of course. Syrus, come here. Be free!   970
SYRUS: O thank you, thank you all, but mostly you.
DEMEA: Delighted.
AESCHINUS: I too—
SYRUS: Yes. To top things off, though.
   If my wife Phrygia could be free as well—
DEMEA: She's a good woman.
SYRUS: And your grandson, sir—
   She's his first nurse.
DEMEA: Why then, I give my word,
   If she's the first, of course she must go free.

MICIO: For that?

DEMEA: For that. I'll pay for her. That ends it.

SYRUS: May heaven grant you everything you pray for!

MICIO: Syrus, a good day's work.

DEMEA: And likewise, Micio,
 If you will do your part and let him have   980
 A little cash to start on, he'll soon pay you.

MICIO: Less than a little.

DEMEA: He's honest.

SYRUS: I'll return it—
 Just give it.

AESCHINUS: Please do!

MICIO: When I've thought it over.

DEMEA: He will.

SYRUS: What a good man!

AESCHINUS: The best of fathers!

MICIO: What is this? Why have you changed your ways so sharply?
 Is this a whim, this sudden lavishness?

DEMEA: Listen. It is to show that what they judge
 To be your inborn lovable good nature
 Comes, not from character or love of justice,
 But from permissiveness, extravagance,
 Indulgence. If you scorn my way of life
 Since I don't always grant my sons' desires,   990
 Aeschinus, then there's no more I can say.
 Pour money forth; buy, do, all that you covet.
 But if you'd have some voice—when you are lost
 For lack of vision, when your appetite
 Is stronger than your wisdom—if a voice
 Can hold you back, correct you, or agree
 If it is right, hear mine.

AESCHINUS: We both bow, father;
 You know what's best. But what about my brother?

DEMEA: I'll let him have his way—but he must know
 It's the last time.

MICIO: Well done.

CANTOR: Applaud, applaud!

HER HUSBAND'S MOTHER

(*HECYRA*)

Translated by Constance Carrier

INTRODUCTION

Her Husband's Mother has always been one of the least popular of Terence's comedies yet it was a play the author thought well enough of to revise and present again after its disastrous debut. In the prologue to the first revival, Terence explains what happened when it was offered to the public at the Ludi Megalenses in 165 B.C.

PROLOGVS (I)

Hecyraest huic nomen fabulae. Hecyra quom datast
novae novom intervenit vitium et calamitas,
ut neque spectari neque cognosci potuerit:
ita populus studio stupidus in funambulo
animum occuparat. nunc haec planest pro nova
et is qui scripsit hanc ob eam rem noluit
iterum referre, ut iterum posset vendere.

.   .   .

alias cognostis eius: quaeso hanc noscite.

FIRST PROLOGUE

This play is styled "The Mother-in-law." On its
first presentation it was interrupted by a strange
and stormy scene, so that it could not be seen or
heard. In fact, the people's thoughts were blindly
preoccupied by a rope-dancer. On this occasion
clearly it is on the footing of a new play. The
author would not have it repeated at the time,
his wish being to have the profits of another performance. . . . You have heard others of
his plays: now be so good as to hear this.[1]

[1] Loeb Classical Library, *Terence*, Vol. II, pp. 126–7.

Disappointed in the audience's preference for louder fun and games, Terence set out to recapture their attention with a second version of *Hecyra* (the Greek term for "Mother-in-law," here "the husband's mother.") At the second performance, to which this Prologue was the preface, the *Hecyra* again met with resistance or indifference. In the Prologue which introduces the version of the play as we possess it today, the distinguished old actor and entrepreneur Ambivius Turpio discusses that second setback, in the process of pleading anew that the play be given a fair hearing. In this prologue to the third version of *Hecyra*, Ambivius (an excellent name for an actor!) sums up the history of his and Terence's efforts to maintain this item on the agenda of the comic muse. Ambivius compliments his audience. Surely they have the judgment and sensitivity to realize that this new comedy by a gifted young playwright is more important than the circus surroundings which have distracted the attention of audiences twice before:

> *eam calamitatem vostra intelligentia*
> *sedabit, si erit adiutrix nostrae industriae*

> If such storms show any signs of rising now, you're
> too worldly not to quell them; you're wise enough
> to value my efforts.

Ambivius reminds them that earlier in his own career he had helped launch the new work of the author Caecilius, as he is now prepared to help Terence. Caecilius too was once young and experimental, but Ambivius had believed in him and recognized his talents; Caecilius had become a favorite with Roman audiences. So with Terence, whose plays are different, Ambivius argues, I come before you to plead the young man's case:

> *orator ad vos venio ornatu prologi*

In the decorative orator's costume of the prologue, Ambivius communicates his message as producer and sponsor: if you honor these hopeful and talented young artists, our theatre will benefit. The poets will overcome their discouragements and disappointments. You, the audience, will be in a position to enjoy more new plays.

So in the canon of Terence's works the *Hecyra* appears three times, first in 165 B.C. a year after the *Andria,* again in 160 on the special occasion of the funeral games for Aemilius Paulus and later the same year at the Ludi Romani when it finally met with success. From a Greek source Terence takes his complicated, mystifying plot and the impulsive actions that lead deeper into its intricacies. He makes his characters Roman in their heady concern for final values and practical decisions. Terence's unique gift for making people more congenial and affectionately understanding of one another by subjecting them to the comic ordeal of an emotional crisis pervades the situation and the progress of its characters. They are interested, worried, active. The young couple, linked by furtive passion and fate but ignorant of their true identity, are brought together in an arranged marriage. The marriage is surprisingly successful until the crisis of the play's opening action. Why has Philumena suddenly left her husband? Terence keeps his audience in long suspense over the embarrassment that has driven her to leave Pamphilus. When her advanced pregnancy is eventually discovered the suspense changes its position and hovers over the identity of her lover. Can reconciliation be expected?

The title of the play, *Hecyra,* "the husband's mother," provides Terence with a character clue of the sort that he so often likes to heed and redeem with a kind of casual grace. Sostrata is the opposite of the conventional harridan mother-in-law. Laches treats her as the stereotyped figure when he accuses her of having driven Philumena away by unkindness. But Terence has reversed the type. Both Sostrata and the other mother-in-law Myrrina help and sympathize with their children; they do not interfere with their lives. Such damage as can be done to the young couple is more likely to come from the stormy fathers-in-law, who show how authority without good sense is weak, without knowledge, inefficient.

The agile slave, for once, is much less helpful than he thinks: like the funambulist Terence shudders at in the "First Prologue." Parmeno's acrobatics keep him more in suspense than they do the audience. The worldly courtesan Bacchis is a gem, bright, hard, valuable. She does not nurse grudges, although she does keep presents. In fact it is this understandable possessiveness that provides the final clue to why Philumena has left her husband.

Characteristic of Terence's dramatic portraiture is the figure of Pamphilus, a lively and congenial study in good behavior. With Bacchis he found pleasure, passion, "fun," leisurely self-indulgence. The marriage of convenience put an end to that freedom. But when Pamphilus comes to us from Terence's pen, his new life with a lovely and loyal companion means much more than he had realized it could. Losing Philumena is an emotional crisis for the young husband, whose nervous confusion and sense of loss threaten his newly won mature identity. He is unable to account for her absence spiritually.

It is a happy stroke of plot fabrication to forge the original identity of these two appealing young people into the hinge on which their ultimate reconciliation with themselves and with their admirable and engaging life turns finally back into place. Philumena, "the girl he loves," never appears on stage but her presence is fully appreciable. In this comedy of seeming cross-purposes and eventual understanding Terence has given us an entertainment in verse which more than justifies his eagerness to have the Romans of his day hear it out from beginning to end.

PALMER BOVIE

HER HUSBAND'S MOTHER

CHARACTERS

LACHES, an old man, father of PAMPHILUS
PHIDIPPUS, an old man
PAMPHILUS, son to LACHES
SOSTRATA, wife to LACHES
MYRRINA, wife to PHIDIPPUS
BACCHIS ⎫
           ⎬ courtesans
PHILOTIS ⎭
SYRA, an old crone
PARMENO, a slave, servant to LACHES and PHIDIPPUS
SOSIA, a slave

SCENE: *A street in Athens. On one side of the stage is old* LACHES'
house, on the other that of old PHIDIPPUS.

Enter the play's producer, L. AMBIVIUS TURPIO, *to speak the
prologue.*

To plead the cause of the play I come dressed as the prologue.[2]
Let me plead it well, and enjoy as a man grown older   10

[2] In the *Hecyra* the first ten lines are fragmentary and conventionally assigned
to the "First Prologue," which we have not translated but referred to in our
introduction.

Those same rights that I had when, as a young play-doctor,
I'd take a play that had failed and give it new life, rewritten,
Rescuing it from oblivion, and along with it the author.
Caecilius,[3] now—those new plays of his I presented
Either were hissed off the stage or played to an empty house.
Though I knew that the odds for success were ninety to one
    against me,
In spite of my doubts I began the work that had to be done.
If I wanted new plays by his hand, I had to produce the old ones,
And this with enough zeal so that he would not be disheartened.
I got them staged at last; reviews were good; we were sold out,   20
And so I brought back to the stage a playwright who might have
    left it,
Discouraged, desperate, driven to abandon the art of the theater
By those, who, hating him, were loud in their criticism.
If I had turned him down, had had no faith in his talent,
Refused to see him, refused to look at what he had written,
Told him to waste his time in anything else but writing,
I would have frightened him off from ever trying again.
So in justice hear me now, and learn what I'm driving at:
This play, *The Mother-in-Law*, has never had a fair hearing—
The storms it stirred up would stop it before it was half-over.   30
If such storms show any signs of rising now, you're too worldly
Not to quell them; you're wise enough to value my efforts.
The first time I put it on, we'd barely got past the prologue
When we were drowned out by the din of wrestlers and chattering
    ladies.
Then, because it was new, I gave it a second production—
If you have any faith in it, you have to give it that chance.
Act One went well till a rumor mentioned gladiators—
Whereupon in rushed the crowd, yelling and pushing for places.
I couldn't hold my own against that deafening uproar.   41
But things go better today; you're all at ease and attentive;
It's my part now to present the play, and yours to grace it

---

[3] Statius Caecilius (d. 168 B.C.), an author of Roman comedies, contemporary with Plautus. Caecilius followed the Greek models, especially Menander, more closely than Plautus. As a comic poet he represents a transition from the style of Plautus to that of Terence.

As a well-bred audience does, to hear it in courteous silence.
Theater exists for all of us, and you must see to it
That we have no coterie-art; you must add your authority
To mine, and we together will keep the drama alive.
If I have never let greed decide what price should be paid me,
If I have always found that my profit lies in your pleasure—   50
Grant me this one request: that the man whose play I present here
Your honor and mine will not permit his haters to silence.
Respect me enough to hear my plea and to heed it—
That authors may write new plays, and that I in the future
May offer at my expense those plays to win your approval.
(*He bows and exits*)

ACT I

Scene 1

Enter the courtesans PHILOTIS *and* SYRA.

PHILOTIS: Syra, how few of us, how very few,
   Have had the luck to find our lovers true!
   Bacchis and her Pamphilus—how he swore   60
   Time and again (you'd have believed him, too)
   He'd never marry—but he's brought a wife home now.
SYRA: I beg you, plead with you, implore:
   Don't pity men; they'll never pity you.
   Be ruthless; shake them down, girl.
PHILOTIS: Every one?
SYRA: Yes, every one. You'll find them at your door
   Wanting one thing alone, and wanting that
   As cheap as they can get it. You're a fool
   To play the mouse when you could play the cat.   70

PHILOTIS: But that seems wrong, they can't be all the same—
SYRA: Wrong to take vengeance? Men are all fair game.
    Catch him who'd catch you, that's the only rule.
    I wish I had your youth and beauty, or
    You had both those and what I've learned of life!

Scene 2

The slave PARMENO *enters from* LACHES' *house, still speaking to those inside.*

PARMENO: If the old man wants me, say that I've gone down
    To see if Pamphilus is back in port.
    You hear me, Scirtus? *If* he asks for *me*.
    But if he doesn't, don't waste the excuse—
    There'll be another time when it will do.   80
    (*Turns, notices "the girls"*)
    Philotis, is that you? You're good to see—
PHILOTIS: Hello.
SYRA: It's Parmeno.
PARMENO: Good-morning, ma'am.
    Where have you been, Philotis? On the town?
PHILOTIS: Out in the wilds of Corinth, for two years.
    My soldier-boss, I stood for his abuse
    So long, I couldn't tell you. It was hell.
PARMENO: I'll bet that you were homesick too, poor kid,
    A girl from Athens, buried 'way out there.   90
PHILOTIS: Nobody knows how glad I am to be
    Back home again, and on my own, and free.
    Out there, I couldn't call my soul my own:
    I had no choice: I did as I was told.
PARMENO: I suppose you had to watch your tongue as well.
PHILOTIS: But what was Bacchis telling me just now?
    No more Pamphilus? I never thought, somehow,
    He'd take a wife unless his girl was dead.   100

PARMENO: A wife?

PHILOTIS: He's married, isn't he?

PARMENO: Well, yes.
But I'm not sure how much stock I take in that.

PHILOTIS: So far so good, where Bacchis is concerned,
Give me a reason, though, for what you said.

PARMENO: I wouldn't dare. Don't ask me any more.

PHILOTIS: You think I'd have to spread it, but you're wrong.
It would be fun to think about, that's all.

PARMENO: No good, my girl: it isn't for your ears,
Your word of honor's not a thing I trust.

PHILOTIS: Come on—I want to hear: You want to tell. 110

PARMENO (*Aside*): She's right. Well, promise, and I'll come across.

PHILOTIS: Now you're my friend again, of course I swear.

PARMENO: Listen.

PHILOTIS: I'm listening.

PARMENO: Well, long before
His father urged this marriage, Pamphilus
Kept Bacchis, till his father got him down
With all their talk of carrying on the line
Since he's the only son. You know the tone.
The boy refused. There was a dreadful fuss, 120
And finally he had to choose between
Duty and love. What else? He went along
And promised marriage to the girl next door.
I think he's never felt, though, it was real,
That it could happen, till the day was here.
Then he broke down. If Bacchis could have seen,
She would have pitied him in his despair.
He'd pour his heart out to me on the sly. 130
"O Parmeno, what have I done?" he'd say.
"I can't go through with it, although I must—
No one will ever know the way I feel—
And my own fault. Leave Bacchis? Why, I'll die!"

PHILOTIS: It was his father should have suffered so.

PARMENO: Well, they were married, and the two returned
Here to this house. He never took her, though;
Call her his wife, but she's a virgin still.

PHILOTIS: You mean even half-drunk he could refuse?
    Impossible! That's not the man I know.   140
PARMENO: Speak from your own experience, but still
    This was a marriage made without his will.
PHILOTIS: And then what?
PARMENO: Well, he told me how things were.
    "Before the wedding night," he said, "I'd learned
    That such a life was more than I could bear.
    What seems my scorn must be a cross to her
    Although the blame must be entirely mine.
    Untouched, intact, for honor's sake," he said.   150
PHILOTIS: That's modesty and manliness, I'd say.
PARMENO: He hadn't finished. "I must not make clear
    My reason—they could only be a slur.
    She has no fault as reason for complaint.
    I only hope that she may recognize
    How hopeless matters are, and so depart."
PHILOTIS: And Bacchis—was he seeing her meanwhile?
PARMENO: O, yes, of course, but Bacchis is no saint.
    He'd left her. Now her favors cost him dear,
    And no more talk of love.
PHILOTIS: That's no surprise.   160
PARMENO: The upshot was, he saw her with new eyes,
    And by comparison his wife began
    To show new virtues that he hadn't known—
    Gentle and modest, sweet and dignified,
    Bearing the insults of this baffling man,
    Her husband, out of pride. So, bit by bit,
    Because her courage touched him to the heart,
    And, too, with Bacchis colder every day—
    Finding his wife's a spirit like his own,   170
    He has begun to fall in love with her.
    But then, some months ago, an uncle died
    At Imbros, and to settle the estate
    His father sent Pamphilus, though by then
    The boy would have been more than glad to stay.
    Since then, the girl's been at her mother-in-law's

In the big town house here. They all prefer
That to the country life my master leads.
PHILOTIS: This marriage, though—you're certain it won't last?
PARMENO: I am, my girl, and I can tell you why—
She and the mother-in-law were going great
For a few days—no words, no trouble—when
All of a sudden, she—the girl, I mean—
Won't stay where Sostrata is, plays dumb,   180
Won't meet her eyes, won't answer her.
PHILOTIS: And then?
PARMENO: Says finally her mother bids her come—
Some ceremony that she must not miss—
And off she goes. A week or so of this.
The note Sostrata, the old lady, sent
Got no reply at all. She sent again
And got excuses: it is all because
The girl is ill, they say. Sostrata went
To see her and they wouldn't let her in.
Then word of all this reached the old man's ears,
He came up yesterday. I know he's been   190
To call on Philumena's father, but
I don't know what they said. The door was shut.
Still, I would be surprised if he succeeds.
I swear I don't know how it's going to end.
That's the whole story: now I've work to do.
(*Starts to go off*)
PHILOTIS: Goodbye. I have to meet a gentleman friend.
PARMENO: Good luck, Philotis. Teach him how to spend.

ACT II

Scene 1

A few minutes have elapsed.
Enter old LACHES *and* SOSTRATA, *the husband's mother, from their house.*

LACHES: Good Lord in heaven, what a tribe they are,
    Wound in a spider-web of wile and plot!
    They have the same desires and the same hates;   200
    They *are* the same, themselves. . . . I tell you what—
    Mothers-in-law do well to stay as far
    As can be from the girls their sons have wed,
    So much dislike between them operates.
    Against their husbands, though, they all unite;
    To the same strain of stubbornness they're bred.
    I think they all have taken special courses
    In mischief-making. They learn every rule.
    My wife could be the head of such a school.
SOSTRATA: I can't see why you say such things as these—
LACHES: You can't?
SOSTRATA: Indeed no, since I am your wife
    And hope to spend with you what's left of life.
LACHES (*Aside*): God save us!
SOSTRATA: Some fine day you're going to find
    That all your accusations have no cause.
LACHES: No cause? What words are harsh enough for you?
    You have disgraced us all, made me a fool,   210
    Given our son a legacy of grief,
    Made his wife's family our enemies

Who thought him safe to trust their daughter to.
If you were not so wilful and so blind,
That marriage would have turned out quite all right.
SOSTRATA: I did this?
LACHES: Woman, do you take me for a stone?
  Out of my sight is not out of my mind.
  Ten miles away I still know very well
  The way my womenfolk have spent the day—
  Know better, even, what is happening here
  Than where the discipline is all my own.
  That sudden dislike of our daughter-in-law's—
  I've known of this for weeks now, never fear.
  Not that I was surprised at all, the shock   220
  Would be to find her fond of you, my dear.
  But here's the fact that really gives me pause:
  There isn't one of us she can bide.
  If I had known, I would have had her stay
  And sent you packing. . . . Sostrata, confess
  How little I deserve to be disgraced.
  I've catered to our whims, moved out of town
  The better to support your idleness;
  Time and again I've worked the whole day long
  (And I'm no longer young) without complaint.
  You might have tried to spare me such distress.
SOSTRATA: It's not my fault she hates us so, I swear.
LACHES: Whose, then? No; you're the one who's liable.
  This house was yours to govern and to guide—
  You and the boy had nothing else to do.   230
  Feuding, at your age, with a girl like her!
  Look, could you call her guilty and be fair?
SOSTRATA: O no, my dear—
LACHES: I'm glad, for our son's sake,
  Though one more lie could not degrade you more.
SOSTRATA: Mightn't her hatred of me be pretense,
  So that she'd see *her* mother oftener?
LACHES: Woman, you'd try the patience of a saint!
  Weren't you refused admittance to their door
  Yesterday?

SOSTRATA: No, my dear, make no mistake—
　　She was not feeling well, could not come down.
LACHES: Sick, was she? I'd say sick of *you*,
　　And I see why. You're all the same, of course,
　　Wanting your sons to marry as you choose,   240
　　Stage-managing—who cares for the expense?—
　　The marriage first and later the divorce.
　　(*As they stand and argue, from the house across the stage, enter*
　　old PHIDIPPUS, *still talking to his daughter who is within*)
PHIDIPPUS: Though I could say what discipline to use
　　To guarantee a child's obedience,
　　I'm far too kind a father not to yield,
　　Too kind to urge you with a show of force.
LACHES (*To* SOSTRATA): Now I can find the truth out. Here he
　　comes.
　　This is pure luck. . . . (*Going to greet him*) Phidippus, I'm
　　aware
　　That I'm as fond a father as the rest,
　　But I'm still master in my house, and there
　　Nobody's spoiled. Now if you'd only learned
　　To follow my example years ago,
　　Life would be easier for all concerned.
　　Your women have you underneath their thumbs.   250
PHIDIPPUS: O really?
LACHES: I was worried and perplexed
　　About your daughter, so I came to ask
　　But not one single reason was revealed.
　　That won't cement relationships, you know.
　　Resentment grows when it must wear a mask.
　　Tell me if we're at fault. I'll make amends
　　So long as I'm convinced the charge is true.
　　Now if the girl is ill, you do us wrong
　　To feel we wouldn't treat her as our own.
　　You're no more anxious for her welfare, sir,
　　Than I am, you may take my word for that,
　　And all because my son's in love with her—   260
　　Really in love—that's what I'm driving at:

He'll take it hard to find his bird has flown
When he comes back. You see how much depends
On her returning.
PHIDIPPUS: You're a man of sense
And kindness, to the best of my belief.
Believe me too, then, when I say that I'm
Equally ready to do all I can
Toward settling matters.
LACHES: Well, then, what prevents
The settling? Is she angry with my son?
PHIDIPPUS: No, no, no. When I tried to set a time   270
For her return to your house, she confessed
She couldn't bear to go without him there.
You'll find some sort of flaw in every man:
Mine, sir, is mildness. Argue I cannot,
Or set my will on others.
LACHES (*To* SOSTRATA):   Do you hear?
SOSTRATA: So there's our last hope gone. O dear, O dear!
LACHES (*To* PHIDIPPUS): Then here we'll have to let the matter
    rest?
PHIDIPPUS: For the time being. Is there anything more?
I must be at the Forum before noon.
LACHES: I'll join you, if I may. (*The two old men walk off stage
    left, leaving* SOSTRATA *alone*)
SOSTRATA: Is this the lot
Of every woman, then! Her husband's hate?
Must thousands suffer so because a score
Deserve the hatred they bring down on all?
The gods themselves warrant my innocence,
But who'll believe me? It's the style of late
To think the worst of every mother-in-law,
Call her a harridan, a heart of stone.
How can they feel so, when I've done my best
To love her as my own dear child?
And all with what reward? To be reviled.
O Pamphilus, I count on you! Come soon!   280
(*She walks back sadly into her own house*)

ACT III

Scene 1

A few minutes have elapsed. Enter young PAMPHILUS *as from the harbor with his slave* PARMENO.

PAMPHILUS: Love has kept all its bitterness for me;
   How could I say that life was worth the cost?
   Why was I eager to come home again?
   Better some mud-hut village than this place
   Where nothing waits me except misery.
   Misery blocks the way before us; then
   Why count the bridges that must be crossed?
PARMENO: Sir, that's one viewpoint. On the other hand,
   Shod, as they say, goes sure: better to chart
   A course across those bridges now, perhaps,   290
   And face resentments that we have to face.
   Both ladies will be glad of your return.
   You'll listen, judge, and make them understand
   (You, too) how slight their differences are.
PAMPHILUS: I know you mean well, but you know I'm lost.
   Nobody lives beneath a blacker star.
   I was in love before they made me wed . . .
   Obey my father or obey my heart:
   That was the choice. I was too much his son,
   But how I grieved was plain to anyone.
   And when I realized that I could learn
   To love my wife—why, then I'm called away,
   And come back now to find that she has fled.
   She or my mother—one must take the blame,

And either way, what's left but one grief more?   300
We're taught that sons should bear their mother's wrongs—
Divided loyalties! How much belongs
To Philumena, who has shown such grace.
Such patience, such forgiveness of my slurs?
It must have been a serious argument
To overthrow that gentleness of hers.
PARMENO: Serious, maybe. Maybe trivial.
    You know, sir, sometimes greater harm is done
    By trifles; some hot-tempered men resent
    What would be laughable to cooler heads.
    They're children too—easily stirred,
    With no more judgment—O they're all the same!   310
    We'll find, as many a man has found before,
    This trouble all stems from a single word.
PAMPHILUS: Well, I suppose it may be as you say.
    Go in; announce me.
PARMENO: Sir, did you hear that noise?
PAMPHILUS: Hush. I hear rustling—what does it mean?
PARMENO: I'll listen closer. . . . Sir, that sound you heard—
PAMPHILUS: Don't tell me what I heard. Did someone shriek?
PARMENO: You talk yourself and you won't let me speak.
    (*The voice of* MYRRINA *is heard from within* PHIDIPPUS' *house,
    calling "Child, child, be still!"*)
PAMPHILUS: That was her mother's voice.
    O this is terrible!
PARMENO: Sir?
PAMPHILUS: Worse than I thought—
PARMENO: Why—
PAMPHILUS: Tell what you're hiding, Parmeno.
    Tell me, with what new grief must I be cursed?
PARMENO: I've heard it's just some kind of chill she's caught—   320
PAMPHILUS: O God! You didn't say—
PARMENO: How could I tell
    Everything in one breath?
PAMPHILUS: What's her disease?
PARMENO: I don't—
PAMPHILUS: The doctor's been here from the first?

PARMENO: I don't—

PAMPHILUS: I must go in and learn the worst.
  How shall I find you, darling? living or dead?
  If you choose death, I have no other choice.
  (*Goes into* PHIDIPPUS' *house*)

PARMENO (*To himself*): Well, should I follow him? No, that's no
    good.
  Nothing but hate between these families—
  Look at the way they locked his mother out.
  Now if the girl gets worse—which for his sake   330
  I hope won't happen—why, they're sure to spread
  All kinds of rumors: that I came to bring
  Some kind of poison to her—anything—
  And I'll get beaten and my mistress blamed.

Scene 2

Enter SOSTRATA.

SOSTRATA: All that disturbance! What's it all about?
  Is Philumena worse? Child, if I could,
  I'd bring the god of healing to your bed.
  All that I can I'll do, and that's inquire.

PARMENO: Please, ma'am—

SOSTRATA: Who's that?

PARMENO: They'll only slam the door
  Right in your face, the way they did before.

SOSTRATA: O Parmeno, it's you! What's to be done?   340
  Why should they make me feel that it's a crime
  To see the girl who's married to my son?

PARMENO: But ma'am, you mustn't go, nor even send
  To ask. Why try to love your enemies?
  Lost effort on your part, disgust on theirs.
  Besides, your son is with her—

SOSTRATA: He's come back?
  He's with her now? You're sure? What a relief!
  Now for a while I can forget my cares.
PARMENO: That's why I think it's wiser if you stay:
  If she feels better, this would be the time   350
  She'd pour her heart out, just the two alone—
  Why she ran home, what made the world turn black—
  Here he comes now, looking as though he'd heard
  His own death sentence.
  (*Young* PAMPHILUS *comes out of* PHIDIPPUS' *house with a sad
  look on his face*)
SOSTRATA: Dearest Pamphilus!
PAMPHILUS: Mother, I hope you're well.
SOSTRATA: Yes, yes indeed;
  And you, dear boy? And Philumena too?
PAMPHILUS: A little better—
SOSTRATA: Heaven favors us,
  And yet, my dear, you're on the verge of tears.
PAMPHILUS: No, I'm all right.
SOSTRATA: Has she been in great pain?
  Those fevers—there are special drugs they need—
PAMPHILUS: Yes, she was feverish.
SOSTRATA: With chills?
PAMPHILUS: Yes, so they said.
  Go in now, mother. I'll come presently.
SOSTRATA: You won't be long?
  (SOSTRATA *goes back into the house*)
PAMPHILUS: Parmeno, find the boys.
  See that they bring the luggage home at once.
PARMENO: What do you mean? That I should show the way
  To our own houseboys, as you'd show a dunce?
PAMPHILUS: Go as I tell you!   360
  (PARMENO *runs off stage right. The young man is now left alone*)

Scene 3

What am I to do?
The thing's incredible, it's all insane!
I learned it half through hearing, half through sight.
When I rushed in, I knew I'd find her ill,
But not from such a cause. When I appeared,
The maids cried out, and happily, "He's here!"
But the next moment I could see them change,
As though they whispered, "But at such an hour!"
I followed one who'd rushed off to report
My coming—followed to the very sill   370
Of my wife's room, and stopped in disbelief.
This was an illness of another sort—
A *birth* there's been no chance yet to conceal!
The cries she could not stifle turned me cold;
All I could do was turn and take to flight,
Denying that such horror could be real
Her mother followed me, and at the door,
Threw herself on her knees and wept. In spite
Of all, I pitied her—humility and pride
Vary so sharply with our circumstance.   380
I stooped to hear the voice that tears made strange:
"You see," she cried, "why she came home to us.
Terrified and hysterical, attacked
By a drunken brute, she came, poor thing, to hide."
(Her words, remembered, make me weep the more.)
"Swear to me," she went on, "swear by the chance
That brought you here today, swear you will keep
Her secret hidden, if the gods permit!
Surely, Pamphilus, you have grown aware
Of her affection for you; now her prayer
Is for your charity in return for it.   390
Whether you'll take her back you must decide—
No one would ever doubt the child is yours:
You're seven months wed, you know; it might have been.

Well, never mind. I have a double aim:
That no one, and her father least of all,
Know of the scandal. If I can't avoid
Their knowledge, then I'll simply lie, bare-faced,
And say that she miscarried. Who would dare
To question that? It's all so possible.
The child must be exposed; [4] once it has died,   400
You'll have no cause for anger, and you will,
Besides, have saved our family's good name."
I gave my promise. I shall keep my word.
But I can't take her back, though, all the same.
It would seem wrong, my honor being at stake—
Although I love her, though the memory
Of our brief time together lingers still.
What life is left for her? Poor girl, almost
I see her, moving through a waste
Of years, timid and transparent ghost.
Changes of fortune! But I've lived with these,
And learned that one can lose a love and live.
Now let me stand and face what must be faced.
(*Looks offstage right*)
Here is Parmeno, now; he must stay clear,   410
Since earlier he was my confidant—
If he comes too close now, he may suspect.
I'll send him off—what errand can I give?

Scene 4

Enter PARMENO *with* SOSIA *and others with luggage.*

PARMENO: Lord, what an awful trip!
SOSIA: You've never had it rough
   Until you've gone by ship.

[4] Abandoned, left to die in some out-of-the-way place. This primitive practise often appears in classical drama as a device that results in the child's being found and taken care of by sympathetic foster parents. Eventually, the child is restored to his true parents and recovers his true identity in a "recognition scene."

PARMENO: That bad?

SOSIA: Just stay on land;
  You'll miss real trouble then.
  One day is bad enough—
  I had a month of hell,   420
  One solid month of storms.
  I'd have been glad to die.

PARMENO: Awful—

SOSIA: Worse than that.
  Try getting me home again
  By boat—I'll run away.

PARMENO: O rot! This kind of fuss—
  I've heard your threats before:
  I'm not fooled, understand?
  But look—there's Pamphilus
  Over there at the door.
  You boys go inside now.
  (*Exit* SOSIA *and porters*)
  I guess I'd better go
  See what he wants of me.
  (*He dashes up to his master*)
  Still here, sir?   430

PAMPHILUS: Waiting for you.

PARMENO: What for, sir?

PAMPHILUS: You must go
  Straight to the Acropolis.

PARMENO: Who? Me?

PAMPHILUS: Yes, right away.
  Find Callidemides—
  We sailed together; I
  Stayed with him as his guest
  A while at Mykonos.

PARMENO (*Aside*): Damn it, you'd think he'd sworn
  I'd get no time for rest
  If he got back home safe.

PAMPHILUS: Be off!

PARMENO: What shall I say?
  Just find him? Nothing more?

PAMPHILUS: No. Tell him I can't come,
   Can't keep the date we made.
   Run! You've no time to waste.
PARMENO: I never saw the man:
   How can I recognize—
PAMPHILUS: O, you can't miss him. He's   440
   Curly-haired and red-faced,
   Blear-eyed, thickset; as pale
   As if he were a ghost.
PARMENO (*Aside*): Hell.
   (*To* PAMPHILUS)   If he doesn't show,
   Must I hang around all day?
PAMPHILUS: Lord, yes. Just use your eyes.
   And now get on your way—
PARMENO: Don't look for any speed.
   I'm all worn out.
PAMPHILUS: O, go!
PARMENO: I've run since dawn. I'm dying on my feet.
   (*He exits at a dogtrot*)
PAMPHILUS: Thank God he's gone. And what do I do now?
   The whole affair's impossible to hide,
   No matter how they want the secret kept.
   I'll do my best, but they must understand
   It's to my parents my first duty lies.
   Father's here with Phidippus. What can I say?   450

Scene 5

Enter the two old men, LACHES *and* PHIDIPPUS, *from stage left.*
They are engrossed in conversation.

LACHES (*To* PHIDIPPUS): You say she's waiting for my son's return?
PHIDIPPUS: That's right.
LACHES: I hear he's come; no more delay.
PAMPHILUS (*Aside*): What reason can I give not to accept—

LACHES: Who's talking there?
PAMPHILUS (*Aside*):   I must be obstinate,
  And they must learn that I will not be moved.
LACHES: Why, it's my son, whom we were speaking of!
PAMPHILUS: Father, hello.
LACHES: And welcome home again.
  It's good to see you, and to see you well—
  Health is the major thing.
PAMPHILUS: You're quite right, sir.
LACHES: Just in?
PAMPHILUS: Yes, father.
LACHES: What did our cousin leave?
PAMPHILUS: He lived too well to leave much, I'm afraid,   460
  And so his epitaph is ready-made:
  His life was all in living.
LACHES: So you bring
  Nothing except the epitaph?
PAMPHILUS: Not quite.
  The little that he left is to the good.
LACHES: No; to the bad, if it's to anything.
  I'd have him back and living, if I could.
PHIDIPPUS: It's safe to wish that, now he's dead and gone
  (*Aside*) And I can guess how honestly you grieve.
LACHES: Phidippus ordered Philumena sent
  To their home yesterday—
  (*Aside to* PHIDIPPUS)   Come on, say yes.
PHIDIPPUS: Don't dig me in the ribs. Of course I did.
LACHES: But now he'll send her back.
PHIDIPPUS: Of course.
PAMPHILUS: I know.
  They told me when I landed.
LACHES: Heaven forbid
  The news has got around!
PAMPHILUS: I think I've made
  Every effort to act, sir, as I should,   470
  And if it seems now that I emphasize
  The gentleness, the kindness, the good faith
  I've shown your daughter—well, I could in truth

Point out these qualities, but I prefer
That she should name them. That's a surer means
Of winning favor from you, since I know,
For all our separation (and I swear
I'm not to blame) she'll speak no ill of me.
She and my mother do not get along,
She cannot tolerate my mother's ways—
And since I think they can't be reconciled,
I must face up to my predicament:
Part with my mother or part with my wife.   480
Surely all sons will place their mothers first.
LACHES: Their mothers would find joy in such a child;
Their fathers too. And yet I half suspect
Something is going on behind the scenes—
Resentment hardening into stubbornness.
PAMPHILUS: I cannot think what there is to resent.
Nothing she did ever deserved my blame;
Over and over she yielded to my will.
I love her, sir; I give her all my praise;
I worship no one else; I found her heart
Mine only. All my prayers will be the same—
That she may find a husband luckier   490
Than I, since fate has driven us apart.
PHIDIPPUS: You could prevent it—
LACHES: If you wanted to.
Beg her to come back.
PAMPHILUS: Father, all my aim
Now is my mother's happiness.
(*He starts to exit, hoping to cut the conversation short*)
LACHES: See here,
Where are you going? Wait, I say! Come back!
(*But the boy has escaped offstage*)
PHIDIPPUS: Obstinate puppy!
LACHES: I said he'd take it hard.
That's why I begged so long for her return.
PHIDIPPUS: I didn't guess that he was quite so mad.
Am I supposed to beg him on my knees?   500
Well, if he wants her back, the door's unbarred;

If not, he has a dowry to repay.

Then he can go to hell in his own way.

LACHES: He may be stubborn, but you're just as bad.

PHIDIPPUS: A mule is better-tempered, Pamphilus,

Than you since you've come back.

LACHES: O that will pass—

Not that he isn't justified.

PHIDIPPUS: Because

You've had a little legacy, you're all Unbearable.

LACHES (*Losing his temper*):

                                        So now it's

all of *us?*

PHIDIPPUS (*Curtly*): Let him decide and send me word tonight.

She'll marry elsewhere if she isn't his.

(*He starts to go*)

LACHES: Phidippus, wait! He's gone. O, let him go!   510

And let them settle this thing as they please—

I wash my hands of it. I've said my say

And no one's heard a word of it. All right:

Where shall I fight my squabble, then? I know—

With Sostrata, since she's the cause of it.

For that and these new insults, let her pay.

(*He goes into his house.*)

ACT IV

Scene 1

The stage is empty for a moment, then enter MYRRINA, *the bride's mother, from* PHIDIPPUS' *house. She is terribly upset.*

MYRRINA: O heaven help us all, where shall I turn?

Why must I suffer so? What can I tell

Her father? I am sure he must have heard
The child cry out, he went at such a rate
Right to her room, and never said a word.
What reason can I give him, if he knows, 520
For having kept it secret? There's the door:
He's coming out. I think I'm going to faint.
(PHIDIPPUS *appears at his own doorway*)

PHIDIPPUS: So—when Myrrina saw me going in
To Philumena's room, she ran outside—
O, there she is. Myrrina? Do you hear?

MYRRINA: Dear husband, did you speak?

PHIDIPPUS: Am I in fact
Your husband? Am I human? What concern
Have you for me, tell me? It must be great,
Considering the tricks you've played so well.

MYRRINA: I? Tricks?

PHIDIPPUS: O don't sound horrified.
Our daughter's borne a child. Well? What have you
To say? You know the father, I suppose?

MYRRINA: Is that a question you should ask me? Who
Else could it be but him she's married to?

PHIDIPPUS: Well, I'll believe it, chiefly since I can't
Bear not to. What I do not understand—
And what you must explain—is why on earth
You took such trouble to conceal the birth. 530
Nothing was wrong; the child's not premature,
And not a monster either. Is your mind
So muddled that you'd rather the child died—
A child you must have known would be a bond
Later between the families—than permit
A marriage that you didn't like to last?
To think that I gave Sostrata the blame!

MYRRINA: I'm miserable.

PHIDIPPUS: If I were sure you were—
And yet I've just remembered what you said
When it was settled he should marry her:
You couldn't bear to see her wed a man
Who'd leave her for a mistress every night.

MYRRINA (*Aside*): Better that he accuse me and suspect   540
　Any cause but the right one for this shame!
PHIDIPPUS: I knew about his habits long ago—
　Those are the wild oats that all young men sow.
　He'll be embarrassed by them soon enough,
　When he looks back upon them. It's not he
　That troubles me; the spirit that you show
　And have shown since the marriage first took place—
　That's the whole cause. You're doing all you can
　To keep your daughter yours; you want to find
　Some way to break up all that I've arranged,
　All I've thought out so carefully. Your plan
　Is quite clear now from all that's happened since.
MYRRINA: There's not a mother, unless she's insane,
　Would treat her child like that, if she were sure
　That such a marriage would be good for us.
PHIDIPPUS: No mother has the wisdom or the wit
　To make decisions, or to prophesy
　What will or will not prove a benefit.
　Some gossip's seen him going to that house   550
　Or leaving it—what if he did? To me,
　Provided that his visits were discreet
　And not too frequent, it would seem quite plain
　The thing to do is wink at them instead
　Of making peccadilloes public talk.
　If we're responsible for his disgrace,
　He'll hate us. Furthermore, consider this:
　He's been in love with her for several years.
　Such an attachment isn't quickly changed;
　Such bonds don't break at someone else's whim—
　Or not at once, or without pain. Indeed,
　That very loyalty that makes him loath
　To leave his mistress gives me confidence
　That we can trust our daughter's heart to him.
MYRRINA: O talk talk talk! Now not another word,
　To me, at least, of him or my offence,
　Go find him. Will he take her back or not?

If he agrees, it's settled; otherwise
The course I've chosen is the one that's right.
PHIDIPPUS: Even assuming that he won't agree   560
  And that your vigilance has seen his flaw,
  Still, I was here. You should have talked with me,
  Not ordered matters with so high a hand.
  This house is mine. I say the child's to stay—
  Those are express commands. (*Aside*) Yet of us both
  I'm the worse fool to think that she'll obey.
  I'd better tell the servants what I've said.
  (*He stalks off into his house*)
MYRRINA: I've never been so wretched in my life.
  How would he bear it if I went beyond
  His guesses to the truth? He's furious
  At what he knows—but if he knew it all!
  How can I tell him? For that matter, how
  Can I allow him in his ignorance   570
  To recognize this child without a name?
  The dark, her terror, let this man escape
  With nothing to identify him by—
  He even snatched away the ring she wore,
  The brute, committing theft as well as rape!
  And Pamphilus—he isn't going to heed
  Any appeal for silence, once we claim
  This misbegotten child is his own son.
  (*She returns to the house as well*)

Scene 2

Enter SOSTRATA *and* PAMPHILUS *from their house.*

SOSTRATA: You've tried to hide it, but without success:
  In your opinion it was I who caused
  Your wife to leave. But O believe me, son,
  I swear by every hope I have of you,

Never once have I ever said or done   580
A word, an act, to make her like me less.
I hoped you loved me; now I have my proof.
Your father's told me that you've made your choice
Between your love and me. Now, for my part,
Let me give such affection its reward.
I've thought this through, my dear, and I conclude
It's best for me, as for your wife and you,
Not to live longer under the same roof.
Your father's at the country place; I'll go
And join him there, so if it's me your wife
Can't bear, she'll have no reason not to come
Back to the house I yield her for a home.
PAMPHILUS: Mother, that's mad, however generous—
Why should you move, to please her foolishness?
I say you shan't, and I'll deny the charge   590
That the suggestion came, not from your grace,
But from my obdurate insistence. NO!
I couldn't give you up, for my sake,
Your friends, or find your pleasures made the less.
SOSTRATA: Pleasures and friends don't matter, by and large—
Not to me, now, as they did long ago
When I was young; I've had my joy of them.
Now what's important is that no one should,
If I can help it, find my life a weight
To hamper him, or wish that I would die.
Innocent though I am, I meet with hate,
Turn where I will, and this I cannot bear.
Best that I leave, and give them no more cause   600
For discontent—cause rather to rejoice.
You know whom it would please. Make no mistake:
They'd set the crowd on those whom they condemn.
PAMPHILUS: With such a mother, such a wife, I'm blessed
In every way but one.
SOSTRATA: How many men
Would count it lucky to be in your place!
Nothing's quite perfect, but if you're so near

Contentment, do one thing for me, my dear—
Let her come back. You have no other choice.

PAMPHILUS: Mother, I'm desperate.

SOSTRATA: Pamphilus, I am too.
If I could bear your grief for you, I would.

Scene 3

Enter LACHES *from their house.*

LACHES: All of this talk of yours I've overheard,
And, Sostrata, believe me, you are right.
You've got to make your mind up. Later on
Perhaps he'll have to do what might be done
Now of his own free will.

SOSTRATA: This is my prayer. 610

LACHES: Well, then, no reason why we shouldn't leave
Together for the country, and despite
Our differences, get on very well.

SOSTRATA: Laches, I'll do my best. I give my word.

LACHES: Before you change your mind, go in and pack.

SOSTRATA: Yes, dear, I'm going.
(*She returns to the house*)

PAMPHILUS: Father.

LACHES: Yes, my son?

PAMPHILUS: Why must my mother go? I can't believe
It's right—

LACHES: Then tell me why you think it's wrong.

PAMPHILUS: Because I'm still not able to decide
About my wife.

LACHES: What except take her back?

PAMPHILUS: That's what I want to do, with all my heart,
But I can't break my resolution, sir.
I'll do what I think right, but even though
I took her back, I doubt that they'd be friends.

LACHES: You can't be sure. And if your mother goes,
  What difference is it what they say, pray tell?
  The young dislike their elders, so it's fit
  The elders should retire—they've had their day.
  Granny and gramp, you know. O here he comes—   620
  Phidippus, in the nick of time. Let's go
  To meet him.

Scene 4

Enter PHIDIPPUS *from his house.*

PHIDIPPUS (*To his daughter, within*): Philumena, heaven knows
  How this will end. I'm furious with you;
  You have disgraced us—still, there's some excuses
  For you: your mother is to blame for it.
  I'll end my days without forgiving her.
LACHES: You're here at the right moment.
PHIDIPPUS: How is that?
PAMPHILUS (*Aside*): What shall I say? How can I keep it dark?
LACHES: Why, Sostrata's decided to leave town.
  Now Philumena can come home again.   630
PHIDIPPUS: O but your wife has never been to blame.
  My wife Myrrina is the one at fault.
PAMPHILUS (*Aside*): I don't care
  Who's made the trouble, just so long as I
  Don't have to take her back.
PHIDIPPUS: My own wish is
  That our relationship remain the same.
  If you feel differently, then take the child.
PAMPHILUS (*Aside*): He's found out the whole story!
LACHES (*Stunned*): Child, child? What child?
PHIDIPPUS: We have a grandson, born today. It seems   640
  That Philumena, when she came to us,

Was pregnant—why they had to keep it hid
I still can't fathom, but somehow they did.
LACHES: Why, that's the best news that you could have brought!
A grandson, eh? Is Philumena well?
Your wife's a most peculiar woman, though—
Such mysteries, such secrets, such extremes!
I'd say she's acted with the worst of taste.
PHIDIPPUS: I disapprove of it as much as you.
PAMPHILUS (*Aside*): No. If I've hesitated up till now,
Here's my decision made. (*Firmly*) She can't return:
I shan't bring up a bastard as my son.
LACHES: So now the matter's settled, Pamphilus!
PAMPHILUS (*Aside*): Damn it—
LACHES: Of all our days no other one
Has brought us better news. How I have prayed
You'd carry on our line!   650
PAMPHILUS (*Aside*):   All over now—
LACHES: You can't refuse your son. No argument.
PAMPHILUS: Father, if she had wished to bear my child
Or to remain my wife—then tell me how
She could have kept from me what she has kept.
And tell me too how I can feel she's mine
When it is clear she wants no more of me.
Are these the terms you want me to accept?
LACHES: It is *her mother's* influence—she's young,   660
You know; there's nothing really strange in that:
Where would you find a woman free from blame,
A man that doesn't sin?
PHIDIPPUS: I don't care how
You settle it, but settle it at last
Between you, whether they are reconciled—
You'll find I'll put no hindrance in your way.
I can't help what my wife does. Still and all,
There is the child. What's to be done with it?
LACHES: What else but hand it to its father here
For us to raise?
PAMPHILUS (*Forgetting himself*): —a child abandoned by   670
The man who fathered it—*I* bring it up?

LACHES (*Hearing only the last*): What are you saying? That we
    should refuse
Our duty? Leave the child to die? You're mad.
Upon my word, I've had enough of this:
Why should I spare your feelings, save your face?
Do you think I'm not man enough to guess
What's at the bottom of your grief? When first
You argued it was for your mother's sake
That Philumena left, your mother vowed
She'd leave the house herself. And when she had   680
And left you with no pretext—what you do
Is fabricate another from the fact
That the child's birth was hidden. O you're wrong
In thinking I can't guess what's in your mind!
(*His anger mounting*) Consider with what patience and how
    long
I've held my tongue and temper, and allowed
Your time and money to be wasted, spent
On that brass-haired, brass-hearted whore of yours—
You would grow bored with her, I thought; once past
That stage, you'd marry well and settle down.
Well, marry you did, at last, but now it seems
You still won't give your mistress up. Of all   690
The insults you could offer, that's the worst.
PAMPHILUS: You think—
LACHES: I know it, and you have no shame;
Nothing but falsehood, quarrels, stubbornness
To break your wife's heart for a hidden cause—
But she's seen through you too. That's why she left.
PHIDIPPUS: He can see through his son, I must confess.
PAMPHILUS: Father, it isn't true. I give my oath—
LACHES: Then take her back, or tell the reason why.
PAMPHILUS: Not here. Not now.
LACHES: The child is not to blame.   700
Take it. The rest we'll argue later on.
PAMPHILUS (*Aside*): No way out, now, and nothing left to say.
I can't refute his anger with the truth—
No point in staying, then; my presence here

Does no one any good, though I still doubt
He'll claim the child if I defy his will—
My mother too—he can't withstand us both.
(*He starts off*)
LACHES: Running away? And with no answer yet?
(*Exit* PAMPHILUS)
The boy's out of his mind. Well, let him go.
As for the child, I'll do my duty there.
PHIDIPPUS: Good. I don't wonder Philumena's vexed—
What woman wouldn't yield to jealousy?   710
She's said herself it's this that she resents.
I couldn't tell you while your son was here—
I've had my doubts, but now the truth is out—
He'll never be content with married life.
LACHES: What's to be done, then? What can you suggest?
PHIDIPPUS: Well, let me see. This . . . woman—could we go
To see her, talk with her, threaten, perhaps,
Make it clear she's got to set him free?
LACHES: That's excellent advice. (*Goes to his door*) Boy!
(*Enter a page*)   Run across
To Bacchis's, and say that she's to come
Here, by my order, and at once. (*Exit page*) One share
Of the responsibility is yours, you know.
You'll have to back me up.   720
PHIDIPPUS: Of course I will.
Our friendship mustn't be allowed to lapse—
Let's keep it living, by whatever means.
Must I be present when you interview
This creature? I'm not very fond of scenes.
LACHES: No. Find a nurse who'll give the child good care.
(*They return to their houses.*)

ACT V

Scene 1

The stage remains empty for a moment. [Perhaps a musical in-
terlude to suggest passage of time.] *Then enter the courtesan*
BACCHIS *with her attendants. At the same moment,* LACHES *enters
from his house to meet her.*

BACCHIS (*To a maid*): It's not for nothing that he's sent for me,
    And I could tell you now what's on his mind.
LACHES (*Aside*): Now keep your temper, Laches; otherwise
    Your words may give you reason for regret   730
    And you end up the loser. Gently now. (*He goes to greet her*)
    Bacchis? How do you do?
BACCHIS: Thank you, I'm well.
LACHES: No doubt you're wondering why I sent for you.
BACCHIS: Since I am what I am, I had some fear
    You might be prejudiced—*ill repute*
    Is just the kindest phrase we get.
    And yet whatever I've done is justified.
LACHES: You're in no danger if you tell the truth.
    I'm too old now to have my faults forgiven,
    And that breeds caution. What cause could I find
    For insult, if your actions are discreet   740
    And you behave as all good women do?
BACCHIS: Thank you. Apologies are little use
    After the insult's given. What's your wish?
LACHES: My son still visits you, I think.
BACCHIS: O—
LACHES: Wait.
    Earlier this was quite forgiveable— (*She tries to interrupt him*)

One moment; I'm not finished. Some time since,
As you no doubt must know, he took a bride.
If I were you, I'd find a substitute
For him, someone perhaps with fewer ties,
Before too late—men's tastes can change, you know,
And all of us grow older every day.

BACCHIS: Who said all this?

LACHES: His mother-in-law.

BACCHIS: Of me?

LACHES: Of you indeed, and with you as excuse
She's carried off her daughter, my son's wife,
And sworn that she would let their baby die.

BACCHIS: If I could give you more than my mere word, 750
More than my oath, I'd give it to you now.
Since your son married, I swear I haven't once
Let him come near me.

LACHES: You're a fine girl. Would you do something more?

BACCHIS: What?

LACHES: Tell these women here what I've just heard
And offer them your oath. Then you'll be cleared
And they'll be satisfied.

BACCHIS: This is a thing
Few women of my sort would undertake—
Coming to talk in such a cause before
A married woman. Still, for your son's sake,
I ought to try. Such rumors, once they're loose,
Could crush his parents and upset his life—
He's treated me too well not to deserve
Some kindness in return. 760

LACHES: Let me repeat:
You're a fine girl, and honest. I admit
I shared the women's view until just now
You've proved me wrong. Let me continue so.
Then you may use our friendship as you will;
Otherwise—no; I'd better hold my tongue
For fear of spoiling matters. I'd advise
Only one thing: try out my character
As friend and not as enemy.

Scene 2

Enter PHIDIPPUS *from off-stage with a nurse.*

PHIDIPPUS (*To nurse*):   —be sure
   You'll be well taken care of, and well fed
   In this house. What I ask you in return
   Is to see that the child is satisfied.
   (*Conducts her to his door. Exit nurse*)
LACHES (*To* BACCHIS): That's my son's father-in-law. He's hired a
      nurse   770
   For our grandchild. (*Calls out*) Phidippus! Bacchis here
   Swears that it isn't true.
PHIDIPPUS: And this is she?
LACHES: Yes.
PHIDIPPUS: There's no truth in women of her kind—
   They have no thought of heaven, nor heaven of them.
BACCHIS: These are my servants. Torture [5] them as you choose,
   Till you're convinced. This is our business now:
   To make Pamphilus' wife return to him.
   If I succeed in this, I think you'll find
   I have no cause for shame at having done
   What others of my station would refuse.
LACHES: Phidippus, now that it's been clearly proven
   The case against our wives is false, we ought
   To test out Bacchis. If your wife finds out
   There was no basis for the accusation brought
   Against her, she'll have nothing to resent.   780
   If my son's anger is at his son's birth
   And all the secrecy surrounding it,
   Why, that's a trifle. As for a divorce,
   There's not a reason in the world for one.
PHIDIPPUS: I hope you're right.

   [5] By Greek law, as by Roman, slaves could be admitted as witnesses only
under torture.

LACHES: Well, cross-examine her.
　　She's here and ready, and she'll answer you.
PHIDIPPUS: Why should I question her? I thought of course
　　You'd heard what I just said, and realized
　. My standpoint. Let the women talk it out—
　　They are the ones she'll have to satisfy.
　　(*He exits into his house*)
LACHES: Bacchis, we'll see now what your word is worth.
BACCHIS: That's what I am supposed to prove?
LACHES (*Pointing to* PHIDIPPUS' *house*):   Go in;
　　Compel them to believe.
BACCHIS: Well, since I must
　　I'll try, although they'll loathe the sight of me—
　　We have a certain natural enmity.
LACHES: O, if they feel that way, they'll come around   790
　　Quickly enough, once you have made it clear
　　Why you have come. You will all three be freed
　　From error and suspicion.
BACCHIS: But O dear
　　It's Philumena I'm ashamed to face.
　　Come with me, both of you.
　　(*She goes into the house with her servants*)
LACHES: What could be better than this favor, done
　　To her as well as me? Who could have found
　　A better method to achieve our ends?
　　If it is true she's broken with my son,
　　She'll be the next thing to a heroine—
　　What feeling can they have but gratitude,
　　And how can she look on us but as friends ?
　　(*He exits.* PARMENO *enters on the run and out of breath*)

Scene 3

PARMENO: I'm not worth much, I'd say—
　　As Pamphilus must think,
　　Sending me off to waste

My time—and what for, pray?   800
To scour the Acropolis:
For nothing, if you please,
Looking for someone who
Doesn't exist, I swear;
Asking, *Sir, do you come
From Mykonos? Are you
Callidemides?*
The answer every time
Was *No.* I'd try once more:
*Sir, do you have a friend
Pamphilus? No* again.
Who'd bawl me out if I'm
Taking no more of that?
It was embarrassing—
But hey, that's Bacchis. She's
Coming out of our door.
What's she been up to there?
(*Enter* BACCHIS, *she spies the slave*)

BACCHIS: I'm glad I've met you, Parmeno. Please go
　　Find Pamphilus at once.
PARMENO: Why Pamphilus?
BACCHIS: Tell him I beg him to come here.
PARMENO: To you?
BACCHIS: To Philumena.
PARMENO: Why?
BACCHIS: No questions, please.   810
　　It's not your business.
PARMENO: What else do I say?
BACCHIS: Tell him Myrrina's recognized the ring
　　He gave me as her daughter's.
PARMENO: Is that all?
BACCHIS: That's all. Just tell him, and he'll lose no time—
　　Go on. Don't loiter.
PARMENO: I'm not loitering.
　　I don't have any chance to loiter—all
　　I ever do is run. Lord, what a day!
　　(*Exit*)

BACCHIS (*To herself*): What I have done just now for Pamphilus
   Ought to ensure his happiness for life:
I've brought him blessings and removed his griefs,
Given him back the son he would have killed,
And too, though he'd rejected her, a wife.
I've cleared his character of everything
His father and his father-in-law despised.   820
How did I come by all this power? The ring.
Nearly ten months ago, as I recall,
Just after dark he ran in, out of breath,
Alone, quite drunk, with this clutched in his hand.
Startled to find him in such state, and filled
With apprehension, all that I could do
Was try to solve the riddle: where and how
Had he come by this ring? He wouldn't say,
And I, alarmed, continued to demand
An answer. Well, I got one, finally:
He'd had a brief adventure in the street,
And in his struggle with the girl he'd pulled
This ring from off her finger. And just now
There at Myrrina's house, she seemed surprised   830
To see me wearing it, and questioned me.
Naturally I told her what I knew—
And there we had the story, all complete.
The girl was Philumena, and the child
Is *his*, no doubt about it! Who'd have guessed
I'd be the one to solve the whole affair?—
And happy to have done a thing which few
Women of my class would consider. We
Are not inclined, quite frankly, to agree
That wives and husbands should be reconciled.
It's taught me one thing: From now on, I swear
I'll be less money-minded and more kind.
I found him as a lover generous
And charming and good-humored, and although
His marrying was inconvenient, still
I hope I've shown today I have a mind
Above revenge. It's really for the best

In any situation to decide
Whether the good outweighs the bad, and then
Bear with the bad.   840

Scene 4

Enter PAMPHILUS *and* PARMENO *who do not see* BACCHIS *at first.*

PAMPHILUS: You're sure you're absolutely certain, Parmeno?
  Because if this is false, all my relief,
  All my rejoicing, would be doomed to death,
  And harder to let die for having lived.
PARMENO: I'm positive.
PAMPHILUS: You give your word?
PARMENO: I do.
PAMPHILUS: I'd walk as a god walks, if it were true.
PARMENO: Of course it is.
PAMPHILUS: But wait—how can I tell
  That while you are reporting one thing, I'm
  Not after all believing something else?
PARMENO: Well—
PAMPHILUS: I'll go through it once more, word for word:
  Myrrina's found that Bacchis has the ring.
PARMENO: That's right.
PAMPHILUS: The ring I gave her months ago.
  And she told you to tell me. Am I right?
PARMENO: You're right.
PAMPHILUS: What man was ever luckier?
  What can I give you, boy, for a reward?
  Nothing's too good. What shall it be? I can't
  Think—
PARMENO (*Pointedly*): But I can.⁶   850
PAMPHILUS: What, then?

  ⁶ Parmeno naturally thinks of his freedom.

PARMENO: Why, nothing, sir.

It doesn't seem to me you're going to find
Anything good in this news, or in me.

PAMPHILUS: What? When I was blind
Dead, buried, and you brought me back to light—
You should go unrewarded? I would be
A monster of ingratitude, to let— (*Suddenly notices* BACCHIS)
Oh, here is Bacchis; I must speak to her,
(*To* PARMENO) But do not be alarmed; I shan't forget.
(*He starts toward* BACCHIS *with open arms*)

BACCHIS: Good day, Pamphilus.

PAMPHILUS: Bacchis, dear Bacchis, you
Have saved me.

BACCHIS: I was glad to be of help.

PAMPHILUS: How could I doubt it after what you've done?
Still the old Bacchis, who could charm a bird
From off a branch! To see you, hear your voice,
To watch you coming toward me, is a joy!

BACCHIS: You haven't changed, yourself—you never will. 860
I've known a lot of men, but never one
As fascinating.

PAMPHILUS (*Laughing*): This from you to me?

BACCHIS: And you're quite right to love your wife, you know.
I couldn't say that earlier, since we met
Only today. But you've made a good choice:
She's a real lady.

PAMPHILUS: So?

PARMENO: O yes, indeed.

PAMPHILUS: Now did my father hear what you explained?

BACCHIS: No, not a word.

PAMPHILUS: No need that he be told.
My life's not like the comedies, with one last act
Where everything's resolved. Here those who should,
Already know. The others we'll ignore.
It's not their business.

BACCHIS: And besides, my boy,
I'll prove to you the secret's being kept.

Myrrina's told her husband she believes   870
My oath, and therefore feels that you are cleared.
PAMPHILUS: I hope this comes out well for all of us. (*Exit* BACCHIS)
PARMENO: You told me, sir, that I had done some good.
I don't know what it's been, though; that's a fact.
May I ask what you talked about with her?
PAMPHILUS: You may not.
PARMENO: I can guess. And furthermore:
—dead, buried, and you brought me back to light—
That's what you said, sir. Just what did you mean?
PAMPHILUS: Parmeno, you don't know all you've done
To save me from the miseries I feared
I'd never see the end of.
PARMENO: But I do,
I know quite well, sir. You can rest assured
I wasn't acting blindly.
PAMPHILUS (*Ironically*): I'll accept
That statement without question.
PARMENO: Have I ever
Failed to do what you bade, sir?
PAMPHILUS: You're a fraud
Who's saved me. Come inside. (*Exit*)
PARMENO: Sir, right away. (*Confused,
to the audience*)
I've done more good, not knowing what I did,
Than when I meant to.   880
(*He runs off*)
(*The orchestra leader turns to the spectators*)
LEADER: Audience, applaud!